THE SOUNDS
OF ENGLISH AND SPANISH

CONTRASTIVE STRUCTURE SERIES

Charles A. Ferguson

General Editor

THE SOUNDS OF

ENGLISH
AND SPANISH

*Robert P. Stockwell
and J. Donald Bowen*

THE UNIVERSITY OF CHICAGO PRESS
CHICAGO AND LONDON

This work was developed pursuant to a contract between
the United States Office of Education and the Center for Applied Linguistics
of the Modern Language Association, and is published with permission
of the United States Office of Education.

Standard Book Number: 226-77503-8
Library of Congress Catalog Card Number: 65-17302

The University of Chicago Press, Chicago 60637
The University of Chicago Press, Ltd., London

© 1965 by The University of Chicago. All rights reserved
Published 1965. Fifth Impression 1970
Printed in the United States of America

GENERAL INTRODUCTION
TO THE SERIES

This study is part of a series of contrastive structure studies which describe the similarities and differences between English and each of the five foreign languages most commonly taught in the United States: French, German, Italian, Russian, and Spanish. Each of the five languages is represented by two volumes in the series, one on the sound systems and the other on the grammatical systems of English and the language in question. The volumes on sounds make some claim to completeness within the limits appropriate to these studies; the volumes on grammar, however, treat only selected topics, since complete coverage would be beyond the scope of the series. The studies are intended to make available for the language teacher, textbook writer, or other interested reader a body of information which descriptive linguists have derived from their contrastive analyses of English and the other languages.

The Center for Applied Linguistics, in undertaking this series of studies, has acted on the conviction held by many linguists and specialists in language teaching that one of the major problems in the learning of a second language is the interference caused by the structural differences between the native language of the learner and the second language. A natural consequence of this conviction is the belief that a careful contrastive analysis of the two languages offers an excellent basis for the preparation of instructional materials, the planning of courses, and the development of actual classroom techniques.

The project got under way in the summer of 1959. The primary responsibility for the various parts of the project fell to specialists of demonstrated competence in linguistics having a strong interest in the application of linguistics to practical problems of language teaching. Wherever possible, a recognized senior scholar specializing in the foreign language was selected either as a consultant or as an author.

Since it did not seem likely that the users of the series would generally read all five studies, considerable duplication was permitted in the material presented. Also, although a general framework was suggested for the studies and some attempt was made to achieve a uniformity of procedure by consultation among those working on the project, each team was given free rein to follow its own approach. As a result, the parts of the series vary in style, terminology, notation, and in the relative emphasis given to different aspects of the analysis.

Some differences in these studies are also due to the wide range of variation in American English, especially in the pronunciation of vowels. No special consideration was given to English spoken outside America since the studies were primarily intended

v

for language teachers and textbook writers in this country. There are also differences in the studies which depend on the structure of each of the foreign languages under comparison. Thus, if a fact of English agrees well with a feature of German it may merit little mention, if any, in an English-German contrastive study, but if the same fact differs in a complicated and highly significant way from a corresponding feature of Spanish, it may require elaborate treatment in an English-Spanish study.

In the course of the project several by-products were produced, two of which are worth noting as of possible interest to readers of volumes in this series. One, Linguistic Reading Lists for Teachers of Modern Languages (Washington, D.C., 1962) was compiled chiefly by linguists working on the project and contains a carefully selected and annotated list of works which linguists would recommend to the teacher of French, German, Italian, Russian, or Spanish. The other, W. W. Gage's Contrastive Studies in Linguistics (Washington, D.C., 1961) consists of an unannotated listing of all contrastive studies which had come to the attention of the Center by the summer of 1961.

Although the value of contrastive analysis has been recognized for some time, relatively few substantial studies have been published. In a sense then this series represents a pioneering venture in the field of applied linguistics and, as with all such ventures, some of the material may eventually turn out to be of little value and some of the methods used may turn out to be inadequate. The authors and editor are fully convinced of the value of the studies, however, and hope that the series will represent an important step in the application of linguistic procedures to language problems. They are also agreed in their expectation that, while in another ten years this series may seem primitive and unsatisfactory, the principles of contrastive analysis will be more widely recognized and appreciated.

Charles A. Ferguson
Director, Center for Applied Linguistics

PREFACE

The justification for a book like this one is the familiar fact that people have trouble learning other languages because they speak their own so well. Teaching another language to an American calls for considerable knowledge about English, because an American's English speech habits are the major inhibiting pressures against the acquisition of second-language habits. Unfortunately, little of this knowledge about English is available in the usual training that language teachers receive.

The absence of systematic training in the structure of English and in the details of how it is different from the structure of Spanish does not, of course, suggest a gap in preparation which cannot be filled in other ways. Many teachers of Spanish are themselves native speakers of English, and in learning Spanish they came up against the very inhibitions they find in their students. They may remember the experience of overcoming their own problems, and they may be skillful at passing this experience on to students. They may, on the other hand, simply have been apt in language learning—good mimics with good memories and a well-developed sense of pattern. Their students may not be as good as they were, so that ways of teaching the less apt must still be sought. Years of experience often lead to the development of ingenious explanations and clever pedagogy to teach one particularly troublesome point or another. Experience varies so much, as does ingenuity, that such devices are difficult to generalize: it is common observation that what works well for one teacher in one situation may not work at all for another teacher in a different situation.

Or if the teacher of Spanish is not a native speaker of English, he may be a native speaker of Spanish. Since it is his language, one might assume he is surely well prepared to teach it, especially if he successfully reversed the process when he learned English himself. But the trip from one language into another is taken on a one-way street. The things that are difficult about English for a Spanish speaker do not necessarily, and certainly do not systematically, reflect the problems that the English speaker will have in learning Spanish. No speaker of Spanish can, merely by pedagogical experience and intuition, develop a full awareness of the ways in which a speaker of English finds Spanish difficult.

In short, necessary as experience in teaching and skillful control of the language are to the teacher of Spanish, these alone are not sufficient to prepare him to meet head-on the obstinate persistence of English speech habits in the production of Spanish sentences by English-speaking students. A particular kind of knowledge—a carefully cultivated kind of awareness—is needed. This knowledge is a practical by-product of a moderately abstract theory of linguistic error. The first two chapters of this book are an attempt to explain the theory, especially as it relates to errors in pronunciation. The main part of the book is an attempt to make the practical applications of the theory available to all interested teachers in the simplest and most usable form we could devise, including in an appendix some suggestions about the presentation of pronunciation to English-speaking students. In another volume, The Grammatical Structures of English and Spanish, we return to the theory again, to examine its implications for the teaching of grammar.

No single particular pedagogy is demanded by this kind of information. This book is not about teaching methods, but about the sources of the problems that must be faced by any teaching method. It is nonetheless true that we have not been entirely impartial about method, nor could we even if we had tried harder. Our combined ten years of experience in the School of Languages of the Foreign Service Institute, Department of State, where intensive language training for immediate use in the field goes on at a pace and on a scale that is almost unheard of elsewhere in the country, have predisposed us to favor what is sometimes called an aural-oral (audio-lingual) approach, sometimes guided imitation, sometimes (quite mistakenly) the direct method. That is to say, we assume that by and large students need to speak a language reasonably well before they can read it well, and that since speaking is an extraordinarily complex set of habits, those methods of teaching which condition habits most effectively are likely to teach language most effectively, all other things being equal. Teachers who share this predisposition will no doubt find this book more useful than teachers who do not, but the nature and variety of the information assembled here are such that we hope even teachers of quite different pedagogical persuasions may not feel their time wasted reading it.

In a work that is derived from as many sources as this one, representing an accumulation of experience, of trial and error, and of linguistic theory as formulated by many different schools, it is impractical to try to acknowledge in a specific way even the individual teachers and colleagues who have been helpful to us, to say nothing of the rich tradition of linguistic and Hispanic scholarship which is embodied, to the extent of our abilities, here. At this point we would have grave difficulty in separating out the things we have learned from this particular experience or that one. Certainly, we are deeply grateful for the exceptional caliber of our former colleagues in Spanish at the Foreign Service Institute, from whom we draw many formulations as well as nearly all our examples. Nor can we fail to mention the linguistic stimulation provided in that organization by the team of linguistic scholars brought together by Henry Lee Smith, Jr., in the ten years after the Second World War: such an environment for productive linguistic labor is rare elsewhere in the academic world. To the Modern Language Association for the opportunity of participating in the College Language Manual project in Spanish and in some of the materials projects of FLES; to the Committee on Language Programs of the ACLS, for their long-continued interest in this project; to individual scholars who have in various ways contributed to whatever quality this project may have—Ismael Silva-Fuenzalida, Guillermo Segreda, Noam Chomsky, Charles A. Ferguson, William E. Bull, A. A. Hill, Stanley Newman, George L. Trager, Clifford H. Prator, John W. Martin, Sol Saporta, to mention but a very few; to William W. Gage, who compiled the Glossary of Terms; to Kenneth Mildenberger and the U.S. Office of Education, who made it possible for the study to be completed—to these and many others, we are pleased to acknowledge a large debt that continues to accumulate.

In spite of all its accomplishments, linguistics is a remarkably primitive science. The ground rules for comparison of two languages, and for evaluating the practical consequences of such a comparison, leave a substantial measure of precision to be desired. Our analysis suffers, no doubt, not only from inadequacies of this general theoretical nature, but also from more purely personal failures of accuracy and fullness of observation. The best we hope is that we have to some extent sharpened the theoretical tools available and displayed with a reasonable degree of clarity some of the more interesting possibilities for the practical application of these tools.

R. P. S.
J. D. B.

University of California,
Los Angeles

TABLE OF
CONTENTS

THE STRUCTURE OF SOUND SYSTEMS

There are several kinds of analogies which throw a certain amount of light on the process of linguistic communication. These analogies may be thought of as models which have certain properties that resemble the properties of language itself. For instance, language has been compared with an electronic circuit. When a signal is fed into the circuit, it goes into a number of channels, is modified by filters, magnified at some points by amplifiers, attenuated at other points by resistors, smoothed out by capacitors, and so on. Various kinds of switching arrangements allow the current to be controlled, allow one channel to be cut out and another to be cut in, allow a variety of choices to be exercised on the part of the user. Each choice that the user makes has certain inevitable consequences on the subsequent flow of current. This difference, between the choices that are free and the events that inevitably follow from a given choice, is one that is a fundamental characteristic of language also. In English, one may choose either a third-person singular subject or not. If he has made the choice of a singular subject, however, it is then inevitable that he choose a singular form for the verb that accompanies it, if the verb has different forms for singular and plural. It happens, however, that English places almost no restrictions on the modifying elements that are associated with the subject—such elements do not, as grammarians say, have to agree in number with a noun. Thus an English speaker can talk about the big house or the big houses, and big is the same in either instance. (The one exception to this generalization, of course, is the demonstrative adjectives this and that, which have plural forms these and those.) Other languages, like Spanish, do place restrictions on the modifying elements associated with nouns: la casa grande, las casas grandes. The particular inevitable consequences of any given choice differ from language to language.

The distinction between choices that can be made freely, which we shall call OPTIONAL CHOICES,[1] and the inevitable consequences of these, which we shall call OBLIGATORY CHOICES, is a fundamental distinction which must be made in some form in order to understand even the most primitive notions about language, to say nothing of the few more sophisticated concepts we have about it. A grammar of a language really consists in describing two things: the optional choices that are available to the speaker of the

---

1. Technical terms are typed in capitals at their first occurrence in this study, and are usually defined or identified at that point. In addition, each such term is listed in the Glossary of Terms at the end of the volume with a brief definition.

language, and the obligatory consequences of each optional choice. Speaking a language may be thought of as picking one's way through a succession of optional choices and then following out the obligatory consequences of them. Suppose, for example, that one has chosen some form of the verb have as an auxiliary verb. This is equivalent to saying that one has chosen to speak of an event completed at least once before some specified point in time, such as the moment of speaking. It is an obligatory consequence of this choice of have as auxiliary that the verb form which follows will be what grammarians call the "past participle": have gone, had worked, had been, and so on. Or suppose that one has chosen some form of be as main verb.[2] This choice imposes not a single obligatory requirement, but a RESTRICTION in the number of choices as to what can follow: in simple, active, declarative sentences, the choices are restricted to a noun phrase, an adjective, or a limited class of adverb phrases: he is a boy, he is nice, he is at home, but not, for example, he is very, since very is a choice that requires a further choice and furthermore restricts the next choice to adjectives and adverbs only: he is very nice, he is very happily reading. Not only does each choice have certain obligatory consequences, then, but it also restricts the variety of optional choices that remain for completing the sentence.

The structure of a language may be regarded as the set of rules which specify what the optional choices are, what their obligatory consequences are, and what the restrictions are that each choice imposes on all the subsequent choices. A substantial body of these choices and restrictions is mastered by a child at an early age. Although rough edges remain to be smoothed off during the rest of his life, the child by the age of six is in rather firm control of the principal choices and restrictions of his language. It is unlikely that even the best four-year college language programs succeed in building in these restrictions as firmly and precisely for a foreign language as the child of six has had them built in for his native language by continuous contact with his linguistic environment.

In a strict sense, these optional and obligatory choices and the restrictions which govern them are unique to each language, but probably no two languages are so completely different that some choices and restrictions are not alike, or at least similar, in them. The fact that there is substantial similarity in the choices and restrictions of related languages makes Spanish easier for a speaker of English to learn than, say, for a speaker of Chinese. But more to the point, the fact that a large number of the restrictions in English and Spanish are different creates most of the problems in the classroom. The speaker of English has mastered the choices and restrictions of English unbelievably well. It does not matter whether we approve of his particular dialect, or whether rhetorical infelicities often occur in his speech, or whether his vocabulary is only a fraction of what we think it ought to be, or whether he uses socially substandard idioms or constructions or pronunciations: what he speaks is a variety of English that is so well entrenched, so thoroughly systematic, and so rigorously demanding in its system that we must start from the fact that its characteristic choices and restrictions are significantly different from those of Spanish at many points, significantly similar to those of Spanish at many others.

---

2. The statement which accounts for all tense, auxiliary, and verb phrase formations in English is actually much more complex, and will be presented in the grammatical discussion. The present simplification is merely for purposes of illustration.

The points of difference are a major source of difficulty. The points of similarity can be used to our advantage.

Our problem as teachers of a second language is to build into the nervous system of each learner a new set of choices and restrictions. It is our impression that it is in the nature of nervous systems that they reject conflict, that they seek unification, orderliness, coherence, and simplicity. In introducing a distinct and separate linguistic organization into a nervous system where one such organization is already comfortably established, we must necessarily encounter stubborn resistance and energetic efforts to amalgamate the new with the old. Perhaps students do not consciously resist the duality we require of them, but they cannot really help themselves. It is quite literally true that as speakers of English they do not feel under any pressure to speak in the English way: they are like a railway engineer who has closed his mind to any way of getting across land except on rails. With the best intention in the world to produce a Spanish vowel, they produce an English vowel. The habitual channels of English choices and restrictions are worn deep, and they fit extremely well: they are comfortable to the point of feeling inevitably right.

The difference between optional choices and obligatory ones extends throughout the structure of a language. The sound system of a language, its PHONOLOGY, may be regarded as a set of rules which specify its pronunciation. Similarly the GRAMMAR of a language may be regarded as a set of rules which specify the grammatical sentences of the language. Since this entire volume is devoted to the differences between Spanish phonology and English phonology, we must devote some discussion to the kinds of rules which are characteristic of phonology in general.

Perhaps the most interesting fact about the pronunciation of language in general is that there are enormous possibilities in the number and variety of sounds that the human vocal apparatus can produce, and yet only a small fraction of this potential variety is actually put to use in natural languages. Which sounds are used in a given language? How can we determine them? Which ones are significant?

When an English speaker says a word like pill, there is a puff of air between the p and the i. (You can test by various means whether the puff of air is present. For example, hold a lighted match two or three inches in front of your lips and say the word pill. The flame will waver and usually be blown out by the puff of air after the p. If a Spanish speaker tries this on a Spanish word like pino, the flame may waver slightly, but will not usually be blown out. Spanish does not have the puff of air after the p.)

How can we know that the puff of air between the p and the i in pill is not one of the significant sounds that the speaker of English reacts to and uses to build words? The most direct way to find this out is to see whether there is any word in English that is different from pill by virtue of lacking the puff of air. We must know, in other words, whether there is a CONTRAST between pill and another word that is exactly like pill except for the puff of air. To determine whether or not there is a contrast, we can use the PAIR TEST. Suppose we wish to test whether p and b are significantly different sounds in English. We will record pairs of words which are exactly alike except for the p vs. b, the difference that we are testing: words like pill vs. bill, pin vs. bin, nip vs. nib, nap vs. nab, and so on. When we play back the recording, any normal native speaker of English should consistently be able to identify the pairs of words as different. If he can do so, then we have proved that there is a PHONEMIC CONTRAST between p and b, and we can say that p and b belong to different PHONEMES in English. But if we try to set up a similar pair test for pill₁ (with a puff of air after the p) and pill₂ (without the puff of air), we will presumably fail. The reason we will fail is that the puff of air is not DISTINCTIVE in English. Its presence or absence is CONDITIONED by the sounds around it; from a knowledge of what the surrounding sounds are, we can predict whether the puff of air will be present or not.

In English, the puff of air is a part of the p. A p with this ASPIRATION—as it is called technically—occurs in pill, but an unaspirated p (no puff of air) occurs in captain. Both these sounds belong to the same p phoneme in English. Which one occurs is determined by what other sounds are around it. A phoneme may be described as a class of sounds which all belong together as a single unit in contrast with other sounds of the language. In writing statements about the phonology of a language, linguists enclose symbols for phonemes in diagonals—for example, the English phonemes /p/ and /b/.[3]

Each variety of the phoneme /p/ is called an ALLOPHONE of /p/, and is written by a PHONETIC SYMBOL placed inside square brackets—for example, aspirated p [pʰ], unaspirated p [p⁼]. Choices between phonemes are optional choices, whereas the conditioned allophones occur as obligatory consequences of the phoneme choices. In English, one can choose between /p/ and /b/ at the beginning of a stressed syllable—pill vs. bill—but if one has chosen /p/ in that environment, it is then obligatory that he use the aspirated allophone of /p/—that is, [pʰ].

It is important to insist that statements about the occurrence of phonemes and allophones must be made in terms of specific ENVIRONMENTS—that is, the surrounding sounds. The occurrence of a particular allophone, such as aspirated p [pʰ] in English, may be conditioned by such factors as the nature of preceding or following consonants or vowels or by the position of stress relative to it.

For example, the English /p/ is regularly aspirated when it is syllable initial followed immediately by a stressed vowel—for example, píll, pórridge, pássionate, appéar. But the English /p/ is unaspirated when it is after s and immediately followed by any vowel, stressed or unstressed—for example, spíll, spárrow, sporádic, whísper.

Linguists have devised various ways of summarizing the facts of the phonology of a language. One way is to write formulas that state the allophones which particular phonemes will have in certain environments. For example, the statement "The phoneme /p/ appears with aspiration in the environment of a following stressed vowel" may be represented:

$$/p/ \rightarrow [p^h] \text{ in env. } -\acute{V}$$

The phoneme being described is given at the left of the arrow, and the allophone and the

---

3. All phonetic symbols used in this book are displayed for convenient reference in the charts on p. 39 (consonants) and p. 41 (vowels). Also, special diacritics and other special symbols are given in the list of Abbreviations and Symbols.

relevant environment are at the right. In formulas of this kind, a dash is used to show the position of the phoneme relative to the environment; symbols like C for consonant, V for vowel, and the acute accent mark for stress are also employed.

The statement "The phoneme /p/ appears without aspiration in the environment of a preceding /s/" may be represented:

$$/p/ \rightarrow [p^=] \text{ in env. } /s/-$$

In addition to knowing what the phonemes of a language are and what their allophones are, it is important to determine the DISTRIBUTION of each phoneme—that is, the positions where it can occur with respect to all other phonemes. Distribution in this sense is an extremely important aspect of the study of pronunciation. We must know in detail the distribution of the phonemes of each of a pair of languages if we are to be able to compare the two. For instance, a phoneme /s/ exists in both English and Spanish. But at one point the distribution is strikingly different: in Spanish, /s/ can never occur before another consonant in the same syllable, whereas in English, it can. This is no mere historical fact or curious detail of observation: it is a psychological fact of great importance to the Spanish speaker. He cannot easily say an English word like speak or smell without putting a vowel in front of the s: espeak, esmell. He has a phoneme /s/, just as the English speaker does, but its distribution is different. Because of this difference, /s/ is not an optional choice for the Spanish speaker in all the same positions where it is an optional choice for the English speaker; at any point where the possibilities of choice differ, a conflict occurs which has consequences for the learning of the two systems.

Before comparing the pronunciation of two languages, four basic questions about each language must be answered. It is part of the duties of the professional linguist to determine the answers to these questions, and the present volume attempts to provide this information for Spanish and English. These are the questions:

1. What are the phonemic contrasts?

One way the linguist answers this question is by seeking out MINIMAL PAIRS, like pill vs. bill, pit vs. bit, rip vs. rib; in instances where he is not sure of the existence of a contrast, he may apply the pair test (he records pairs that he thinks may be minimal, and tests them to see whether native speakers distinguish them consistently). To establish contrasting segments is to establish phonemic contrasts, with each pole of the contrast represented by a phoneme.

The consonant phonemes of Spanish and English are listed on pages 116-17. The vowel phonemes of the two languages are listed on pages 117-19.

2. What are the allophones of each phoneme, and to what environments are the allophones restricted?

The linguist answers this question first by determining that two given phonetic entities are not in contrast, and then by examining the difference in environment that may be presumed to account for the difference between the phonetic entities. A clear instance of this kind of description is the $[p^h]$ vs. $[p^=]$ of pill and spill discussed above. Sometimes, however, he finds two (or more) different phonetic entities occurring indiscriminately in precisely the same environment (that is, when a pair test is set up, native speakers do not distinguish between them consistently). For instance, the phoneme /p/ after a vowel at the end of an English word can be either released (the lips open after closure) or unreleased (the lips simply remain closed). Thus, he went up can be ended with [pˈ] (released) or [pˈ] (unreleased), and the difference will not be noticed unless special attention is called to it. There is no contrast between them. Such a situation is FREE VARIATION. There are, then, two kinds of allophones in a phoneme: (a) those that are conditioned by the environment, and (b) those that are in free variation. The point about allophones is that the various allophones of a phoneme do not contrast with each other. They make up a single unit: from the point of view of the native speaker of English, the differences between varieties of /p/ that we have pointed out are unimportant, since in his language they do not make a difference that he notices in the sound of utterances. The difference between these allophones is nonetheless real: [pʰ] and [p⁼], and also [pˈ] and [pˈ], are physically different from each other, just as each is different from [b]. But the difference is one which the English speaker has learned to ignore, to pay no mind whatever. These allophonic differences are of no strictly linguistic (communicative) importance; free variation, though not phonemic, may have stylistic importance (e.g., oratorical vs. casual speech).

The allophones of Spanish and English phonemes are described in detail throughout Chapters 5 and 7.

3.   What is the distribution of each phoneme?

It is this question which makes clear the fact that differences in pronunciation amount to differences in choice and their consequences. After a vowel, for instance, the Spanish speaker can choose in the same syllable either a single consonant or none at all; he cannot choose two or more consonants as the English speaker can.[4] The English speaker can choose a single consonant phoneme (e.g., limb /lim/), two consonants (e.g., limp /limp/), three consonants (e.g., limps /limps/), or—under very tight restrictions—four consonants (e.g., glimpsed /glimpst/). Thus, even though we may feel that two sounds—one in English, the other in Spanish—are much alike and should not be a source of difficulty, it is nonetheless true that if their distributions are not also similar they may in fact be a major source of difficulty.

The distribution of the phonemes of Spanish and English is described throughout Chapters 5, 6, and 7. Most of the distribution of consonants is summarized in Chapter 6.

4.   What is the frequency of each phonemic contrast?

When a contrast is extremely frequent—that is, when it makes the difference between large numbers of utterances—it is said to have a HIGH FUNCTIONAL LOAD. When it is only rarely important, it is said to have a LOW functional load. The functional load of of a contrast can sometimes be extremely important in determining the stage at which it

---

4. To this generalization about Spanish there are several exceptions (largely confined to highly literate speech) like Ajax /áhaks/.

should be taught or the amount of emphasis which should be placed on it. Let us take an example from English.

The phonemic contrast between /p/ and /b/ is important: it has a high functional load, with hundreds of minimal pairs, such as:

/p/	/b/
pill	bill
patter	batter
sopping	sobbing
nipple	nibble
ape	Abe
rip	rib

On the other hand, the phonemic contrast between /ž/ (the consonant sound spelled s in pleasure) and /ǰ/ (the j sound in jet) has a low functional load. It takes a great deal of searching to find minimal pairs such as pleasure vs. pledger or lesion vs. legion. Accordingly, it may be important in teaching English to give much more emphasis to the /p/ vs. /b/ contrast than to the /ž/ vs. /ǰ/ contrast, depending on the sound system of the learner's language.

Information on the frequency of occurrence of individual phonemes is not provided in this study, but some information on the frequency of occurrence of certain phonemic contrasts is included where this is appropriate to the discussion.

In discussing these four questions, we have talked as though a language were spoken in the same way by all its speakers. In fact, however, for both English and Spanish there are important DIALECT DIFFERENCES—for example, between British and American English, and between Peninsular and American Spanish. Such differences must be taken into account for both languages: learners with different backgrounds in their English speech habits may encounter different problems in studying Spanish. On the other hand, different groups or classes of learners may study different varieties of Spanish. Dialect differences may affect the answers to each of the four questions. We will give illustrations for each point with Spanish or English examples.

1. Phonemes. One of the best known dialect differences between varieties of Spanish is that speakers of Castilian Spanish make a distinction between words in each of the following pairs: sona, zona; casa, caza; vos, voz. In general, non-Castilian speakers do not distinguish between the two sounds (spelled s and z). Castilian has two phonemes (which will be written /s/ and /ş/ when these sounds are under discussion); other dialects have only one phoneme (/s/) occurring in words of both types.

A parallel instance involving dialects of American English is illustrated by the pairs of words stock, stalk; knotty, naughty; collar, caller; pa, paw. Many Americans pronounce the two words in each of these and similar pairs the same way. Thus, some speakers have only one and the same vowel phoneme at the beginning of each of these words, whereas others—the majority—have two different vowel phonemes there.

2. Allophones. Some allophones of the /r/ phoneme are different in British and American English: for example, the kind of r between vowel sounds in words like very, sorry, courage.

Different allophones of the Spanish /r/ phoneme are heard when speakers from different areas pronounce ir, hablar, leer, or other words ending in r.

3. <u>Distribution</u>. Some American English dialects have a sequence of phonemes /hw/ at the beginning of words like which, whether, whale, white. Other American dialects never have the cluster /hw/; speakers of such dialects will pronounce the words listed above exactly like the words witch, weather, wail, Wight.

In Spanish, some speakers of some dialects have the sequence of phonemes /ps/ at the end of a word (e.g., clubs /klups/); other speakers do not have /-ps/, but say /klúbes/.

4. <u>Functional Load</u>. This is a more complex point to illustrate. There are a considerable number of speakers of American English who pronounce differently the words bomb and balm not, as some do, by having any l sound in balm or by having a vowel of markedly different quality in the two words, but by having a longer vowel sound in balm than in bomb. In some dialects, the difference between a long and a short vowel of the same quality has a low functional load. In others, the same kind of difference has a much higher functional load, being used also to distinguish pairs like harmony vs. hominy. The teaching of this difference would be more important in trying to teach a dialect where it has a higher functional load than one in which it has a lower functional load.

Differences between dialects of Spanish will be alluded to frequently throughout our comparison of the sound systems. A notable example is pp. 63-65. Dialect differences in English are also mentioned from time to time (e.g., pp. 92-93).

These, then, are the four basic questions we must consider in comparing the pronunciation of English and Spanish.

1. What are the phonemic contrasts?
2. What are the allophones of each phoneme, and to what environments are the allophones restricted?
3. What is the distribution of each phoneme?
4. What is the frequency of each phonemic contrast?

By comparing the answers to these questions, and giving consideration to dialect variation, we will discover the differences between the languages. We then need a reasonable way to establish a hierarchy of difficulty among these differences—a scale from most difficult to least difficult. Such a hierarchy will provide us with a basis for deciding how much drill is needed on each point, and will be one of the major factors in deciding what the optimum order of presentation will be.

SOUND SYSTEMS IN CONFLICT: A HIERARCHY OF DIFFICULTY $\boxed{2}$

In attempting to arrive at a reasonable hierarchy of difficulty, we must take into account information from what psychologists have developed as LEARNING THEORY.[1] There are no doubt many aspects of learning theory from which we might benefit, but one concept in particular seems promising: the notion of transfer—negative transfer, positive transfer, and zero transfer. A student may have some habitual responses which are contrary to the responses required for a new skill which he is trying to master (negative) or which are similar to the new responses (positive), or which have no relation to them (zero). This notion of transfer is applicable throughout the structure of the language: the sound system, the grammar, the vocabulary. Let us use illustrations of transfer based on the relation of pronunciation to spelling.

Suppose, for instance, that a student is trying to learn to pronounce Spanish by using Spanish orthography as a guide. He sees the word Habana, spelled (as in English) with an initial h-. But the h- is "silent" (i.e., represents no phonological reality) in Spanish orthography. The student's literacy habits have conditioned him to produce the initial sound of have, hold, her, him when he sees h-. These are the conditions of negative transfer—a familiar response to a familiar stimulus is carried over where a new response to the stimulus is wanted. The effect of the old response is negative: he pronounces the Spanish word with an h-. On the other hand, to continue with orthographically conditioned transfers, the existence of ch in both Spanish and English orthographies with approximately the same sound values is a condition for positive transfer: the familiar ch of church carries over to Chile, leche, lechuga with positive effect. Finally, the symbol ñ might lead to zero transfer—but in fact, since the student is familiar with n but not with ñ, he often ignores the tilde and hence encounters negative transfer. An unarguable instance of zero transfer for the reader of English does not exist in Spanish orthography; we must look instead to a symbol system like those of Korean or Chinese to find true instances of zero transfer for him.

---

1. For a convenient summary of learning theory as relevant to linguistics, see James J. Jenkins, "The Learning Theory Approach," in Psycholinguistics: A Survey of Theory and Research, ed. Charles E. Osgood (Ind. Univ. Pubs. in Anthropology and Linguistics, Memoir 10), pp. 20-35, Baltimore, 1954.

The conditions of negative, positive, and zero transfer by themselves would enable us to set up a reasonable hierarchy of difficulty. We could safely assume that instances where conditions for positive transfer existed would lend themselves to mastery more readily than instances where conditions for negative or zero transfer existed. It is probable that we should have somewhat more difficulty determining whether the instances of negative transfer were more difficult than those of zero transfer: does the student have more trouble mastering gender concord in Spanish (el muchacho mejicano, but la muchacha mejicana), an instance of zero transfer, or with por/para, where the phonetic similarity of por and English for seems to set up an instance of negative transfer? Indeed, we would have no little difficulty deciding exactly which instances involved negative transfer and which ones zero: it is not at all clear, for example, whether ser/estar is difficult because of negative transfer from is to es, or because of zero transfer from lack of distinction between such verbs in English to presence of it in Spanish, or because of both factors together.

It seems that we may get around the difficulties inherent in the question of types of transfer by focusing our attention on the kinds of choices that exist at any given point in the two languages. We have already seen that the pronunciation of a language may be characterized as a set of choices, plus obligatory consequences, or, as we might say, optional choices and obligatory choices. We can add to these a third set; zero choices—those which exist in one language but not at all in the other. An example is the phoneme /ž/—the middle consonant of pleasure—which exists in English but not in Spanish. We can now set up the following three-way correspondences between English and Spanish. (Op optional, Ob obligatory, Ø zero).

There are eight possible situations, not counting the theoretical ninth possibility of zero choice in both languages:

	English choice	Spanish choice
1.	Op	Op
2.	Ob	Op
3.	Ø	Op
4.	Op	Ob
5.	Ob	Ob
6.	Ø	Ob
7.	Op	Ø
8.	Ob	Ø

In this method of comparison of sound systems, "optional choice" refers to the possible selection among phonemes. For example, the English speaker may begin a word with /p/ or with /b/. "Obligatory choice" refers, for one thing, to the selection of conditioned allophones. For example, when the English speaker has /p/ at the beginning of a word, the structure of the language requires the aspirated allophone [pʰ] in that environment. Also, "obligatory choice" refers to limitations in distribution of phonemes. For example, before /m/ at the beginning of a word, English has only /s/, never /z/. The term "zero choice," which is meaningful only when two languages are being compared, refers to the existence of a certain sound in one language which has no counterpart at all in the other. Let us see what sort of examples might exist for each type.[2]

1. English Op, Spanish Op. Both languages allow certain consonants to appear at the beginning of a word before a vowel. There are words like me, knee, tea; mí, ní, tí; and others. We can symbolize this fact in a general way:

$$
\left\{ \begin{array}{l} \text{English} \\ \text{Spanish} \end{array} \right\} C \rightarrow \left\{ \left\{ \begin{array}{l} /m/ \\ /n/ \\ /t/ \\ . \\ . \\ . \end{array} \right\} \text{ in env. } -V \right\}
$$

That is, initially before a vowel, English and Spanish share the possibility of choosing such consonants as /m, n, t/. Although this description is obviously incomplete, since the full list of possible consonants is not specified, the mere fact that the two languages share a specifiable list of pre-vocalic consonantal possibilities is a huge source of positive transfer. One can barely imagine how much more difficult Spanish would be to teach if this set of choices were not held in common.

2. English Ob, Spanish Op. Examples for this comparison are scarce. If we limit our coverage of English to a particular dialect, however, an example can be found. In the dialect that is sometimes called southwest midland (Oklahoma, Arkansas, southern Missouri, southern Kansas, northwest Texas), the vowels of pin and pen are identical. That is, speakers of this dialect have no choice between /ɪ/ and /ɛ/ before /n/. They can of course choose other vowels, like those of pat, pot, bought, heat, but the only vowel they can choose in the area of /ɛ/ and /ɪ/ is a vowel which is really neither one of these but more or less midway between. It is a well-known joke that they can distinguish between pin and pen only by specifying a "stickin' pin" or a "writin' pin." For these speakers it is clear that there is no choice between /ɛ/ and /ɪ/ in the environment: —n. Faced with a Spanish item like lento, the conditions of negative transfer exist for them: they will regu-

---

2. In the discussion of optional vs. obligatory choices on the level of phonology, we are reversing a familiar use of these terms. There is a sense in which nearly all phonological choices are obligatory: if one has in mind, so to speak, a string of words, then the distinctive phonological shape of each word is obligatory; that is, if one wishes to utter the word in English which has the meaning "one plus one" or "four minus two," he must say something which can be written phonetically [tʉw], or (in a more detailed phonetic writing) [tʰʋ˜u]. In other words, the physical shape of the word two is established by lexical rule—any other sequence of sounds will presumably be some other word. But if he wishes to say the word which means "dealing with monetary problems" (i.e., economic), he may say either [ɛkɨnámɨyk] or [ɪ̆ykɨnámɨyk]—that is, the first syllable may rhyme either with Tech or with teak. This is free variation on a specifiable level of analysis—the choice may be considered entirely optional. This usage of the terms optional vs. obligatory is possible—and quite proper—if, and only if, the phonology is viewed within the context of a complete set of rules of sentence formation (i.e., a complete grammar). But in the present situation, where only phonology is under consideration, and where the purpose is to specify the possibilities of combining sounds to produce words—where the words cannot be said to have been selected before the phonological rules—then the usage of optional and obligatory must be reversed, because the matters that are optional are the minimally significant phonological elements, and the matters that are obligatory are the phonetic consequences of choosing one or another combination of these minimal elements.

larly produce the only vowel their dialect allows in the general phonetic area of /ɛ/ or /ɪ/, and it is not very similar to the correct vowel.[3]

3. English θ̣, Spanish Op. This correspondence characterizes the classic difficulty the English speaker has with the erre of Spanish perro, or the jota of Spanish hijo. In neither instance does the sound exist in English, although both sounds represent optional choices of considerable frequency in Spanish. From the English speaker's point of view, they are new sounds.

4. English Op, Spanish Ob. This correspondence characterizes one of the more difficult problems of Spanish phonology for the English learner. Take, for example, the pronunciation of items like dado and dedo in isolation. The d at the beginning is pronounced differently from the d in the middle. The initial d is much like the initial d of English den, doll, door. (It is not exactly the same, but the difference is irrelevant for this purpose.) We will write it with the phonetic symbol [d]. The middle d of dado, dedo, on the other hand, is conspicuously different—to the English ear—from the initial d. It sounds more nearly like the initial th of then, there, those. We will write it with the phonetic symbol [ð]. Dado and dedo can now be written phonetically as [dáðo], [déðo]. For the Spanish speaker, the pronunciation of [ð], rather than [d], in the middle of these words is obligatory. He will not ordinarily even be aware that he pronounces two quite different sounds for the d's of dado and dedo. To use the technical terminology introduced earlier, [d] and [ð] are allophones of a single phoneme /d/ in Spanish. Among the consonants of Spanish, /d/ exists as one possible optional choice, which may be symbolized:

$$\text{Spanish C} \rightarrow \left\{ \left[\begin{array}{c} /p/ \\ /t/ \\ /k/ \\ /b/ \\ /d/ \\ /g/ \\ . \\ . \\ . \end{array} \right] \text{ in env. } -V \right\}$$

There is then a subsidiary rule about /d/ (illustrated, incompletely, below):

$$/d/ \rightarrow \left\{ \begin{array}{l} [d] \text{ in env. } \left\{ \begin{array}{c} /l/ \\ /n/ \\ \# \end{array} \right\} - \\ [ð] \text{ in env. } \quad V \quad - \end{array} \right\}$$

That is, if /d/ is preceded by silence (a break in utterance continuity symbolized in the formula by #) or an /n/ or /l/, it is pronounced as [d]. If it is preceded by a vowel, it is pronounced as [ð]. The phonetic difference between [d] and [ð] is CONDITIONED by this

---

3. Of the writers, R.P.S. has been plagued by this disability since his first exposure to Spanish. He can testify to its persistence. Even as a trained phonetician, he can avoid the obligatory vowel of his native dialect only with concentrated effort.

rule—a rule which merely describes a set of conditions to which Spanish speakers habitually, and unconsciously, conform. Because of this rule, [đ] is for them simply a kind of /d/. But for the English speaker, the conditions are different. For him [d] and [đ] are IN CONTRAST—that is, they belong to different phonemes, /d/ and /đ/. The fact of contrast is proved by pairs such as dine/thine, dare/there, dough/though. [d] and [đ] exist as two possible choices among the consonants of English:

$$\text{English C} \;\rightarrow\; \left\{ \left\{ \begin{array}{l} \text{/p/} \\ \text{/t/} \\ \text{/k/} \\ \text{/b/} \\ \text{/d/} \\ \text{/g/} \\ \text{/v/} \\ \text{/đ/} \\ \cdot \\ \cdot \\ \cdot \end{array} \right\} \;\text{in env.} -V \right\}$$

In English, unlike Spanish, /d/ and /đ/ are in contrast: they are both optional choices, and their distribution cannot be predicted. Predictability is at the heart of the matter: the occurrence of Spanish [d] and [đ] can be predicted by writing merely one symbol, /d/; given this symbol in an environment, it is possible always and infallibly to predict whether it will be pronounced [d] or [đ]. The difference between them is obligatory.

This correspondence between English optional choices and Spanish obligatory choices is so important in its consequences that another example may clarify it still further. Suppose we consider the possibilities of nasal consonants ([m] as in ham, [n] as in hen, [ŋ] as in hang) in the environment of following stop consonants ([p] as in up, [t] as in putt, [k] as in puck, [b] as in tub, [d] as in dud, [g] as in dug). The phonetic symbols needed for this discussion are all familiar letters of the alphabet in familiar values, except for [ŋ]. Note that the letters ng are used to spell both /ŋ/ and /ŋg/ in English: words like singer and banging have /ŋ/, whereas words like finger and younger have /ŋg/.

Certain articulatory facts about these consonants must be briefly explained in order to make the point clear. In terms of the place in the mouth at which the sound is articulated, the nasal and stop consonants fall into three classes: those made at the lips ([m p b]); those made by the tip of the tongue at or just behind the upper teeth ([n t d]); and those made toward the back of the mouth, with the tongue touching the back part of the roof of the mouth (the VELUM) ([ŋ k g]).

Lips	Teeth	Velum
m	n	ŋ
p	t	k
b	d	g

It is characteristic of Spanish that in a sequence of nasal consonant plus stop consonant, the point of articulation of BOTH consonants is fixed by the stop consonant. This can be formulated:

$$\text{Spanish N} \rightarrow \begin{cases} [\text{m}] \text{ in env. } - \begin{Bmatrix} /\text{p}/ \\ /\text{b}/ \end{Bmatrix} \\ [\text{n}] \text{ in env. } - \begin{Bmatrix} /\text{t}/ \\ /\text{d}/ \end{Bmatrix} \\ [\text{ŋ}] \text{ in env. } - \begin{Bmatrix} /\text{k}/ \\ /\text{g}/ \end{Bmatrix} \end{cases}$$

That is, a nasal (N) can be only [m] if the following consonant is [p] or [b], only [n] if the following consonant is [t] or [d], only [ŋ] if the following consonant is [k] or [g]. This restriction remains valid regardless of word boundaries and spelling: hombre, un beso; endosar, un día; inglés, un gato. It is optional whether a nasal be chosen at all; but if one is chosen, it is obligatory that its point of articulation be the same as that of a following stop consonant. In English, on the other hand, no such restriction exists: [mb] lumber, [nb] unbend, [ŋb] kingbird; [md] lambda, [nd] under, [ŋd] kingdom; [mg] Baumgardner, [ng] ingrown, [ŋg] finger. In English, not only is the choice of a nasal consonant optional, as in Spanish, but so is the choice of a particular nasal, regardless of the following stop consonant, which is not true in Spanish.

5. English Ob, Spanish Ob. It is here that we get maximum positive transfer. Any English pattern that is obligatory is necessarily one to which the speaker gives no thought—it is an area where he has no choice. If the same pattern is obligatory also in Spanish, there should be no problem—indeed, there will not normally even be any awareness that there might have been a problem. These instances are more frequent than we realize: comparison between Japanese and Spanish, on the one hand, and between English and Spanish, on the other, will reveal that the English speaker is not so bad off for Spanish-like habits as we who are faced with the student's errors are prone to think. To take a simple instance: given the consonantal sequence /s/ plus /w/, both languages require that a vowel be chosen in the next position—swear, suerte. This is not a trivial observation: if the consonantal sequence is /p/ followed by /r/, English requires a vowel, as in pray, but Spanish allows /y/ or /w/, for example, prieto /pryéto/, pruebo /prwébo/.[4] Thus the fact that the Spanish speaker has a different range of choice after /pr/ constitutes a problem for the English speaker, even though the sequence /pr/ itself does not.

6. English Ø, Spanish Ob. This correspondence is the extreme of the scale. In English, a given habit does not exist at all; in Spanish, it is obligatory and hence normally outside the speaker's conscious control—it is a habit which he internalized at an early age and has given no thought to since. Zero may be viewed as a kind of negative obligation: to say that a pattern is zero is about the same as saying that it is obligatory that the speaker not conform to the pattern. We have, as it were, an absolute negative restric-

---

4. The semivowels /y/ and /w/ are definitely different from ordinary vowels (even though they are spelled with the same letters), because they are not syllabic.

tion in the one instance, an absolute positive restriction in the other. An example is to be found in the middle consonant of Spanish words like haba, leva, avance. Although spelled with b or v, this sound is different from anything represented by b or v in English. The phonetic symbol we will use for it is [ƀ]. It is articulated by bringing the lower lip up toward the upper lip, as if for b, but without touching, so that the air produces a friction noise, as if for v. In Spanish, the difference between [b] and [ƀ] is closely parallel to that between [d] and [đ]. The two sounds are allophones of a single phoneme, predictable from a single symbol in the following way (this formulation of the rule is illustrative only, not complete):

$$
\text{Spanish } /b/ \;\rightarrow\; \left\{ \begin{array}{l} [b] \text{ in env. } \left\{ \begin{array}{l} /m/ \\ \# \end{array} \right\} \;- \\ [ƀ] \text{ in env.} \quad V \quad - \end{array} \right\}
$$

That is, [ƀ] normally occurs after vowels, [b] elsewhere. The situation of [b]–[ƀ] is different from that of [d]–[đ] in only one significant respect: [ƀ] does not exist in English at all (a zero category), but [đ] does (an optional category). But this is a big difference pedagogically. In the instance of [đ], the English speaker must transfer a familiar sound and redistribute it with respect to other sounds; in the instance of [ƀ], he must learn a new sound as well as a new distribution.

7. English Op, Spanish Ø. This particular correspondence is a frequent one in going from English to Spanish pronunciation. English has several vowels, for instance, that are entirely lacking in Spanish. The vowel of American English grass, symbolized by [æ], does not exist in Spanish. Partly because of negative transfer from the spelling a, words like gracias are often pronounced with this vowel in early stages of learning. The problem is merely to reduce the range of choice that the English speaker is accustomed to exercising.

8. English Ob, Spanish Ø. An English obligatory pattern of pronunciation can be difficult to get rid of. For instance, it is obligatory in most English dialects that items with t or d between syllables, where the first syllable is stressed (butter, shudder, splatter, Betty, patty), have an allophone of /t/ (or /d/) that is rather like the Spanish r of para, pero. It is a voiced tongue-tip FLAP. Faced with Spanish words like foto, beta, pita, the English speaker of most dialects will produce the obligatory English flap rather than the fully articulated /t/ of Spanish. Another example also involves allophones of English /t/: in items like mountain, button, latent, the English speaker of most dialects has a variety of /t/ for which instead of dropping the tongue tip as he usually does to release a /t/, he maintains the tongue tip in the same position for the following /n/. Such an articulation does not exist under any conditions in any dialect of Spanish. Words like quitan, meten, which always have a normally released /t/ and a full vowel, are subject to this kind of transfer.

Having at least an idea, now, of the eight kinds of differences that a comparison can reveal when it is based on the different possibilities of choice in the two languages, we can attempt to rearrange the comparisons in an order which will constitute a HIERARCHY OF DIFFICULTY. We must know which kinds of differences will be most difficult to master and which will be easiest, in order to grade our teaching materials, arrange them into an effective sequence, and determine how much drill is needed on each point. The hierarchy suggested below is by no means final; further experience with it may well result in readjustments in the relative position of one category of difficulty or another.

Difficulty		Comparison		Type	Examples (from preceding discussion)
Magnitude	Order	Eng.	Span.		
I	1	Ø	Ob	6	[ƀ]
	2	Ø	Op	3	erre, jota
	3	Op	Ob	4	[d]/[đ]
II	4	Ob	Op	2	i/e before n
	5	Ob	Ø	8	flap /t/ between vowels
	6	Op	Ø	7	[æ]
III	7	Op	Op	1	List of prevocalic consonants
	8	Ob	Ob	5	sw—plus vowel

Given such a hierarchy, we must examine several other criteria that will enter into the grading and sequencing of materials designed to eliminate these difficulties.

The most important of these is FUNCTIONAL LOAD—that is, the extent to which a given sound is used in Spanish to distinguish one word from another, the quantity of distinctive information that it carries. The Spanish ñ belongs in Group I in the hierarchy of difficulty (Ø in English, Optional in Spanish). But its functional load is almost zero. There are about a dozen words in which ñ carries the burden of contrast with the cluster [ny] (spelled -ni-): uñón (big toenail) vs. unión and the like.[5] An American can speak Spanish for a long time without ever needing this contrast. For ñ he can substitute [ny], modifying a cluster he controls from his English habits only to the extent of being careful not to make the syllable division between [n] and [y]—that is, he must say [u.nyón] rather than [un.yón]. The ñ would, therefore, in spite of its relatively high rank in the hierarchy of difficulty, be placed very late (indeed, almost last) in a reasonable pedagogical hierarchy.

A less important additional criterion is POTENTIAL MISHEARING. Spanish initial [t⁼]—the variety of /t/ that appears before vowels—provides an example. This sound is very difficult, Group I (Ø in English, Obligatory in Spanish), in our hierarchy above. But failure to produce it correctly (with the tongue tip against the back side of the upper teeth, without a puff of air) will rarely cause misunderstanding. However, the Amer-

---

5. The word unión is to be transcribed as [unyón]. In the view of other analysts, it is better transcribed as [unión], which would alter the example. The comparison to be made with English still stands, because in the English pattern the syllable division would obligatorily be [un.yón].

ican who is listening rather than speaking—receiving rather than producing—will often hear a Spanish initial [t⁼] as being a [d]. One good way for him to learn to hear it correctly is for him to produce it correctly. We would therefore place the [t⁼] fairly high in a pedagogically oriented sequence even though when evaluated as to its effect on the production of Spanish, it will only add American accent to the student's pronunciation—not unintelligibility at any point.

The final additional criterion is PATTERN CONGRUITY. The sounds of a language pattern themselves in groups or sets. In Spanish, /b/, /d/, and /g/ constitute a set. /b/ and /d/ are high in difficulty, in functional load, and in potentiality for mishearing. There is no doubt they must appear early in a pedagogical sequence. /g/ is also difficult, but it is considerably lower in functional load and has less potential for mishearing. Because it patterns like /b/ and /d/, we feel it would be incongruous to place it out of sequence with them even though it does not constitute a problem of the same order.

These, then, are the criteria which have determined the sequence of our presentation:

1. Hierarchy of difficulty
2. Functional load
3. Potential mishearing
4. Pattern congruity

Matching these criteria against one another is no easy task, and there is clearly no single "right" or "best" sequence of presentation. Our own procedure has been, in general, to put those things first that were most important in the task of communication, either because mishandling of them could easily result in misunderstanding or because they carried a heavy functional load and would therefore be especially obvious and frequent sources of accent. In order to get similar problems together, however, we have violated the mixed criteria of importance. Our preferred pedagogical sequence is:

1. Basic intonation features and patterns
   (including stress, pitch, juncture, and rhythm)
2. Weak stressed vowels
3. Strong stressed vowels and diphthongs
4. Voiced stop-spirants
5. Vibrants and liquids
6. Voiceless stops
7. Spirants
8. Nasals and palatals
9. Semivowels
10. Consonant clusters
11. Other intonation features and patterns.

The above order is not identical with the order of presentation in this volume. We have arbitrarily followed intonation with consonants, on the assumption that the familiarity of teachers with the problems of the vowels might justify our leaving the vowels until after the matters that showed the more interesting details of dialectal variation had been described. The above order is, however, identical with that adopted for our text on pronunciation.[6]

---

6. J. Donald Bowen and Robert P. Stockwell, Patterns of Spanish Pronunciation (Chicago: University of Chicago Press, 1960).

STRESS, RHYTHM, AND INTONATION PATTERNS

3

   When one approaches a new language like Spanish with the intention of learning how to speak it, the first thing he notices and the last thing he masters is the inflection of the voice: the complex rise and fall, the rhythm, the lilt, the various kinds of signals that mark what is emphasized, what parts are joined together, what parts are explicitly disjoined. It has often been noted that a child masters several of these features in his native language before he is in really good control of vowels or consonants or meanings. It is curious that these are the last parts of the structure that linguists have succeeded in analyzing—they are learned earlier, are not much discussed in school, are further below the level of awareness, are more difficult to verbalize about. We shall begin with these overriding features of the structures of Spanish and English and work down to the smaller details. No utterance can be made in either language without its carrying an intonation pattern, the components of which are STRESS (relative prominence of syllables), PITCH (highness or lowness of tone), and TERMINAL JUNCTURES (certain features which signal the phrasing in speech).[1]

   The flow of speech in any language is broken by pauses—short or long periods of silence—which usually come at the ends of whole utterances or at the ends of large parts of utterances such as "sentences," "clauses," and the like. Immediately before such pauses there are often special features of pronunciation, such as a slight drawling of a vowel or a certain kind of change in pitch, which themselves signal the presence of the boundary just as much as the pause does. In fact, speakers often do not make any appreciable pause at all at these important boundaries, but use only the other signaling features we have mentioned.

   These features, wherever they occur (with or without pause, even with or with-

---

   1. We are going to proceed to discuss stress, pitch, terminal junctures, and associated matters without first identifying the vowel-consonant sequences which carry these elements. We will use traditional spelling until we are ready to analyze vowels and consonants. We will therefore be writing some items which are neither fish nor fowl: traditional spelling on the line, modified by accentual and other non-traditional diacritics above the line. This will cause no trouble for English, since everyone knows accents are not written on English words. But on Spanish words, it is not by mistake or faulty printing that we write tiene as tiéne, or él as el, depending on the actual presence or absence of strong stress in the utterance.

out an important grammatical boundary), are the terminal junctures, and the stretch of speech between the beginning of an utterance and the first terminal juncture or between two terminal junctures is called a PHRASE. The concept of the phrase in Spanish and English pronunciation is of considerable importance because most of the overriding phenomena of stress, pitch, and rhythm in these languages operate in terms of phrases and are best described relative to phrases.

STRESS

Stress is what makes the difference between ésta and está in Spanish or between the noun tórment and the verb tormént in English. In the first of each of these pairs, the first syllable is more prominent ("accented"); in the second, the last syllable. Often when these words are said, there are features in the rise and fall of the pitch—the pitch contour—which contribute to the prominence of the accented syllable. It can be shown, however, that there are contrastive levels of prominence not obligatorily associated with the shape of the contour itself. This means that we must pay attention to stress as an independent feature of the language.[2]

This independent importance of stress is demonstrated by finding examples where the pitch contour, as contour, plays no important part in the prominence we observe. Items for such a pair test are:

| Sí, ésta. | Yes, this one. | Sí, está. | Yes, he is. |
| Sí, ábra. | Yes, open up. | Sí, habrá. | Yes, there will be. |

Each of these utterances can be said with a pitch contour which goes approximately as indicated by the line above the words:

Sí ésta.   Sí está.

Sí ábra.   Sí habrá.

---

2. It has been seriously doubted by some investigators that pitch, stress, and juncture can be treated independently. Cf. Dwight L. Bolinger and Lewis J. Gerstman, "Disjuncture as a Cue to Constructs," Word, XIII (1957), 246-55, where they describe some interesting experiments (using English examples such as light house keeper) which indicate that loudness (intensity) as a cue to relative prominence can easily be overridden by relatively slight pitch changes and differences in pacing, such as putting light and house closer together in one instance and further apart in another. These experiments and others devised by Bolinger have raised questions about the viability of an analysis that separates pitch and stress as independent entities. But though the questions have been raised, no one has yet come forth with a new analysis of Spanish (one which does not make this separation but still accounts for all the observed data). Bolinger has proposed a partial theory of pitch-accent in English (one which raises many new questions but fails to provide a basis for a full transcription of intonation), and some investigators (including R. P. S.) have come to favor a type of intonational analysis that combines pitch and stress in a way suggested by Henry Sweet in the last quarter of the nineteenth century. But for the purposes of this volume, the more familiar analysis is retained, since it is essentially the one found widely in the texts on descriptive linguistics that teachers are likely to consult. The differences between various intonational analyses are much more trivial than they appear on the surface: any system which enables one to deal conveniently with the differences between Spanish and English in any case serves the present need. Finally, it should be noted that a treatment of intonation within the context not simply of phonology but of a total grammar would be quite distinct from any of the alternatives referred to above.

When each utterance of either pair is said with this contour, we still have, as the distinction in each pair, a stress difference between the last two syllables, a stress difference which is associated with the point at which the skip down occurs in the contour—the contour itself is independent.

This difference in relative prominence can be viewed in two ways: (1) the more prominent syllable can be said to have a stress, whereas the less prominent one has no stress at all; (2) both syllables have a stress, with the more prominent syllable having a STRONG STRESS and the less prominent one having a WEAK STRESS. In the first instance, one can then speak of the POSITION of stress, the contrast being between its occurrence in one or more positions and its absence in all other positions. In the second instance, one can speak of the position of strong stress and the position of weak stress, both being viewed as positive entities. The two views are entirely interchangeable—there is no reason to argue about either choice. Since it is useful to be able to talk about, and to symbolize, weak stress, we will hereafter speak in terms of the second alternative, and will assign the symbols /´/ (acute accent) to strong stress and /˙/ (dot accent) to weak stress. The weak stress will be marked only when necessary. The dot accent will be used when pitch contours are being shown.

Spanish has only the two degrees of stress, strong and weak, that were demonstrated by the pair test above. English, however, has three degrees of stress: STRONG, MEDIAL, and WEAK. The vowels of English weak-stressed syllables have certain special characteristics. For one thing, the vowel qualities found in weak-stressed syllables are noticeably different from those in syllables with greater stress, so that it is difficult to compare them directly. Also, there are many differences among speakers of English as to what vowels actually occur with weak stress. These problems will receive fuller treatment in the discussion of vowels in Chapter 7.

Although these factors make it difficult to find sets of words to construct a pair test establishing the difference between strong and weak stress in English, two sets which in some dialects meet the requirements of the pair test are:[3]

> díffer   vs.   defér
> pérvert   vs.   pervért

Such examples establish the two extremes, STRONG /´/ and WEAK /˙/. The MEDIAL stress /`/ (grave accent) is most readily established by comparing compounds with phrases that have the same lexical units:

---

3. <u>Differ</u> and <u>defer</u> do not have the same vowel in the first syllable among many speakers, in which instance they are not a perfect minimal pair. We have in mind the following pronunciations for the pair: [dífɨr] vs. [dɪfɨr]. Likewise, although the two forms spelled <u>pervert</u> have identical vowels, in most dialects the first one does not have weak stress on the second syllable. The pair is more often pronounced [pɨrvɨrt] vs. [pɨrvɨrt] instead of [pɨrvɨrt] vs. [pɨrvɨrt]. It is probably true that a great many dialects of English have <u>no minimal contrasts at all</u> between strong and weak stress; in such dialects, there is always a difference between the phonetic quality of the vowels of the strong-stressed syllables and the phonetic quality of the vowels of the weak-stressed syllables of the contrasting items. Chapter 7 discusses this problem more fully.

Lòng Ísland vs. lóng ísland
Nèw Yórker vs. néw Yórker

These four examples can have identical pitch contours:

```
    ┌───┐ ┌──────
────┘   └─┘
```

long is   land
new   Yor ker

One of the functions served by this contour is to make the second of the two strong stresses in the right-hand column stronger than the first. Further evidence for /ˇ/ is to be seen in these examples:

White Hòuse vs. Whíte hoúse   (the house owned by the White family)

The intonation contour intended is:

```
    ┌──┐
────┘  └──────
```

White   house

Thus, the first /´/, rather than the second /´/, in White hoúse is stronger. The pattern of stress that contrasts with this one, the pattern of Whíte Hòuse, the president's residence, is the usual compounding stress sequence of English.[4] Notice:

> pláygroùnd
> bláckbòard
> chímney sweèp
> róad tèst
> ápple pòlisher
> Spánish teàcher
> trúck drìver

The other common source of medial stress in English, aside from compounds, is in polysyllabic words, which have strong and medial stress along with weak stresses in a variety of sequences:

> appréciàte
> nécessàry
> respònsibílity
> ìncompátible

The usual pattern of English disyllabic words is "strong + weak," as in happy, sorry; less frequent is "weak + strong," as in belied, attack; a relatively small number have medial stress on one of the two syllables:

---

4. The details of the contrast between strong and medial stress vary somewhat from one dialect to another; then too, speakers of English sometimes pronounce the same sequence with different stress patterns. For a fuller discussion of this point, see A. A. Hill, Introduction to Linguistic Structures (New York: Harcourt, Brace & Co., 1958), pp. 14-21.

cómbàt
élbòw
ùnkémpt
rèspéll

The distribution of stresses within any one item is different in the two languages. As we have seen, patterns of stress in English words are varied. Some instances
of minimal or near minimal pairs of words which contrast in stress involve pure vocabulary differences, such as reéfer vs. refér, bíllow vs. belów, and the like. Stress alternation may serve also to distinguish pairs of nouns and verbs, such as ínsult vs. insúlt, or
pérmit vs. permít; probably most minimal or near-minimal stress pairs are nouns and
verbs, similar to the examples we have given. In Spanish, on the other hand, the patterns
of word stress are less varied, and the minimal pairs exemplifying stress contrasts are
of different kinds. Probably the commonest source of such pairs is provided by certain
verb endings, like -o (first person singular present) and -ó (third singular preterite), or
-e (first singular present subjunctive) and -é (first singular preterite). For example:

háblo	I am speaking
habló	he spoke
háble	(that) I speak
hablé	I spoke

Spanish regularly has relatively long sequences of weak-stressed syllables uninterrupted
by strong stress. In English, there is a fairly regular alternation between syllables under
weak stress and syllables under one of the stronger stresses—thus, English prèsentátion,
Spanish presentación; English commúnicàte, Spanish comunicár. This distributional difference is further complicated by the fact that in dozens of borrowings from one language
to the other or from a common source, difficulty arises when the strong stress in Spanish
is on a syllable which is adjacent to the syllable that receives the strong stress in English—although whenever it is not on the immediately adjacent syllable, the difficulty is
much less—thus, English télephòne, Spanish teléfono, English dífficùlt, Spanish difícil;
English híppodròme, Spanish hipódromo.

PITCH CONTOURS

The rise and fall of the pitch through a phrase is important among the overriding features of the sound systems of Spanish and English.

At first glance, these phrase melodies seem to be almost infinite in number
and impossible of description and codification. However, linguistic investigations have
discovered certain important facts which make it possible to provide systematic statements about the structure of Spanish and English pitch contours.

The first important fact about the range of possibilities for pitch contours is
that it is sufficient to know the pitch at only certain points in the phrase. When the speaker chooses the pitch at these points, the variations at other points are either conditioned
or make no difference.

For Spanish we need to specify the pitch at: (1) each strong stress in the phrase; (2) the end of the phrase; and (3) the beginning of the phrase, but only if there are any weak stressed syllables before the first strong stress. Since the phrase may contain only one strong stress and may begin with it, the minimum number of points in a phrase at which pitch must be marked is two. Also, since there are apparently never more than three strong stresses in a phrase in Spanish, the maximum number of points in a phrase at which pitch must be marked is five.

The English situation is similar in that certain strong stresses, the end, and often the beginning of a phrase are places where the choice of pitch is optional; however, certain other complications are involved, to which we will return later.

The second major fact about pitch contours is that only a few pitch levels are significant. That is, at the points where the choice of pitch is optional, the speaker chooses between only a few different heights of pitch. By one type of analysis (but see footnote 2), these significant pitch levels are phonemes. English has four such significant pitch levels, and Spanish has only three. Using the lowest number for the lowest pitch, and the highest number for the highest pitch, we will number these /1/, /2/, /3/, and /4/ for English, and /1/, /2/, and /3/ for Spanish.

We also use a system to represent intonation in which the various accent marks indicating stress phonemes are placed at appropriate relative heights over the vowel, as on a musical staff. Both manners of transcription are illustrated below:

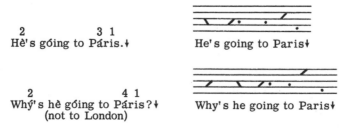

English equivalent	Spanish spelling with pitch numbers	Spanish spelling with relative height
Isn't that true?	2 22 Nó es verdád.↑	no es verdad↑
It isn't true.	2 11 Nó es verdád.↓	no es verdad↓
It isn't <u>true.</u>	2 31 Nó es verdád.↓	no es verdad↓

English examples, illustrating the use of the highest pitch level, /4/, are:

2   3 1
Hè's góing to Páris.↓   He's going to Paris↓

2   4 1
Whý's hè góing to Páris?↓   Why's he going to Paris↓
(not to London)

Besides the difference in the number of pitches—three levels in Spanish against four in English—there is an important phonetic difference that throws the two badly out of congruence. The three in Spanish are spaced closer together than the four in English, in a fashion analogous to the musical notation below.

1 2 3 4   1 2 3
  English   Spanish

TERMINAL JUNCTURES

As mentioned above (p. 19), the phenomena which characterize phrase ends are analyzed as terminal junctures. In English, the terminal junctures are three, each of which involves, in addition to other features, a different amount of slowing down in the part of the phrase preceding it.

The three terminal junctures of English are:

1. TERMINAL FALLING, symbolized by an arrow pointing downward /↓/. Its presence results in the maximum degree of slowing down. The preceding syllable diminishes rapidly in intensity, with a drop of pitch, although not a drop all the way down to the next lower phonemic pitch level.

2. TERMINAL RISING, symbolized /↑/. Its presence results in an intermediate degree of slowing down. The preceding syllable rises noticeably in pitch, with a slight increase in intensity before its final cessation.

3. TERMINAL LEVEL, symbolized /|/. Its presence results in less slowing down than for the other two terminal junctures. The occurrences of /|/ produce the effect of internal breaks or pauses <u>within</u> an utterance.[5]

All three terminal junctures are illustrated in the examples below:

Traditional punctuation	Analytic marking of stress, pitch, and juncture	Pedagogical marking of stress, pitch, and juncture
1. He decorated the girl with the flowers.	Hè décoràted the gírl 3 1 with the flówers↓	He decorated the girl with the flowers↓

This sentence is ambiguous in meaning: it can mean either that a girl was decorated with flowers as a means of decoration or that a girl identified by the fact that she had some flowers was decorated with something else.

5. Cf. George L. Trager and Henry Lee Smith, Jr., <u>Outline of English Structure</u> (Studies in Linguistics, Occasional Papers, III), Washington, 1951, pp. 44-49, where the symbols /#/, /||/ and /|/ are used for terminal falling, rising, and level, respectively.

2. He decorated the girl with the flowers.

Hè décoràted the gírl
²
with the flówers↑
³ ³

He decorated the girl with the flowers↑

This is a question containing the same ambiguity as the example above.

3. He <u>decorated</u> the girl with the <u>flowers</u>.

Hè décoràted|the gírl
² ⁴   ²   ²
with the flówers↓
³ ¹

He decorated|the girl with the flowers↓

This is no longer ambiguous: it can mean only that the girl who was identified by the fact of having flowers was decorated with something else.

4. He decorated the <u>girl</u> with the <u>flowers</u>.

Hè décoràted the gírl|
²   ⁴²
wìth the flówers↓
²   ³ ¹

He decorated the girl|with the flowers↓

Nor is this ambiguous: it can mean only that the flowers were used as the decoration that was awarded.

In Spanish, the terminal junctures are also three—definable and transcribable the same way as those of English. The problem is that they are distributed differently. Terminal level /|/ occurs much more frequently in Spanish than in English. Terminal rising /↑/ (which is shorter and faster than in English /↑/) rarely occurs except before pause, while in English it often appears internally not before pause. A sampling of data relevant to the three terminal junctures in Spanish appears below:

English equivalent	Spanish traditional spelling except for stress, pitch, and juncture	Intonation shown analytically with numbers
Is Mary coming yet?	Ya viene Maria↑	Yá viéne María↑ ² ² ²²
Are you coming yet, Mary?	Ya viene|Maria↑	Yá viéne|María↑ ² ²² ² ²²
Mary's coming now.	Ya viene Maria↓	Yá viéne María↓ ² ² ¹¹
He's coming now, Mary.	Ya viene|Maria↓	Yá viéne|María↓ ² ³ ¹ ¹ ¹¹

VOCAL QUALIFIERS

Much confusion about intonation results from the fact that there is another kind of intonation-like behavior which must be clearly separated from intonation itself. This is the system of vocal qualifiers. The criterion that justifies analyzing them as a separate system separately describable is that in any given utterance they may be present or not; they are not compulsory within the linguistic pattern; they are something added to the utterance, over and above the linguistic structure, rather than part of the structure.

The kinds of phenomena that properly fall under the category of vocal qualifiers can be observed in the differences that attach to the utterance of the single item "No" in the following sequences. Note that the differences are not stress, pitch, or juncture: these features—the intonation features—are constant. In each instance of the item "No," the pitch contour can be /21↓/ or /31↓/.

1. Has your father come in yet?
   No. (uncolored: no vocal qualifiers)
2. You know what? Ann just came back!
   No! (spoken with OPENNESS and DRAWL: surprise)
3. Please, Dad, let me take the car.
   You heard me. No! (spoken with OVERLOUDNESS: anger)
4. Well, then, did you do it after all?
   No! (spoken with CLIPPING: annoyance)
5. Didn't he give it back even then?
   No! (spoken with RASP: disgust)

Whereas any utterance in either Spanish or English must have features of stress, pitch, terminal juncture, and the usual segmental material (vowels and consonants), it may or may not have features like OVERLOUDNESS, OVERSOFTNESS, RASP, OPENNESS, OVERHIGHNESS, OVERLOWNESS, DRAWLING, CLIPPING, or any of the other features of this type—they constitute a system in themselves unobliged by what goes on in the linguistic structure.[6]

The systems of vocal qualification in English and Spanish—indeed, throughout all the languages that have for convenience been labeled "Standard Average European"—are sufficiently similar that they give the student little trouble if he masters the linguistic systems first. The difficulty with them is that they are a severe stumbling block for the teacher explaining or demonstrating intonation to his students, since he must keep them carefully separated or end in a morass of undistinguishable contours.

INTONATION PATTERNS

Each phrase—the stretch of speech bounded by terminal junctures—has an INTONATION PATTERN; The intonation pattern consists of the pitch contour of the phrase and the concluding terminal juncture. The pitch contour, as discussed above, con-

---

6. Cf. Robert P. Stockwell, J. Donald Bowen, and I. Silva-Fuenzalida, "Spanish Juncture and Intonation," Language, XXXII (1956), 641-65.

sists of a series of significant pitch levels occurring at certain points in the phrase. In both English and Spanish, these points are at the beginning of the phrase, at certain strong stresses, and before the concluding terminal juncture. In Spanish, as pointed out above, every strong stress (up to the maximum of three) is a place where the pitch level must be specified.

There are important differences between the English and the Spanish situations. In English, there is an optional choice of one strong stress to serve as the CENTER of the phrase. No strong stress after the center is a significant pitch point, unless of course it happens also to be the last syllable. In English, we may say:

2   31
Hè wórked thrée dáys.↓
2   3   1
Hè wórked thrée dáys.↓
2   3   1
Hè wórked thrée dáys.↓

The strong stress at the intonational center (the middle number) of a phrase is the most prominent syllable in the phrase. In Spanish, the last strong stress of the phrase is the most prominent, except under some special circumstances.

An intonation pattern, when being discussed as a grammatical unit in the languages, is symbolized by a root sign (√), a sequence of pitch numbers, and a terminal juncture symbol. In writing Spanish intonation patterns, four pitch numbers appear, with the first two customarily written in parentheses, since under certain conditions (e.g., no initial unstressed syllables, only one strong stress in the phrase) the first two pitches may not be present. For example, a common Spanish intonation, that of the normal, uncolored statement, is √(12)11↓. This symbolization means that the pattern has pitch level one on initial unstressed syllables in the phrase (if there are any), pitch level two on the first strong stress (if the phrase has more than one strong stress), and pitch level one on the last strong stress of the phrase and on the last syllable of the phrase; the whole pitch contour is then followed by a terminal falling juncture.

In writing English intonation patterns, three pitch numbers appear, with the first customarily written in parentheses. The pitch number in parentheses refers to whatever precedes the center of the phrase: if the intonational center comes at the beginning of the phrase, this first pitch is of course not present. For example, the normal, uncolored statement pattern of English is symbolized by √(2)31↓.

USAGE OF INTONATION PATTERNS

A. Normal (uncolored by special emphases) statements and information questions

    1.   Single-phrase utterance

        Spanish √(12)11↓:   English √(2)31↓:

```
1 2   1 1                          2         31
Había múchos↓                      Thère were lóts↓

2       1 1                        2           3   1
Sóy de Colómbia↓                   I'm from Colómbia↓

1   2    11                        2            31
Para dónde vá↓                     Whére're you góing↓

2        1 1                       2           31
Cómo se lláma↓                     Whát's your náme↓
```

    2.   Two-phrase utterance

        Spanish √(12)22 | and √(12)11↓:   English √(2)32 | and √(2)31↓:

```
2          2 2 1     2 1 1         2       3 2  2          31
El es estudiánte|del primér áno↓   Hè's a stúdent|in his fírst yéar↓

2     2 2 1 2      1 1             2        32 2     31
Qué hiciéron|allá en la fínca↓     Whát did you dó|at the fárm↓
```

B. Yes-no questions and echo-information questions

        Spanish √(12)22↑:   English √(2)33↑:

```
1 2      2 2                       2          3 3
Ustéd tiéne ótro↑                  Hàve you gót anóther↑

2     2 2                          2                33
Vá al céntro↑                      Àre you góing dòwn tówn↑

2        2 2                       2        33
Cómo se lláma↑ (after not hearing  Whát's your náme↑ (after not hearing
               the answer to this                    the answer to this
               query the first                        query the first
               time)                                  time)
```

        Spanish √(12)31 |: (alternate for yes-no questions)

```
1 2      3 1
Ustéd tiéne ótro|

2     3 1
Vá al céntro|
```

C. Emphatic or contrastive statements of information questions

        Spanish √(12)31↓:   English √(2)41↓:

```
2          1 1 2     3      1      2              31 2         4    1
Nó sóy de Chíle↓ Sóy de Colómbia↓  I'm nót from Chíle↓ I'm from Colómbia↓

2   2   21 2        3 1            3    3     31 1 2      4 1
Sábado↑ Nó↓ Hóy es domíngo↓        Sáturday↑ Nó↓ Todáy is Súnday↓

21  2 11 1     3   1               31 2 31     2    41
Sí↓ Yá sé↓ Pero cuándo↓            Yés↓ I knów↓ But whén↓
```

D. Vocative and other utterance modifiers

Spanish √(11)11↓:

2 1   1 11
Hóla│María↓

1 2   11   1   1 1
Estóy bién│muchas grácias↓

21 1 11
Sí│senór↓

English √(2)22↓:

32 2 2
Hí│Máry↓

2   32   2   2
I'm fíne│thánk yòu↓

English √(1)11↓: (alternate used only in
certain status contexts)

31 11
Yés│sír↓

E. Greetings

Spanish √(12)21↓ or √(12)31↓:

1 21
Adiós↓

2   2 1
Hásta manána↓

2   31
Buénos días↓

2 31   2 11
Qué tál↓ or Qué tál↓

English √(2)31↓ or √(2)32↑ or √322↑:

2   32   3   22
Goòd-býe↑ or Goòd-býe↑

2   3 2
Seè you tomórrow↑

2   3 1   3   2 2
Goòd mórning↓ or Goòd mórning↑

2   3 1
Hów's it góing↓

F. Listing

Spanish √(1)22↑:

1   2 2 1 22   2 2
Hay bláncas↑azúles↑vérdes↑

2 1 1
y rójas↓

English √(2)33│ or √(2)22↑:

2   33 33   33 2   31
Thèy're white│blúe│greén│and réd↓

2   22 22   22 2   31
Thèy're white↑blúe↑greén↑and réd↓

Some of the more obvious reactions that will be caused by the application of English patterns to Spanish utterances are the following. The pattern √(2)31↓ occurs on normal, uncolored utterances in English; Spanish utterances meant to be non-contrastive or normal will sound strangely insistent if uttered with the equivalent √(12)31↓ pattern, since it marks a statement as emphatic or contrastive in Spanish. If one answers the question "¿De dónde es usted?" by saying:

2   3 1
Sóy de Colómbia↓

his interrogator may well think he is irritated by the question. In the examples of Spanish questions above, the proper intonation will not come easily or naturally to an English speaker, because the correct Spanish pattern √(12)11↓ has the meaning of annoyance, disinterest, or disgust in English utterances, as in:

2   1 1
Whát's fòr dínner↓

```
2    11
Cóme ón↓

2                    11
Whát are you dóing nów↓
```

The last thing a student wants to do is to sound disinterested or disgusted: he will avoid
the familiar pattern which has that meaning for him. He must be shown the difference between the two patterns, and be assured that it is normal to say,

```
2      1  1
Sóy de Colómbia↓
```

in Spanish. Occasionally, when a student finds it difficult to master the pattern, it helps
to ask him to say it as if he were a little angry. Then he may be assured that he is not
sounding angry in Spanish; Spanish speakers show anger (as we also do) by adding the vocal qualifiers of overloudness, rasp, overhigh pitch, and/or others.

When a student wants emphasis in Spanish, he will likely have the /3/ in the
pattern √(12)31↓ too high, using the English pattern √(2)41↓. This will sound strange but
will not be misunderstood.

In yes-no questions, the terminal pitch of the Spanish pattern √(1)222↑ will
likely be too high, influenced by the similar English pattern √(2)33↑. This will sound
overemphatic. Thus,

```
2      2  2
Nó tiéne ótro↑
```

would translate Don't you have another? but

```
2      3  3
Nó tiéne ótro↑
```

would be Don't you even have another?

English students will have a strong tendency to avoid the Spanish vocative and
utterance-modifier pattern √(1)11↓ as being too servile. The utterances

```
31  11
Yés|sír↓

31  1   1
Nó|thánk yòu↓
```

are normal under certain circumstances (the first, for example, when a private standing
at attention replies to an officer), but are considered highly inappropriate in situations
where there is no comparable status relationship; they would then be considered curt,
abrupt, discourteous. An appropriate polite pattern of English is the one seen below:

```
33   2    2
Nó|thánk yòu↑

3    2  2      22
Cértainly|Mìster Smíth↑
```

A student who wants to avoid the impression of brusqueness also avoids the √(11)11↓ pattern and substitutes the polite English pattern. He must be assured it is normal to say,

```
21 1 11
Sí|sènór↓
```

in Spanish. As in the instance of the √(12)11↓ pattern, it may be useful to help him master the pattern by suggesting that he say it as if he were annoyed. When he gets it right, he may be assured that it does not express annoyance in Spanish.

Greetings are also a problem to most students, who want to be especially polite when using them. Although the √(12)31↓ pattern is not inappropriate on some salutations as

$$
\begin{array}{cc}
2 & 31 \\
\end{array}
$$
Buénos días↓

it is rarely found on leave-takings, where the customary pattern is

$$
\begin{array}{cc}
1 & 21 \\
\end{array}
$$
Adiós↓

and, of course, the regular English patterns

$$
\begin{array}{cccc}
2 & 32 & 3 & 22 \\
\end{array}
$$
Gòod-býe↑ or Gòod-býe↑

sound sing-songy and unnatural when applied to "Adiós," and must by all means be avoided.

The listing intonations are sufficiently similar not to cause any special difficulties; the different analyses (Spanish √(12)22↑ and English √(2)22↑) are adopted because of considerations of the internal consistencies of two different language systems rather than because of the phonetic difference in this situation.

EMPHASIS

Many of the details of English intonation which must be avoided in Spanish concern EMPHASIS. One of these is the fact that the location of the center of an intonation pattern is an optional choice. Whenever we wish to point out a contrast, we put the center at the point that will show this.

$$
\begin{array}{ccc}
2 & 3 & 1 \\
\end{array}
$$
Hè's a fírst-yéar stúdent. (that is, not second or third.)

This mechanism has no regular counterpart in Spanish.

Furthermore, in a contrast-showing situation, words which do not ordinarily receive a strong stress may receive a strong stress and also be made the center of the intonation pattern. (In the examples cited here, the syllable at the center is underlined. In Spanish examples, we underline the syllable which, obligatorily, is the most prominent. Pitch-level numbers are not shown, since any of several pitch contours might be used to express the contrast.)

Do you wánt a róom wíth méals|or withóut méals?↓
Quiére un cuárto con comídas|o sin comídas?↓

Spanish only rarely puts a special stress on con or sin, whereas English must stress the prepositions if they appear in contrast, as above.

To represent in Spanish the contrast of

Thát ìsn't mý wórk|ìt's hís↓

we must recast the sentence:

Ése trabájo nó es <u>mío</u>| es <u>súyo</u>↓

Spanish does not have sentences like:

*Nó es <u>mí</u> trabájo| es <u>súyo</u>↓

(When we wish to discuss sounds or groups of sounds, words or groups of words, which do not actually occur in a language, we adopt the linguists' convention of marking them with an asterisk *.)

Similarly,

<u>Hé's</u> a <u>fírst</u>-yéar stúdent| and <u>shé's</u> a <u>thírd</u>-year student↓

may be mistranslated by the unwary as:

*<u>Él</u> es estudiánte del pri<u>mér</u> áño| y <u>é</u>lla del ter<u>cér</u> áno↓

Rather, it should be:

Él es estudiánte del primér <u>á</u>ño| y élla del tercér <u>á</u>ño↓

An additional habit of emphasis not used in Spanish is the shift of the center of intonation to a different syllable of a word when pointing out a contrast. For instance, a word like disad<u>ván</u>tage may become <u>dís</u>advantage.

It was bóth an ad<u>ván</u>tage| and a <u>dís</u>advàntage↓

Compare the Spanish sentence

Tódos tiénen sus ven<u>tá</u>jas| y desven<u>tá</u>jas↓

It is not normally altered to have a contrastive stress on <u>des</u>-:

*Tódos tiénen sus ven<u>tá</u>jas| y <u>dés</u>ventajas↓

RHYTHM

There are certain correlations that pitch, stress, and terminal juncture have with vowels and consonants. These correlations are different in English and Spanish, with the result that they produce totally different rhythmic effects. The most important of these is that syllable length in Spanish is not correlated with stress in the same way it is in English. The unit of tempo in Spanish is the SYLLABLE; the unit of tempo in English is the STRESS GROUP. The rhythm of an English sentence may be represented graphically, the length of underline indicating syllable duration.

What do you think he'll do?
<u>   </u> <u> </u> <u> </u> <u>   </u>   <u>   </u>

The same sentence pronounced with Spanish rhythm would be rather more like this:

What do you think he'll do?
<u> </u> <u> </u> <u> </u> <u> </u> <u> </u> <u>   </u>

In Spanish, then, syllables are not regularly longer simply because they are under a strong stress or at the center of an intonation pattern; in English they are. To drawl an English strong stressed syllable at the center requires that it be considerably lengthened, since it will normally be longer than the other syllables of the phrase anyway. To drawl the most prominent syllable in a Spanish phrase requires far less actual length before one must recognize the presence of a vocal qualifier. Suppose we compare the pronunciation of these two sentences, listening only for relative syllable length of <u>dos</u> vs. <u>dose</u>.

$$\begin{array}{cc} 2 & 31 \\ \text{Tiéne dós}\!\downarrow \end{array}$$

$$\begin{array}{cc} 2 & 31 \\ \text{Táke a dóse}\!\downarrow \end{array}$$

In the Spanish sentence, <u>dos</u> is short—noticeably shorter than <u>dose</u> in the English sentence. If the Spanish sentence is drawled, the item <u>dos</u> comes out approximately as long as <u>dose</u> in the undrawled English sentence. If then the English sentence is spoken with drawl, <u>dose</u> is substantially longer than <u>dos</u> can be in any normal Spanish manner of speaking the sentence. The ear of an English-speaking student, accustomed to correlating weaker stresses with shorter syllables, will receive the impression of machine-gun-like rapidity from hearing Spanish. This is simply because of the relative regularity of syllable length—the fact that one syllable comes at him right after another at what is to him a disconcerting speed. He misses the rather long English stressed syllables that give him a chance, as it were, to catch up.

THE ARTICULATION
OF CONSONANTS
AND VOWELS

4

The description of the sounds of a language falls most naturally into two parts: that covered by Chapter 3; and the rest, consisting of the vowels and consonants and certain boundary elements involving the vowels and consonants. These three types of sounds—vowels, consonants, and boundary elements—grouped together, are referred to as SEGMENTAL ELEMENTS. In arriving at a description of them for the purpose of comparing Spanish and English (or any other pair of languages), a phonetic frame of reference is necessary.

The most usual point of departure for such a description is the ARTICULATORY BASIS of the sounds—the way they are formed—which is in point of fact a part of physiology. The convenience of formulating terminology on this basis stems from the fact that it yields a reasonably simple set of terms for the objective discussion of differences among human speech sounds.[1] In addition, we can become sufficiently conscious of the similar articulatory equipment that each of us carries inside his head, so that we can easily compare notes and check observations.

CONSONANTS

The articulation of consonants can be described, and a given consonant can be reasonably well identified, by the use of four principal dimensions:

1. THE ARTICULATORS

Articulators are the doers of articulation, so to speak: the organs and parts of organs that move freely enough to be active in speech. One articulator is the LOWER LIP, which can be moved toward or away from the upper lip and upper teeth, as in producing p, b, m, f, v, the initial sounds of pit, bit, mit, fit, very. Another is the TONGUE, which is extremely versatile; for our purposes, at least three parts of the tongue are important—

---

1. Other bases of description are sometimes used, such as the auditory impressionism of terms like "heavy," "sharp," "muffled," and the like. The past few years have seen rapid developments of the ACOUSTIC basis, which promises to contribute greatly to the understanding of speech sounds; but the terminology growing out of the development, although in certain respects potentially superior to that of the articulatory basis, is not yet as simple or as widely used.

tip, middle, and back. The tip can articulate freely in the area of the teeth and for a considerable distance behind the upper teeth. The initial sounds of <u>thin</u>, <u>then</u>, <u>tin</u>, <u>din</u>, <u>line</u>, and <u>nine</u> are tongue-tip articulations. The middle of the tongue—the area behind the tip extending back about three-quarters of an inch—usually articulates farther back of the upper teeth. The initial sounds of <u>sin</u>, <u>chin</u>, and <u>join</u> are predominantly middle-tongue articulations, although in some articulations of these items the tongue tip may participate or even predominate. The back of the tongue is utilized in the initial sounds of <u>goal</u> and <u>coal</u>. It is clear that the tongue and lower lip are the most important articulators. There are, however, other articulators; for example, the vocal cords, the two flaps of tissue in the Adam's apple which are responsible for voicing (see p. 37), may be closed to make the catch in the throat of items like <u>uh</u>-<u>uh</u> or <u>oh</u>-<u>oh</u>.

2. THE POINTS OF ARTICULATION

Clearly, any point in the mouth that can be reached by an articulator can, in theory, be used as a point of articulation. Proceeding from the front of the mouth to the back, the most frequently used points of articulation are: the upper lip—as in the initial sounds of <u>pill</u>, <u>bill</u>, <u>mill</u>; the lower edge of the upper front teeth, with the lower lip as articulator—the initial sounds of <u>fan</u>, <u>van</u>; the area at the cutting edge of the upper and lower front teeth, with tongue tip as articulator—the initial sounds of <u>thin</u>, <u>then</u>; the back side of the upper front teeth—in the Spanish articulation of the initial sounds in <u>tiene</u>, <u>dos</u>; the gum ridge (the alveolar ridge) behind the upper front teeth—the initial sounds of English <u>ten</u>, <u>den</u>, <u>sin</u>, <u>let</u>, <u>nine</u>, <u>chin</u>, <u>join</u>; the hard palate—the initial sounds of <u>kill</u>, <u>gill</u>; and the soft palate (velum)—in the initial sounds of <u>coal</u>, <u>goal</u>. We need not consider, for our purposes, the possibility of articulation farther back in the mouth, but for other languages (e.g., Arabic, Tagalog) we would need to.

3. MANNER OF ARTICULATION

The different manners of articulation are somewhat more difficult to grasp than are the articulators and points of articulation. Essentially they are of two types: those in which the air flow is stopped momentarily, and those in which the air flow is impeded or restricted in some way without actually being stopped. The basic dichotomy is therefore between STOPS and CONTINUANTS. The stops include the initial sounds of <u>pill</u>, <u>bill</u> (stopped at the lips—BI-LABIAL stops), <u>till</u>, <u>dill</u> (stopped at the teeth or alveolar ridge—DENTAL or ALVEOLAR stops), <u>coal</u>, <u>goal</u> (stopped at the velum—VELAR stops). Note that POINT OF ARTICULATION was used in the parentheses above to classify the stop types. It is equally possible to use the ARTICULATOR: labial stops, apical (tongue-tip) stops, dorsal (back-of-tongue) stops. Or, to be absolutely precise, they can be combined: bilabial stops, apico-dental stops, apico-alveolar stops, dorso-palatal stops, dorso-velar stops, and so on. There is no uniform practice in terminology: one describes a sound to the degree of precision that is useful and necessary in a particular discussion for a particular purpose. We will return to this question of precision after we have looked somewhat further into the terminological possibilities of articulatory description.

CONTINUANTS are of various kinds. Continuants produced with friction are called FRICATIVES or SPIRANTS. Instead of stopping the flow of air up from the lungs, it is possible to squeeze it at some point so that it is forced to flow rapidly through a small area. The effect is much the same as that which occurs when a broad river is forced through a narrow channel: <u>rapids</u> are generated by friction between the water and the surfaces over and through which it is passing. Typical fricatives are heard in the initial sounds of <u>fan</u>, <u>van</u>, <u>seal</u>, <u>zeal</u>, <u>shill</u>. Since more than one type of fricative may be produced at the same point of articulation by the same articulator, we must distinguish between at least two types: SLIT FRICATIVES, and GROOVE FRICATIVES. Slit fricatives are those in which the air column is squeezed through a slit opening—relatively broad from side to side, but narrow from top to bottom. Slit fricatives include the initial sounds of <u>fan</u>, <u>van</u>, <u>thigh</u>, <u>thy</u>, and the jota of Spanish <u>gila</u>, <u>Jaime</u>. Groove fricatives are those in which the air column is squeezed through a more or less rounded opening formed by a trough in the tongue. Groove fricatives include the initial sound of <u>seal</u>, <u>zeal</u>, <u>she</u>, <u>genre</u>, and the Spanish <u>s</u>, particularly the Castilian variety of <u>s</u> heard in <u>sí</u>, <u>será</u>.

The other classes of continuants in English and Spanish are not so numerous as the fricatives. They include the LATERAL CONTINUANTS, in which the air is forced around one side, or both sides, of the tongue, as in the initial sound of <u>let</u>; the NASAL CONTINUANTS, in which the air column is closed off at some point in the mouth and allowed to pass through the nose, as in the initial sounds of <u>me</u> and <u>knee</u>; the RETROFLEX CONTINUANTS, in which the air column is forced over and around a hump in the tongue, as in the initial sound of <u>run</u>, <u>rear</u>; and the VIBRANTS, in which the air column is interrupted by a rapid motion of the tongue across it, as in the TRILL <u>rr</u> of Spanish <u>perro</u> (two or more interruptions) or the FLAP <u>r</u> sound of Spanish <u>pero</u> (a one-tap interruption).

The semivowels, such as the English <u>y</u> sound of <u>yes</u> or the <u>w</u> sound of <u>win</u>, are a special type of continuant. As their name suggests, they are in some respects closer to vowels; they are explained again below under vowels (pp. 88 ff.).

Finally, there are sounds which combine the beginning of a stop with the ending of a fricative. Any given sound may be divided into three phases; ONSET, HOLD, and RELEASE, corresponding to beginning, middle, and end. In the type of articulation known as an AFFRICATE, the onset and hold are as in a stop but the release is as in a fricative. Thus, the initial sound of <u>chill</u> begins like the <u>t</u> of <u>till</u>, but ends like the <u>sh</u> of <u>shill</u>. Other affricates include the initial sound of <u>Jill</u>, German <u>pferd</u>, <u>zwei</u>, and the like.

4. VOICING

When the vocal cords vibrate during the articulation of a sound, the sound is said to be VOICED. When the vocal cords do not vibrate during a sound, it is said to be VOICELESS. This difference can easily be heard by covering the ears and saying the initial sound of <u>seal</u>, <u>sssss</u>, and then the initial sound of <u>zeal</u>, <u>zzzzz</u>. In the latter instance, a distinct buzzing should be noted, which is absent in the former instance.

One other aspect of articulation needs to be noted before charting the symbols that we will use for consonants. This is the question of relative FORCE of articulation. If, in a given articulation, the muscular tension is considerable and a substantial measure of lung pressure is used, the sound is said to be FORTIS. The initial sounds of <u>pill</u>, <u>till</u>, <u>kill</u>, fill, sill, and shill are fortis in English. If the muscular tension and lung pressure are relatively relaxed and unforced, the sound is said to be LENIS. The initial sounds of bill, dill, gill, very, and zeal are LENIS in English. It is generally true in English that voiced consonants are lenis, voiceless consonants are fortis; but this is a habit in English, not an articulatory necessity.

Given a repertory of terms like the ones that have been introduced and briefly discussed above, it is possible to achieve varying degrees of precision in describing consonants. We may, if necessary, be extremely precise: the initial sound of English tool may be described as a "voiceless fortis aspirated (i.e., having a puff of air during release) apico-alveolar stop," or it may be described simply in terms of the three features of its articulation that are critical in distinguishing it from other English consonants: "voiceless alveolar stop," or (equally well) "voiceless apical stop." In either instance, it is inconvenient to repeat such heavy terminology often—we need abbreviations. The abbreviations are PHONETIC SYMBOLS. These symbols usually look like letters of the alphabet which have in some instances been modified in order to get additional symbols. The only significant difference between using these symbols in alphabetical writing and using them in phonetic writing is that a symbol in the former usage may mean many things (compare the values of ough in tough, though, through, hiccough, cough), or, conversely, several symbols may be used for the same sound (compare b and v in tubo and tuvo, cabo and cavo); but in phonetic usage they have a consistent, fixed, explicitly defined value in any one discussion.

Figure 1 presents the symbols for consonants that we have used in the subsequent discussion. It is extremely important that the precise meaning of each symbol be understood by anyone reading further in this book; the chart should be studied in terms of the general discussion of consonants in the preceding pages. It should also be noted that our symbols are not necessarily those of the International Phonetic Association or of any single American tradition. On the phonetic level, symbols can be chosen pretty much in terms of printing and/or typing convenience. In our opinion, there can be no legitimate criticism of any given set of symbols which meet the following criteria: (1) precise definition of each symbol in terms of all the intersecting categories which it represents; (2) consistency of signification of a given symbol throughout the system; (3) relative simplicity and/or familiarity in the shape of the symbols.

The symbols in Figure 1 can be modified by various diacritic markings to indicate finer shades of phonetic differentiation. For example, [y] with heavy palatal friction can be marked [y̆]; [w] with velar friction [w̆]; the aspiration of initial [p], [t], and [k] in English [p^h], [t^h], and [k^h]; all the items placed in the DENTAL column are marked by a fronting diacritic placed after the basic alveolar symbol [t$^<$]; symbols for voiced consonants may be shown as voiceless or semivoiced (meaning occasional loss of voicing in the course of pronunciation) by the addition of the symbol [˷] under the letter: [d̨], [b̨], and so on. Consonants are normally non-syllabic—that is, they do not constitute the nucleus of a syllable. Sometimes, however, a continuant is syllabic—for example, the final sound of English hidden. A syllabic continuant is symbolized by the appropriate consonant letter with a small circle beneath it—for example, [n̥].

Figure 1. POINT OF ARTICULATION

MANNER OF ARTICULATION	Lips (labial)	Lips-teeth (labio-dental)	Between teeth (interdental)	Teeth (dental)	Alveolar ridge (alveolar)	Hard palate (palatal)	Soft palate (velar)	Glottis (glottal)
Stops	p b			t< d<	t d		k g	?
Slit fricatives*	ꝑ ƀ	f v	ş đ				h g	h
Groove fricatives				s< z<	s z	š ž		
Retroflex					ɹ			
Affricates						ch ǰ		
Nasals	m	ɱ		n<	n	ny / ṇ	ŋ	
Laterals				1<	l	(l)y		
Vibrants					r rr / ṭ			
Semivowels	(w)					y	w	
	Lower lip		Tip and/or middle of tongue				Back of tongue	Glottal bands

Symbols in the left half of a box are voiceless, those in the right half voiced.

Other than [h], a superscript symbol represents weak pronunciation of a sound.

*The term fricative is interchangeable with the term spirant.

VOWELS

The description of the articulation of VOWELS is simpler than that of consonants with respect to the number of dimensions needed to classify them, but it is more complex in that many persons find these categories more difficult to understand than such categories as stop or fricative.

The essential fact about the articulation of vowels which differentiates them from consonants is that when a vowel is produced, the air column is neither stopped nor squeezed, nor is the flow of air in any way hindered, whereas all consonants are produced by some kind of interference in the air column. For this reason it is more difficult to become aware, kinesthetically, of what the tongue is doing to produce vocalic differences.

The quality of vowels can be described with reasonable accuracy by two basic dimensions; the HIGH-LOW, and the FRONT-BACK. The HIGH-LOW dimension refers to how close the tongue is to the roof of the mouth—that is, how high or low in the mouth it is. For example, the vowel of pit is higher than the vowel of pot. The FRONT-BACK dimension refers to where, for the production of a given vowel, the air passage between the tongue and the roof of the mouth is narrowest. For example, the vowel of <u>pit</u> is farther front ("fronter") than the vowel of <u>put</u>. These two dimensions are illustrated in Figure 2.

Figure 2

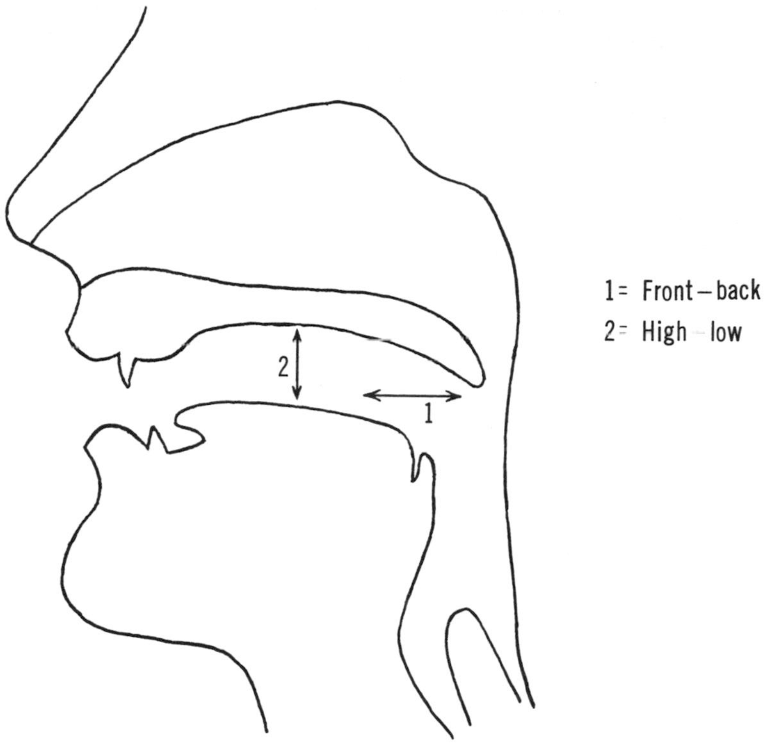

1= Front – back
2= High – low

        A useful chart of vowel differences can be constructed by dividing both the <u>front</u>-<u>back</u> and <u>high</u>-<u>low</u> dimensions into three segments each:

Front-Back (1)

Front	Central	Back

High-Low (2)

High
Mid
Low

Combined into a single chart, these appear:

	Front	Central	Back
High			
Mid			
Low			

It will, however, develop that we will need to divide up some of these categories into smaller categories. All the vowel qualities that will be needed for discussion in this study are shown in the chart below, with the symbols we are using for them.

	Front	Central	Back
High	i ɪ	ɨ	ʋ u
Mid	e ɛ	ʌ	o
Low	æ	a	ɔ

The value of each symbol is most readily remembered through a key word:

[i]	si	(Spanish)
[ɪ]	sit	(English)
[e]	se	(Spanish)
[ɛ]	set	(English)
[æ]	sat	(English)
[a]	sot	(English), sala (Spanish)
[ʌ]	shut	(English)
[ɨ]	. . .	
[u]	su	(Spanish)
[ʋ]	soot, foot	(English)
[o]	lo	(Spanish)
[ɔ]	sought	(English)

The one symbol above for which no example was cited needs special comment. [ɨ] is frequent in English weak-stressed syllables: rose̱s, hit 'em, hurried pronunciation of ju̱st a minu̱te, and so on, but it is rare in syllables under strong stress.

Besides the two principal dimensions—high-low and front-back—probably the most important additional dimension is that connected with the rounding or spreading of the lips. This is not an important dimension for English and Spanish, however, since back vowels are all rounded in both languages (but more so in Spanish than in English), and front and central vowels are all unrounded (spread). Another dimension of some value is TENSE-LAX, corresponding to fortis-lenis among consonants. A tense vowel is articulated with greater muscular tension of the tongue than the corresponding lax vowel. For example, the vowels [i, e, u] are usually tense, whereas the vowels [ɪ, ε, ʋ] are usually lax.

Vowels are normally syllabic—that is, they constitute the nucleus of a syllable. Sometimes, however, a vowel is non-syllabic—for example, the u̲ sound in Spanish causa. A non-syllabic vowel is symbolized by the appropriate vowel letter with a small arc beneath it—for example, [u̯] indicates only a glide—that is, a movement of the tongue toward the position symbolized by the vowel letter. Non-syllabic vowels and glides are often called semivowels, and may be represented by consonant letters such as [y] and [w]. Since semivowels sometimes have consonantal features such as friction noise and since semivowel phonemes in a given language may have a distribution similar to that of consonants, they were listed among the consonants of Figure 1.

BOUNDARY ELEMENTS WITHIN A PHRASE

The difference between the pronunciations of night rate and nitrate, as said by many speakers of English, consists not in differences in which vowel and consonant phonemes occur, but rather in the ways of passing from one of them to the next.

In careful listening to differences of this sort, listeners often have the impression of a momentary hesitation in certain forms (night rate, beeline) not present in others (nitrate, feline). This apparent brief hesitation in night rate and beeline is called a BOUNDARY ELEMENT or OPEN TRANSITION. Below are further pairs which, in the pronunciation of many speakers, illustrate this contrast between presence and absence of the boundary element.

showcase	locate	daylight	halite
ore trade	portrait	door fee	morphine
carbarn	carbon	seesaw	Esau
		indoor	Endor

The words which are intended to illustrate the absence of the boundary element may sometimes be said with it, especially when someone is striving for clarity of pronunciation. Most speakers of English should find that at least some of our examples do illustrate the contrast in their speech.

The name BOUNDARY ELEMENT is used because this phenomenon occurs mostly at the boundaries of words or between important parts of words. The name OPEN TRANSITION indicates that the sounds on each side of this element seem not so closely connected to each other as two adjacent segmental elements usually are.

In our phonemic transcription, the boundary element is written either by leaving a space between adjacent symbols for vowels or consonants or by the symbol /+/.[2]

There are also boundary-element phenomena in Spanish which constitute a Spanish phoneme /+/. However, compared to the situation in English, Spanish makes much less use of its boundary element; the listener's perception of word boundaries is much more dependent on context. Little consideration is given in this book to the Spanish use of /+/, since the details are neither clear nor unarguable; nor is the question of boundary elements within phrases important to pedagogy. A few discussions have been published elsewhere.[3]

TRANSCRIPTION

No <u>absolute science</u> of articulatory phonetics exists, and the accuracy of a phonetic transcription depends on the experience and skill of the transcriber. Even two experts will rarely, if ever, agree on all the details of such a transcription. But if they are linguists as well as phoneticians they know that it is not important for them to agree on all details; the differences are resolvable by the technique of PHONEMIC ANALYSIS, which by the pair-test systematically seeks out the significant contrasts in the sound system of the language. The subsequent discussion will confine itself to these contrasts as they are analyzed for the two languages in question, dipping below the phonemic level only to get at specific problems; but the PHONEMES thus discussed are rooted in PHONETICS, for which at least the above minimal frame of reference is needed. In accord with now well-established procedure, PHONEMIC TRANSCRIPTION is placed within diagonals: /#/; it is given for English only to make special points. Otherwise we have assumed that the pronunciation of the English items by the reader will be close enough to our own to make the point clear. PHONETIC TRANSCRIPTION is placed within square brackets: [#]. In no instance is our phonetic transcription closely refined: it is precise enough not to mislead, broad enough to be interpreted easily. For all Spanish items we have cited either a phonetic or phonemic transcription—sometimes one, sometimes the other, sometimes both, depending on the point in question. Still a third kind of transcription—a MODIFIED PHONEMIC FOR PEDAGOGICAL PURPOSES—will be discussed in the Appendix.

---

2. Other names for the phenomenon are "internal open juncture" and "plus juncture," the latter from the symbol sometimes used to write it.

3. Cf. Robert P. Stockwell, J. Donald Bowen, and I. Silva-Fuenzalida, "Spanish Juncture and Intonation," <u>Language</u> XXXII (1956), 641-65.

THE CONSONANT SYSTEMS OF SPANISH AND ENGLISH

The complete consonant structure of each of the two languages will be stated (pp. 116-17) after the details of each have been examined for the problems which they create in the classroom. For comparative purposes, the consonants may be divided into two groups: (1) Those which easily lead to misunderstanding whenever the most nearly similar English consonant is transferred to replace a Spanish consonant; and (2) those which produce a heavy foreign accent, but are understandable, when so transferred.

In the discussion of these points, illustrations are frequently given in the form of lists of similar-sounding Spanish and English words. The manner of using such lists in teaching will be discussed hereafter in the Appendix. The English items in the left-hand column, it should be remembered, are not translations (no translations are given—they are not pertinent to the problem of pronunciation). They are simply <u>similar-sounding</u> English words which represent the kinds of English sequences that cause the Spanish items of the right-hand column to be mispronounced.

SPANISH CONSONANTS WHOSE MISPRONUNCIATION BY ENGLISH INFLUENCE CAN CAUSE MISUNDERSTANDING—/d/

The first of these is the consonant spelled <u>d</u>, which is also the phoneme /d/. This phoneme has three principal variants (allophones) in Spanish. One of these is [d^ʿ], which will be pronounced [d] by English speakers: slight accent, but no misunderstanding. A second is [đ], which also exists in English, but is unrelated to the /d/ phoneme: it is a different phoneme in contrast with /d/, as in <u>den</u>, <u>then</u> (phonemically, /dén/-/đén/). A third allophone is [ḍ], occurring only in final position. The English speaker's problem is to redistribute his /d/ and /đ/ so that they occur in limited positions not in contrast, in accord with the pattern of Spanish. This pattern is to pronounce [d^ʿ] after pause, after /n/, after /l/, and after a boundary element, as in:

[díle]	dile
[dónde]	donde
[fálda]	falda

44

but to pronounce [d] in all other internal positions, irrespective of word boundaries (word boundaries are only rarely marked by boundary elements),

[ládo]	lado
[dedonde]	de donde

and to pronounce [d] in final positions (i.e., before a boundary element or pause):

[ustéd]	usted
[berdad]	verdad

Put another way, the choice of [d] vs. [d] is optional in English but obligatory in Spanish. Two /d/ phonemes in two successive Spanish syllables may sound to the speaker of English quite different from each other, in accord with the distribution stated above, and still be identified as the "same" sound by speakers of Spanish. Note the lists below, which contain items from both languages where /d/ phonemes appear in a sequence of syllables but are phonetically quite different:

English	Spanish	
daddy	[dádo]	dado
deader	[dédo]	dedo
doddering	[dormído]	dormido
doodle	[dolído]	dolido

Misunderstanding most easily arises in the Spanish environment /CV́dV/, phonetically [CV́dV]—that is, a two-syllable sequence with /d/ initial in the second syllable and the strong stress on the first syllable. The English speaker will tend to use the /d/ of shudder, daddy, ladder, and this /d/ will be misunderstood as the Spanish /r/. Thus, the words of the first column below will be heard as if they were those of the second column if the English speaker uses his own /d/ instead of the correct [d]:

1.		2.	
[tódo]	todo	[tóro]	toro
[káda]	cada	[kára]	cara
[óda]	oda	[óra]	hora
[séda]	seda	[séra]	sera
[módo]	modo	[móro]	moro
[mída]	mida	[míra]	mira
[pída]	pida	[píra]	pira
[lódo]	lodo	[lóro]	loro
[kódo]	codo	[kóro]	coro
[múdo]	mudo	[múro]	muro
[áda]	hada	[ára]	ara
[padeşér]	padecer	[pareşér]	parecer

Actually, the distinction between [d] and [r] is not difficult either to hear or to imitate, in a contrast paired off as above, but the tendency to use the English [d] where the Spanish [d] belongs is reinforced by the writing system and by the American's thoroughly conditioned habits acquired through years of speaking and reading English. At this point the Spanish writing system, in many ways one of the best in the world, for pedagogical purposes among English speakers does more harm than good.

Some sequences in which /d/ participates are markedly unlike in the two languages. In the sequence /V́dVn/, English speakers have phonetically [Vd⌐n̥] (phonemically /Vd+n/) as compared with Spanish [VdVn]. The English /d/ is released nasally, the tongue tip remaining in position for the syllabic /n/.

English		Spanish	
[ɔ́ɹd⌐n+l]	ordinal	[órdenes]	órdenes
[spíyd⌐n̥]	speedin'	[píden]	piden
[wɔ́ɹd⌐n̥]	warden	[gwárdan]	guardan
[áɹd⌐n̥]	Arden	[árden]	arden

Similarly, the sequence /V́dVl/ gives [Vd⌐l̥] (phonemically /Vd+l/) in English, the [d] having only a lateral, not a tongue tip, release; as against [VdVl] in Spanish, with full apical release of the /d/.

English		Spanish	
[bád⌐l+y]	bodily	[badelía]	badelía
[ríd⌐lɹ]	riddler	[rredolór]	redolor
[réd⌐l+nt]	redolent	[rredolénte]	redolente

So much for the major problems that arise from the differences between Spanish /d/ and English /d/. A few further phonetic refinements may be noted.

The stop allophone of Spanish /d/, which is dental [d⌐] as in donde, is not only articulated farther forward than the English alveolar /d/ but is also more lenis: it is not released as forcefully.

The voiced spirant allophone of Spanish /d/, which is the inter-dental or post-dental [đ] as in lado, sido, differs from the [đ] of English father, either, bathe, in being considerably more lenis and farther back. In final position, in free variation with the voiced spirant, the voiceless allophone [đ̥] is so lenis in many dialects that it disappears altogether: usted becomes [usté]; the voiced allophone may disappear medially, but in dialects where the slightest trace of it remains it carries the entire functional load of distinguishing certain items from others, as in the lists below:

[púa]	púa	[púđa]	puda
[mía]	mía	[míđa]	mida
[bóa]	boa	[bóđa]	boda
[ka(l)yáo]	Callao	[ka(l)yáđo]	callado
[béa]	vea	[béđa]	veda
[kréo]	creo	[kréđo]	credo
[pío]	pío	[píđo]	pido
[séa]	sea	[séđa]	seda
[lewéle]	le huele	[leđwéle]	le duele

The same is true of the voiceless allophone:

[sé]	sé	[séd̪]	sed
[rré]	re	[rréd̪]	red

One of the interesting consequences of the extremely lenis articulation of the Spanish [d̪] is that in learning English many Spanish speakers say words like father, mother, with such a lenis [d] that they sound almost as though the speakers were under the influence of alcohol. It is possible to take advantage of this fact by suggesting to Americans whose [d] is too fortis in Spanish that they should weaken it somewhat as if they were saying father in a drunken fashion: [fáᵈɨɹ].

SPANISH CONSONANTS WHOSE MISPRONUNCIATION
BY ENGLISH INFLUENCE CAN CAUSE
MISUNDERSTANDING — /b/

Like the Spanish /d/, the /b/ appears in three variants: a stop [b] identical with that of English; a bilabial spirant [ƀ] (this is most likely to be heard by an English speaker either as [v] or as [w], the latter especially when /b/ is between vowels the second of which is /o/ or /u/, since the rounding of the vowel will be anticipated); and a voiceless spirant [ƀ̥] in the rare instances when it is in final position. The pattern of the distribution of the variants of /b/ is similar to that of the /d/; [b] is pronounced after pause, after [m] and after a boundary element, but [ƀ] occurs in all other positions except absolute final: compare [bómba] bomba with [káƀo] cabo and [álƀa] alba. In some dialects, [b] occurs after [l] instead of [ƀ]: [álba]. English [b] thus occurs in several positions where only [ƀ] can occur in Spanish: compare [béƀe] bebe with baby.

Since [ƀ] and [ƀ̥] do not exist at all in English, the English speaker's problem is learning to produce these sounds so that they even reasonably approximate the Spanish ones. He will frequently try substituting a [w] for [ƀ], and since there are numerous minimal contrasts between [ƀ] and [w] in Spanish, the substitution is not satisfactory:

[áƀa]	haba	[áwa]	agua
[náƀas]	nabas, navas	[náwas]	naguas
[léƀa]	leva	[léwa]	legua
[aƀánte]	avante	[awánte]	aguante
[unaƀélga]	una belga	[unawélga]	una huelga
[ésteƀéso]	este beso	[éstewéso]	este hueso
[unaƀéka]	una beca	[unawéka]	una hueca

Failing this substitution, the English speaker may be led, either by the spelling system or by misinformation from a Spanish speaker who acquired it from the spelling system and hypercorrection in his own school system, to try a contrast between his own /b/ and /v/. There is of course absolutely no correlation between the occurrence of [b] and [ƀ] in Spanish and the occurrence of b and v in the spelling system beyond the fact that b and v represent any variant of the /b/ phoneme, so that the pairs of words below are pronounced exactly alike:

baca	vaca	cabo	cavo
barón	varón	Cuba	cuva
basta	vasta	tubo	tuvo

The [v] sound is alien to Spanish phonological structure except as a syllable-final variant of /f/ preceding a voiced consonant, and should be avoided even though it will not produce misunderstanding.

Finally, the [ƀ] is often quite lenis, and may not be heard at all by the English speaker. He may try to drop it altogether, especially between vowels, and again the result is unsatisfactory because of the minimal contrasts that exist:

[bóa]	boa	[bóƀa]	boba
[lóa]	loa	[lóƀa]	loba
[búa]	bua	[búƀa]	búba
[kúo]	cúo	[kúƀo]	cubo
[día]	día	[díƀa]	diva
[ausár]	ahusar	[aƀusár]	abusar
[salía]	salía	[salíƀa]	saliva
[pulikaría]	pulicaría	[puƀlikaría]	publicaría
[dóndestáustéḍ]	Dónde está usted?	[dóndestáƀaustéḍ]	Dónde estába ustéd?

SPANISH CONSONANTS WHOSE MISPRONUNCIATION BY ENGLISH INFLUENCE CAN CAUSE MISUNDERSTANDING—/g/

Since language is structured, we may expect, from our knowledge of the facts about /b/ and /d/, that /g/ in Spanish will be remarkably similar. There are two variants: a stop [g], and a spirant [g̃]. The stop appears after pause, after /n/ (which will be phonetically [ŋ]), and after a boundary element; the spirant appears elsewhere: compare [gáŋga] ganga with [ág̃o] hago and [sálg̃o] sálgo. English [g] appears in positions where [g̃] is normal in Spanish: compare [gíg̃i] guigui with giggle.

The failure of the English speaker to master the variants of this sound only rarely gives rise to misunderstanding. We have treated /g/ along with /b/ and /d/ only because of the similar pattern of their variants.

There are two possibilities of misunderstanding from mishandling of the [g] and [g̃]. One is confusion of [g̃] and [ƀ] whenever the vowel /u/ follows. The [ƀ] and [g̃] sound somewhat alike in this instance, because they both tend to be pronounced with rounded lips in anticipation of the rounded vowel.

[ag̃uṣár]	aguzar	[aƀusár]	abusar
[lag̃úla]	la gula	[laƀúla]	la bula
[ezg̃úrḍo]	es gurdo	[ezƀúrḍo]	es burdo
[múchog̃ústo]	mucho gusto	[múchoƀústo]	mucho busto

The other is the tendency of the English speaker to miss hearing the [g̃] altogether since it is quite lenis. This is especially likely between vowels and results in the confusion of items like:

[léo]	leo	[légo]	lego
[bóa]	boa	[bóga]	boga
[día]	dia	[díga]	diga
[béa]	vea	[béga]	vega
[mía]	mia	[míga]	miga

SPANISH CONSONANTS WHOSE MISPRONUNCIATION BY ENGLISH INFLUENCE CAN CAUSE MISUNDERSTANDING—/r/

In the description of /d/ above, it was mentioned that /d/ can be misunderstood as /r/ in words like cada if one uses the English variety of /d/ which exists in words like coddle. This suggests that Spanish /r/ is markedly different from the English /r/.

In English, /r/ is most frequently produced by the articulation that is known as RETROFLECTION: the tongue tip is turned upward and back toward the roof of the mouth without making contact. This is the allophone that appears between vowels in American dialects and that appears before consonants and boundary elements in all but the so-called "r-less" dialects—that is, dialects in which /r/'s are absent before consonants and boundary elements.

Other allophones of /r/ exist in English, such as the varieties of retroflex spirants which occur initially and after consonants; the ones after consonants are partly or wholly voiceless when the preceding consonant is voiceless. These kinds of English /r/ are heard in words like dream, tree, broad, fry, run.

In Spanish, there is one pronunciation of /r/ which closely resembles the retroflex spirant of English, but it is limited to a few regions in the Spanish-speaking world. In parts of Chile and Peru this pronunciation is used after consonants, in words like tres.

The pronunciation of /r/ that appears in most dialects—and that is unquestionably the standard variety—is an alveolar FLAP, produced by a rapid motion of the tongue tip upward from behind the lower teeth across the alveolar ridge with no stop-phase between, merely touching against the alveolar area in passing on to the next sound. When a consonant follows the flap, there may or may not be a slight friction during part of the flap. Before a terminal-rising or a terminal-falling juncture the friction is much more noticeable, the /r/ is generally voiceless, and there may even be several voiceless flaps together, especially if the syllable is stressed.

Between vowels, Spanish /r/, unlike most other consonants of the language, may occur either single or doubled. The single /r/ is the alveolar flap just described; the double /rr/ is a tongue-tip trill[1]—examples /káro/ caro: /kárro/ carro.

---

1. We, at least, are satisfied that the analysis of the trill as in perro is best

In all other positions, there is no contrast between /r/ and /rr/. At the beginning of an utterance, after a boundary element, or after /n/, /l/, or /s/, only the trill /rr/ occurs. Spanish orthography spells /rr/ in this position with a single r—examples: /rrópa/ ropa, /rréy/ rey. It is to be noted that when words are pronounced in CLOSE TRANSITION —that is, without a boundary element between them—the /rr/ spelled r at the beginning of words is still pronounced as the trill /rr/—examples: /larrópa/ la ropa.

In many dialects, this initial /rr/ begins the first tap from a position in which the tongue tip is making contact with the alveolar ridge or the upper teeth. This results in a stoplike beginning of the trill which we might symbolize [^{d}rr-].

In absolute-final position, the pronunciation of /r/ is highly variable. It may be a single flap or a succession of them; it may be partly or wholly voiceless; it may have a considerable amount of friction noise, giving it something of a spirantal quality. This final /r/ is spelled with a single r. When a word ending in r is pronounced in close transition with a following word beginning with a vowel, the /r/ is pronounced like the usual flap /r/ between vowels—examples: /bér/ ver, /bérahwán/ ver a Juan.

A comparison of items that contain /r/ in English with items that contain /r/ in Spanish is of considerable pedagogical interest, since from such a list a student can perceive more easily than in any other way the tremendous gap between the English and the Spanish manners of articulation.

English /r/	Spanish /r/	
airway	/éroe/	héroe
Karo	/kyéro/	quiero
Sarah	/ṣéra/	cera
very very	/beribéri/	beriberi
corral	/korál/	coral
ear	/ír/	ir
car	/kár/	car
lay air	/leér/	leer
soar	/sór/	Sor
bravo	/brábo/	bravo
train	/trén/	tren
frock	/frák/	frac
fresco	/frésko/	fresco
Arta	/árta/	harta
Herbert	/yérba/	yerba
parquet	/parkeé/	parqueé
Gargantua	/gargánta/	garganta

---

as /rr/, not as a separate phoneme /R/ or /r̄/ or however one might choose to write it. There are, in fact, dialects in which other continuants are doubled: /kánne/ for carne, /kállos/ for Carlos, though this is not in general true of standard Spanish.

English /r/	Spanish /rr/	
harrow	/hárro/	jarro
borrow	/bárro/	barro
sorrow	/sárro/	sarro
Pharoah	/férro/	ferro
Korea	/korría/	corría
Ravel	/rrabél/	Ravel
rascal	/rrásko/	rasco
race	/rrés/	res
roan	/rrón/	ron
Rhea	/rría/	ría
ray	/rréy/	rey

We have included /r/ among the critical consonants, because English /r/ is unlike either /r/ or /rr/ in Spanish and cannot be associated with either one. Also, if the English speaker fails to distinguish Spanish /r/ and /rr/, a vast number of minimal pairs will be pronounced alike.

/káro/	caro	/kárro/	carro
/kóro/	coro	/kórro/	corro
/péro/	pero	/pérro/	perro
/pára/	para	/párra/	parra
/bára/	bara	/bárra/	barra
/ʒéro/	cero	/ṣérro/	cerro
/yéro/	yero	/yérro/	hierro
/fóro/	foro	/fórro/	forro
/fyéro/	fiero	/fyérro/	fierro
/amára/	amara	/amárra/	amarra

Indeed, at least as a point of departure, the English speaker may do well to associate the English /r/ between vowels with English /t/ or /d/ between vowels (if the stress is on the first of the two syllables):

English /t/	Spanish /r/	
photo	/fóro/	foro
auto	/óro/	oro
Otto	/áro/	aro
rotter	/rráro/	raro
motor	/móro/	moro
meadow	/méro/	mero
Buddha	/búra/	bura
coda	/kóra/	Cora
solder	/sára/	Sara
leader	/líra/	lira

Speakers of the "r-less" dialects of English will experience difficulties mastering contrasts like those listed below (including taboo items which should serve to point up the utility of the contrasts):

/bárba/	barba	/bába/	baba
/barbéro/	barbero	/babéro/	babero
/kúrba/	curba	/kúba/	Cuba
/bárbaro/	bárbaro	/bábaro/	bavaro
/karbón/	carbón	/kabón/	cabón
/árda/	arda	/áda/	hada
/fárda/	farda	/fáda/	fada
/emfardár/	enfardar	/emfadár/	enfadar
/lárdo/	lardo	/ládo/	lado
/perdón/	perdón	/pedón/	pedón
/hwérga/	juerga	/hwéga/	juega
/árgo/	argo	/ágo/	hago
/bárgas/	Vargas	/bágas/	vagas
/kárga/	carga	/kága/	caga
/lárgo/	largo	/lágo/	lago
/amór/	amor	/amó/	amó
/kolór/	color	/koló/	coló
/kalór/	calor	/kaló/	caló
/bibír/	vivir	/bibí/	viví
/estribór/	estribor	/estribó/	estribó

Most English speakers of "r-less" dialects do contrast such pairs as /háəd/ hard and /hád/ hod; but the lengthening off-glide /ə/, which constitutes the minimal difference in English, does not exist in Spanish and will go unnoticed if the English speaker tries to substitute it for /r/.

SPANISH CONSONANTS WHOSE MISPRONUNCIATION
BY ENGLISH INFLUENCE CAN CAUSE
MISUNDERSTANDING—/t/

The /t/ phoneme in English has a rather large number of relatively easy-to-distinguish allophones.[2] In spite of this fact, the English speaker can get by with substituting an English allophone of /t/ in almost all Spanish items. There is, however, one environment in which this is not true. Because of this one environment, /t/ is included as the last of the consonants which will cause outright misunderstanding if pronounced in Spanish as though they were English.

A glance at any list of Spanish words containing /t/ makes it evident that /t/ occurs at the beginning and in the middle of words, but rarely at the end of them. This

---

2. Cf. George L. Trager, "The Phoneme 'T': A Study in Theory and Method," American Speech, XVII (1942), 144-48.

suggests, rightly, that /t/ nearly always begins a syllable in Spanish. In English, /t/ occurs also at the end, and is by no means regularly first in a syllable.

The phonetic differences between English and Spanish /t/ in any position are considerable. Spanish /t/, like /d/, is dental in articulation; the tongue stops the air column at the back side of the upper teeth rather than at the alveolar ridge, as in English. It never has the puff of air on release (ASPIRATION) which English has whenever it is initial in a syllable that is under one of the higher levels of stress. It is never flapped as the English /t/ is between vowel nuclei before a weak-stressed syllable. The Spanish /t/ is, in short, a phoneme with little variation in phonetic shape. English speakers who are trying to master it have a built-in set of complex conditioned variations in the phonetic shape of their own English /t/.

The following list contains items with the aspirated allophone of the English /t/ in comparison with the unaspirated Spanish /t/.

English /t/	Spanish /t/	
too	/tú/	tú
tea	/tí/	ti
ton	/tán/	tan
toss	/tás/	tas
tall	/tál/	tal
ten	/tén/	ten
taboo	/tabú/	tabú
trace	/trés/	trés
tuna	/túna/	tuna
atune	/atún/	atún
attire	/atár/	atar

The following list, on the other hand, includes a different allophone of the English /t/; the voiced flap indicated phonetically as [ṭ] in comparison with the /t/ of Spanish in the same situation.

English /t/		Spanish /t/	
[fówṭow]	photo	/fóto/	foto
[bɛ́yṭɨ]	beta	/béta/	beta
[píyṭɨɹ]	Peter	/píta/	pita
[mɛ́yṭɨɹ]	mater	/méta/	meta

The situation at this point, then, before we go further into the allophones of English /t/, is precisely the reverse of the earlier situation in which Spanish showed two allophones of the /d/ phoneme in comparison with only one for English: [dáðo] compared with [dǽdɨy]. That is, there are several varieties of /t/ in English, essentially only one in Spanish. (Phonetic details are indicated only for the /t/'s.)

English [tʰ] and [t̪]		Spanish [t̪]	
[tʰɨ́yt̪ɨr]	teeter	[t̪ít̪o]	tito
[tʰɛ́yt̪ɨr]	'tater	[t̪ét̪a]	teta
[tʰát̪ɨr]	totter	[t̪át̪a]	tata
[tʰówt̪ɨm]	totem	[t̪ót̪em]	totem

Examples of this kind are the ones which give cause for concern about the pronunciation of /t/ in Spanish. Just as English /d/ is misheard as Spanish /r/ in this intervocalic position, English /t/ will also be misheard as Spanish /r/, with the result of confusing such Spanish items as the following:[3]

/át̪a/	ata	/ára/	ara
/bét̪as/	vetas, betas	/béras/	veras
/kót̪o/	coto	/kóro/	coro
/pít̪a/	pita	/píra/	pira
/t̪ít̪o/	tito	/t̪íro/	tiro
/pát̪a/	pata	/pára/	para

Besides the confusion of English /t/ with Spanish /r/, there is another potential confusion resulting from the multiplicity of allophones that /t/ has in English—a confusion whose potential is only barely realized in the classroom, because the sequence happens to occur infrequently in Spanish. This is the matter of the lateral release of /t/ when it precedes /-ɨl/ after stress in English. A few examples will suffice, since it is a minor problem.

English	Spanish	
futile	/inút̪il/	inútil
petal	/pét̪ulo/	pétulo
mottle	/nat̪át̪il/	natátil
rattle	/dát̪il/	dátil

Much more serious is the allophone of English /t/ that appears before /-ɨn/ after a stressed syllable. This allophone, a /t/ released glottally into the following syllabic nasal, cannot be confused with anything that occurs in Spanish. It is simply so different from a voiceless dental stop that a Spanish speaker has great difficulty deciding what sound the American has in mind. Notice the wide phonetic gap:

English	Spanish	
kitten	/kít̪an/	quitan
matin	/mét̪en/	meten
Latin	/lát̪en/	laten
batten	/bát̪en/	baten

---

3. Many English speakers have no contrast between /t/ and /d/ in this position; for both the /t/ and /d/ of other speakers, they use a voiced flap which is close to the Spanish /r/.

SPANISH CONSONANTS WHOSE MISPRONUNCIATION
BY ENGLISH INFLUENCE RESULTS IN
A HEAVY FOREIGN ACCENT

The division we are making among the consonants is an arbitrary one. Some of the mispronunciations we have been discussing might not, in a specific instance, lead to confusion; some of those we are about to discuss might well do so. Any mispronunciation can lead to confusion; whether it does or not in any specific instance will depend on the context, the existence and frequency of similar items, the aptitude of the audience for making the right phonetic analogies, and so forth.

Our real point is to establish a hierarchy of importance so that a teacher may pay first attention to errors that are most likely to disrupt communication. It is pedagogically impracticable to try to correct everything at once, and the focus of correction at any one stage should not be an accident of experience; it should be, as it were, an educated focus. All the errors discussed so far can be corrected simultaneously, from the beginning: stress, intonation, and the consonants / d b g r t /. Those about to be discussed move into critical focus after the first priorities have begun to be mastered—or have at least been brought thoroughly into the student's awareness.

SPANISH CONSONANTS WHOSE MISPRONUNCIATION
BY ENGLISH INFLUENCE RESULTS IN A
HEAVY FOREIGN ACCENT—/p/

Spanish /p/, like Spanish /t/, is unaspirated. It is usually syllable-initial, but it may appear at the end of a syllable if the next one begins with a voiceless dental stop: /séptimo/ séptimo, /septyémbre/ septiembre; but it rarely appears in final position. English /p/ is regularly rather heavily aspirated in initial position and is much more forcefully articulated (fortis). English /p/ occurs of course in a large number of positions where Spanish /p/ never occurs, but this is not a source of trouble for the English speaker learning Spanish (in reverse, for the Spanish speaker learning English, it is a severe problem indeed.)

The two /p/'s may be compared in the following lists:

English /p/	Spanish /p/	
pace	/péş/	pez
pone	/pón/	pon
Peru	/perú/	Perú
pawn	/pán/	pan
pore	/pór/	por
par	/pár/	par
pooh	/pú/	pu
papa	/pápa/	pápa
plan	/plán/	plan
pus	/páş/	paz

There is one environment shared by /p/ in both languages where for all practical purposes the /p/'s are identical: between vowels after a stressed syllable.

English	Spanish	
popper	/pápa/	papa
copper	/kápa/	capa
sopper	/ṣápa/	zapa
soaper	/sópo/	sopo
opera	/ápoda/	ápoda
apical	/épiko/	épico

SPANISH CONSONANTS WHOSE MISPRONUNCIATION
BY ENGLISH INFLUENCE RESULTS IN A
HEAVY FOREIGN ACCENT—/k/

Spanish /k/ is like Spanish /p/ and /t/ in that it is unaspirated in most dialects and usually syllable-initial. There are, however, some dialects which aspirate /k/. Unlike /t/, but like /p/, /k/ may appear at the end of a syllable if the next one begins with a voiceless dental consonant—/akṣyón/, /lekṣyón/, /aktíbo/—but it rarely appears in final position. Its distribution is thus more limited than that of English /k/, but it occasions few pedagogical problems. The two may be compared in the following lists:

English /k/	Spanish /k/	
coal	/kól/	col
Conn	/kán/	can
Kay	/ké/	qué
quarrel	/kwál/	cuál
cone	/kón/	con
kilo	/kílo/	kilo
call	/kál/	cal
coo	/kú/	cu
café	/café/	café
cocoa	/kóko/	coco
accord	/akórde/	acorde
akin	/akyén/	a quién
a key	/akí/	aquí
Achilles	/akíles/	Aquiles
acre	/éko/	eco
apical	/épiko/	épico
cockle	/káko/	caco
cocoa	/kóko/	coco
poker	/póko/	poco

SPANISH CONSONANTS WHOSE MISPRONUNCIATION
BY ENGLISH INFLUENCE RESULTS IN A
HEAVY FOREIGN ACCENT—/l/

The mispronunciation of /l/ marks the English accent in Spanish more clearly than any consonant but /r/, although it does not lead to the same degree of misunderstanding. In the production of both the English /l/ and the Spanish /l/, the air passes around the sides of the tongue. To make /l/ as Spanish speakers do, the tongue is high and front in the mouth, tense, with the tip and front in contact with the alveolar ridge as though for the production of English /d/, and the back of the tongue is held as though for the vowel /i/. There is so little room left at the sides for the air to pass that friction noise may often be heard. The /l/ is in effect almost a laterally released [d]. The following pairs illustrate this similarity:

English	Spanish	
wheedle	/híl/	Gil
a kettle	/akél/	aquel
addle	/ál/	al
chattel	/chál/	chal
saddle	/sál/	sal
bottle	/bál/	val
coddle	/kál/	cal
mottle	/mál/	mal
toddle	/tál/	tal
poodle	/púl/	pul
tootle	/túl/	tul

English syllable-initial /l/, especially before high front vowels such as /ɪ/ and /ɛ/, is sometimes fairly similar to the Spanish /l/, and carrying over the English /l/ to Spanish in this position rarely creates a heavy foreign accent. (Compare English lay and Spanish ley.)

English /l/ before a consonant or at the end of a syllable is, however, quite different. English speakers often make this /l/ with the tip of the tongue in the same position as in Spanish, but that is the end of the similarity except for the fact that the air column escapes laterally around the sides of the tongue. There is a much smaller area of tongue contact with the alveolar ridge; there is little tension and no friction; and the center and back of the tongue are about as for the vowel [ʌ]. It may be said that the Spanish /l/ in all positions is "i-colored," whereas the English syllable-final or pre-consonantal /l/ is "ʌ-colored."[4] Compare these lists:

---

4. For a fuller description of the allophones of English /l/, see Daniel Jones, An Outline of English Phonetics, 8th ed. (Cambridge: Heffer, 1957), pp. 173-76.

English /l/		Spanish /l/
feel	/fíl/	fil
seal	/síl/	sil
hotel	/otél/	hotel
el	/él/	el
dell	/dél/	del
tall	/tál/	tal
Saul	/sául/	sal
coal	/kól/	col
soul	/sól/	sol
tool	/túl/	tul
salvo	/sálbo/	salvo
folder	/fálda/	falda
vulgar	/wélga/	huelga

SPANISH CONSONANTS WHOSE MISPRONUNCIATION BY ENGLISH INFLUENCE RESULTS IN A HEAVY FOREIGN ACCENT—/s/

Spanish /s/ presents a highly complex problem of description, because of the allophonic variation it has as well as the great amount of dialectal variation it shows throughout the Spanish-speaking world. The most important allophonic variation is the occurrence of special variants before voiced consonants. The most important dialectal variations are: the special tongue-tip pronunciation of /s/ heard chiefly in the northern part of Spain, and the h-like pronunciation of /s/ heard especially in coastal areas of the New World.

The Spanish /s/ in Latin America is not much different from the English /s/; but before voiced consonants in dialects that do not use the h-like allophone, it is voiced—that is, it sounds like English /z/.[5] This may be summarized by the formula

$$\text{Spanish } /s/ \; \rightarrow \; [z] \text{ in env. } \underline{\hspace{1cm}} \; \left\{ \begin{array}{l} /b/ \\ /d/ \\ /g/ \\ /m/ \\ /n/ \\ /\text{ny}/ \\ /l/ \\ /(l)y/ \\ /rr/ \end{array} \right\}$$

5. In addition, [z] occurs before /+w/ and /+y/ as in:

[loz wébos]	los huevos	[loz yúgos]	los yugos
[dez wéso]	deshueso	[dez yélo]	deshielo

We have, of course, in one example ignored the dialects which have the /ş/ [z̨] in an item like juzgar. In our modified phonemic transcription used for teaching, we mark all these possible interdentals by a hook placed under the z if voiced or the s if voiceless: [z̨], [ş].

z		s	
[ezbóso]	esboso	[espóso]	esposo
[rrazgár]	rasgar	[rraskár]	rascar
[ezbélta]	esbelta	[espélta]	espelta
[ázno]	asno	[ásko]	asco
[mízmo]	mismo	[místo]	mixto
[huzgár]	juzgar	[buskár]	buscar
[dezdenyár]	desdeñar	[destenyír]	desteñir
[dizgústo]	disgusto	[diskúrso]	discurso
[dézde]	desde	[déste]	de este
[ézde]	es de	[éste]	este

In one of these clusters, /srr/, the s is usually ASSIMILATED to the following /rr/ in point of articulation and the /rr/ is stronger and somewhat spirantized. The auditory effect is almost as if the /s/ were dropped completely and the /rr/ pronounced as a long, strong spirant.

/isrraél/	Israel	/losrrícos/	los ricos

In parts of Spain, including areas of Castilian pronunciation, the /s/ is articulated as a tongue-tip groove spirant which resembles the English /š/, although it is by no means identical with it.

The other dialect variation of importance is the h-like pronunciation of /s/. In southern Spain and throughout the coastal areas of Latin America, the pronunciation of Spanish /s/ before consonants and finally as a weak aspiration [h] is common. It is limited to syllable-final position. Since English speakers may always use their /s/ or /z/ sounds for the [s] and [z] allophones of Spanish /s/ and be perfectly understood, the use of the [h] pronunciation of Spanish /s/ is not a major problem for speech production. It is, however, a serious problem for hearing, since the English speaker often fails to hear the [h] at all. If students are being trained to work with a dialect that uses the [h], they will have to have special practice in contrasts that are very numerous in Spanish, such as the singular and plural of nouns and adjectives ending in a vowel (gato - gatos [gáto - gáto[h]]) or the second and third person forms of verbs (comes - come [kóme[h] - kóme]). Other similar examples are:

[té[h]]	tez	[té]	te
[bú[h]]	bus	[bú]	bu
[bé[h]]	vez	[bé]	ve
[mé[h]]	mes	[mé]	me
[nó[h]]	nos	[nó]	no

The examples of /s/ before consonants in the lists illustrating [s] vs. [z] given earlier in this section would all have the [h] pronunciation in the dialects under consideration. Some Argentine dialects have [h] in those words, even though they regularly have

[s] on the words in the list immediately below. The following list shows the occurrence of [s] and [^{h}] in syllable-initial and syllable-final positions:

[é^h]	es	[sé]	sé
[ló^h]	los	[sól]	sol
[nó^h]	nos	[són]	son
[lí^h]	lis	[síl]	sil
[ó^h]	hoz	[só]	so
[lá^h]	las	[sál]	sal

One problem which an English speaker learning Spanish will face results from the fact that many English words with /z/ or /ž/ have Spanish counterparts with /s/. The student has difficulty learning to pronounce the Spanish words with [s] instead of [z] or [ž]. This difficulty is reinforced by the fact that English spelling of these words is often with s(i) representing the /z/ or /ž/, whereas the Spanish word is also spelled with s pronounced with the phoneme /s/.

English		Spanish	
/prɛ́zɨnt/	present	/presénte/	presente
/prɛ́zɨdɨnt/	president	/presidénte/	presidente
/prɨyzɛ́nt/	present	/presentár/	presentar
/prɛ̀zɨntéyšɨnz/	presentations	/presentasyónes/	presentaciónes
/vízɨt/	visit	/bisitár/	visitar
/dɨvížɨn/	division	/dibisyón/	division
/dɨváržɨn/	diversion	/dibersyón/	diversion
/ɨnvéyžɨn/	invasion	/inbasyón/	invasion
/sǽntɨ rówzɨ/	Santa Rosa	/sántarrósa/	Santa Rosa
/ròwzɨlíndɨ/	Rosalinda	/rrosalínda/	Rosalinda
/pràpɨzíšɨn/	proposition	/propósito/	propósito
/prɛ̀pɨzíšɨn/	preposition	/preposisyón/	preposición
/ríyzɨn/	reason	/rrasón/	razón

SPANISH CONSONANTS WHOSE MISPRONUNCIATION
BY ENGLISH INFLUENCE RESULTS IN A
HEAVY FOREIGN ACCENT—/h/

The Spanish /h/ is articulated with friction noise created by raising the back of the tongue toward the velum. In English, /h/ before vowels is rarely more than a voiceless onset to the vowel with only slight friction. Even when there is some friction, it is not localized in the velar area as it is in Spanish.

Some areas of the Spanish-speaking world have varieties of /h/ which are markedly more fricative than those of other areas. Chile at one geographic extreme and

Madrid at the other characteristically have heavily fricative /h/'s. In careful speech, however, all areas have the tense and highly fricative variety.

The difference between /h/ in English and /h/ in Spanish can be observed from
these lists:

English /h/		Spanish /h/
hoe	/hó/	jo
he	/hí/	gi
hey	/hé/	ge
hymen	/háyme/	Jaime
heater	/híra/	gira
hurrah	/hurár/	jurar
holly	/hále/	jale
hotter	/hára/	jara
hoosegow	/huşgádo/	juzgado
Hilda	/hílda/	Gilda
aha	/ahá/	ajá
Mohican	/mohíka/	Mojica

The position in which /h/ is usually most difficult for the English speaker to
master is between vowels after the stressed syllable:

[méhiko]	México
[déhese]	déjese
[kéhense]	quéjense
[krúhalo]	crújalo
[alóha]	aloja

SPANISH CONSONANTS WHOSE MISPRONUNCIATION
BY ENGLISH INFLUENCE RESULTS IN A
HEAVY FOREIGN ACCENT—/n/

The pronunciation of Spanish /n/ does not ordinarily cause an English speaker much trouble, but there are a few special instances which are potential sources of foreign accent.

/n/ in Spanish before vowels differs from /n/ in English by its dental articulation: like /t/ and /d/, the tip of the tongue touches the back side of the upper teeth,
whereas in English the tip of the tongue makes its closure against the gum ridge (alveolar
ridge) behind the upper teeth. In both instances, of course, the air passes freely through
the nose.

/n/ has a wide range of variation when it appears before consonants. It is regularly assimilated to the point of articulation at which the next consonant is made. Accordingly, /n/ never occurs before the labial consonants /p/, /b/, and /f/: it always becomes
/m/. It does, curiously, occur before /m/ itself, as in /in medyáta/ inmediata, but there

are cogent reasons for describing this sequence as containing a boundary element between the /n/ and the /m/—for example, some speakers do say /immedyáta/.

/n/ occurs before all but labial consonants. Before the Castilian /ş/, the /n/ can actually be articulated against the lower edge of the upper teeth. Before the dental consonants /t/ and /d/, it is articulated against the back side of the upper teeth. Before the alveolar consonants /s/ and /r/, it is articulated against the alveolar ridge. Before the palatal consonants /ch/ and /y/, it is farther back, still articulated with the tip of the tongue, against the hard palate. The fact that it is articulated with the tip of the tongue is of great importance in distinguishing /n/ plus /y/ from /ɲy/ ṉ̃. (This detail will be discussed at greater length below.) Before the velar consonants /k/, /g/, /h/, and /+w/, it is articulated all the way back against the soft palate and is phonetically [ŋ]. In several dialects of the Caribbean area, [ŋ] is the only allophone of /n/ that occurs before the boundary element or a terminal juncture. For this reason, there have been competent authorities[6] who have assigned [ŋ] the status of a phoneme, because it has such contrasts as [eŋóhas] en hojas "on pages" [enóhas] enojas "you anger." We prefer to handle this contrast and many others of a similar order by the use of a boundary element (internal open, or plus, juncture): /en óhas/ in contrast with /enóhas/. (Further discussion of this point will be presented later.)

It is obvious that the single phoneme /n/ in Spanish covers the same phonetic area as the two phonemes /n/ and /ŋ/ cover in English, and that furthermore the /n/ area is split midway by a different phoneme; the eñe which we write /ɲy/ for pedagogical reasons that will subsequently become clear. These facts cause almost no difficulty to the English learner, because English /n/ and /ŋ/ are distributed in a manner that closely resembles the distribution of [n] and [ŋ] in Spanish.[7] The two breaks in the congruence of the distribution of the two sounds in Spanish and English are before /h/ and /+w/, where [ŋ] is the Spanish allophone. It will have to be drilled in such words and phrases as the following:

/nh/		/n + w/	
[estraŋhéro]	extranjero	[sáŋ wiche]	sandwich
[naráŋha]	naranja	[uŋ wéso]	un hueso
[fiŋhír]	fingir	[uŋ wéƀo]	un huevo
[uŋ hésto]	un gesto	[uŋ wérto]	un huerto
[uŋ hárro]	un jarro	[uŋ wérfano]	un huérfano

The difference between the characteristic sounds of /n/ in Spanish and /n/ in English can be heard when /n/ occurs before or after vowels, with its articulation uninfluenced by any following consonant. It may also be pointed out that the Spanish /n/ is markedly longer than the English /n/ between vowels.

---

6. Notably, O. L. Chavarría-Aguilar in "The Phonemes of Costa Rican Spanish," Language, XXVII (1951), 248-53.

7. Students of the history of English will recognize that this congruence is due to the historical development of English during most of which time [n] and [ŋ] were allophones much as they are in Spanish today.

English /n-/	Spanish /n-/	
knee	/ní/	ni
no	/nó/	no
known	/nón/	non
novella	/nobéla/	novela

English /-n-/	Spanish /-n-/	
Lana	/lána/	lana
pony	/póne/	pone
Anna	/ána/	Ana

English /-n/	Spanish /-n/	
seen	/sín/	sin
sown	/són/	son
pawn	/pán/	pan
dawn	/dán/	dan
Bonn	/bán/	van
ten	/tén/	ten
pone	/pón/	pon
Ben	/bén/	ven

SPANISH CONSONANTS WHOSE MISPRONUNCIATION BY ENGLISH INFLUENCE RESULTS IN A HEAVY FOREIGN ACCENT—/y/

/y/, like /s/, presents a complex problem of description, because of the extraordinarily wide range of phonetic variation it undergoes both within and between dialects. The range of variation extends all the way from an [i̯] that is essentially identical with the /y/ of English yes, through the /ž/ of English measure, to the /ǰ/ of English juice. The distribution of these variants within the over-all pattern of Spanish structure is:

/y/ appears as [ǰ], [ž], [y̆], or [i̯] in all syllable-initial positions, including those after a boundary element and between vowels.

/y/ appears as [i̯] in all positions where it is not syllable-initial, including those post-consonantally, pre-consonantally, and before a boundary element.

If English /y/ is used in the same syllable after a vowel, it will fall short of Spanish /y/ in that it may not glide to a sufficiently high-front position. This is because the English /y/, which is always frictionless, and which after a vowel glides toward a higher and fronter position than the vowel which it follows, does not always reach the position of [i] —it may reach only the position of [e] or even lower, depending on the height of the preceding vowel. If any variety of English /y/ is used before a vowel in the same syllable, it will fall short of being satisfactory in the amount of friction and tension of articulation. The amount of the friction in the /y/ varies from one dialect area to another (maximum in the River Plate area, minimum in urban Colombia and Mexico), but in all areas it exceeds the friction of the English /y/.

English speakers may well be confused by the range of variation that /y/ has in Spanish. The Spanish words in the left-hand column below will be heard sometimes to resemble the items of the first English column, sometimes those of the second. But the difference is subphonemic, and the English speaker must learn to ignore it.[8]

Spanish		English	
/yéso/	yeso	Jess	yes
/yó/	yo	Joe	yo-yo
/yélo/	hielo	Jello	yellow
/yáka/	yaca	Jack	yak
/yá/	ya	jaw	yaw
/yána/	llana	John	yawn
/yúte/	yute	jute	Ute
/yábe/	llave	jabber	yabber
/yé/	ye	Jay	yea
/yérno/	yerno	germ	yearn
/yúgo/	yugo	juke	uke

The intervocalic /y/ in Spanish also corresponds to several contrasting phonologic elements in English; the English speaker must learn to ignore this subphonemic variation.

Spanish		English		
/méya/	mella	major	measure	mayor
/áya/	aya	agile	azure	eye 'er
/éya/	ella	aged	Asia	Ayer
/pláya/	playa	plagiary	pleasure	player
/líyo/	Lillo	legion	leisure	lea 'er

SPANISH CONSONANTS WHOSE MISPRONUNCIATION BY ENGLISH INFLUENCE RESULTS IN A HEAVY FOREIGN ACCENT—/w/

Any given sound in a language is phonetically definable in terms of the intersection of several categories of articulation: for example, a [t] may be defined as the intersection of dental, stop, and voiceless articulation. Each one of these categories is needed in order to completely define the sound, but they are not all on the same level of importance in determining how that sound will interact with neighboring sounds. It is sometimes true that in defining a given sound one of its intersecting categories is more

---

8. While discussing /y/, we do not transcribe ll by /(l)y/ as we do elsewhere, but merely by /y/, in order to avoid dialect confusion.

important than the others. This is true of the English and Spanish /w/'s. Both of them are labial, velar, and gliding; but in defining the English phoneme the labial quality is more important than the velar quality, whereas in defining the Spanish phoneme the velar quality is more important. A clear illustration of this difference is the way in which nasals are assimilated before /w/ in each language: in English, the word <u>sandwich</u> by some speakers is pronounced as /sǽmwich/; in Spanish, the same word (borrowed) is [sáŋ wiche].

Another example of the importance of the velar quality of the Spanish /w/ is the confusion which occurs in some areas between /w/ and the sequence /gw/. In the sequence /gw/ between vowels, the spirant allophone of the velar /g/ is especially weak and the /gw/ often sounds like [w] to the English speaker. Some speakers of Spanish even drop the /g/ completely in this position. For example, <u>agua</u> may be said /ágwa/ [á^{g}wa] or /áwa/. Sometimes, especially in parts of Mexico, there is even confusion at the beginning of certain words between /gw/ spelled <u>gu</u> and /w/ spelled <u>hu</u>. In fact, many Spanish dictionaries give double entries for a number of items, especially those which are recent borrowings:

guaca	huaca
guasca	huasca
güipil	huipil

This confusion shows up also in the dialogue in novels or plays where the author is presumably trying to indicate non-standard pronunciations:

güevos	for	huevos
güesos	for	huesos
güeno	for	(b)ueno
agüelo	for	a(b)uelo

The difference between English /w/ and Spanish /w/ can be heard by comparing the following lists of English and Spanish items:

English	Spanish	
west	/wéste/	hueste
wave	/wébo/	huevo
walk	/wáka/	huaca
wasp	/wáso/	huaso
wake	/wéka/	hueca
weigher	/wé(l)ya/	huella

SPANISH CONSONANTS WHOSE MISPRONUNCIATION BY ENGLISH INFLUENCE CAUSES LITTLE DIFFICULTY IN COMPREHENSION AND LITTLE DISTRACTION OF ATTENTION TO ACCENT

As we have remarked, there are no perfect equivalents to be found in the matching of English speech sounds to those of Spanish. Nonetheless, there are several pairs which are either close enough or of such low frequency of occurrence as to warrant little attention in a classroom. The available time can be much more profitably spent correcting the errors that result from the differences which have already been discussed. The following description of the consonants is included to complete the pattern and for the use of those whose desire is to refine even the smallest details of pronunciation.

SPANISH CONSONANTS WHICH PRESENT NO REAL DIFFICULTY TO THE ENGLISH LEARNER—/ch/

The English affricate /ch/, characteristically at the onset of stressed syllables, is heavily aspirated and fricative. The Spanish /ch/ is unaspirated and markedly less fricative. For obvious pedagogical reasons we avoid the conventional phonetic symbol /č/ and use the digraph ch, since the usage is almost perfectly consistent in both English and Spanish spelling traditions. The following paired lists serve to illustrate the difference between the /ch/'s of English and Spanish:

English		Spanish
choppy	/chápa/	chapa
chaw	/chál/	chal
cheese	/chís/	chis
check	/chéke/	cheque
chore	/chórro/	chorro
achieve	/archíbo/	archivo
catcher	/kácha/	cacha
filcher	/fícha/	ficha
anchovy	/áncha/	ancha
cinches	/sínchas/	cinchas

SPANISH CONSONANTS WHICH PRESENT NO REAL DIFFICULTY TO THE ENGLISH LEARNER—/m/

The /m/ in Spanish is somewhat more tensely articulated than the /m/ of English. In clusters with labial stops (/mp/, /mb/), the Spanish /m/ is fully articulated as a continuant before the stop begins. The same clusters in English are more usually realized by heavy nasalization of the preceding vowel with relatively little continuation of the /m/ itself. The following examples will serve for illustration:

English		Spanish
me	/mí/	mi
may	/mé/	me
moo	/mú/	mu
meal	/míl/	mil
camper	/kámpo/	campo
ambers	/ámbos/	ambos
tempo	/témplo/	templo

English	Spanish	
ember	/émbra/	hembra
limpid	/límpio/	limpio
timber	/tímbre/	timbre

The Spanish cluster /mf/ may be realized phonetically in one of four ways: as labio-dental [ɱ] plus [f], as [m] plus bi-labial [ɸ], or as nasality of the preceding vowel followed immediately either by the spirant [f] or by the spirant [ɸ]. We have heard all four articulations in abundance. One mistake which the English learner is likely to make is to use /n/ followed by /f/, which is an impossible Spanish sequence. If he does manage to produce some variety of /m/ before the /f/, he must avoid inserting a [p] by analogy with the structure he has in English words like emphasis /ɛ́mpfɨsɨs/. The differences of articulation may be examined by listening to items like the following:

English	Spanish	
infirm	/emférmo/	enfermo
infernal	/imfyérno/	infierno
informal	/imfórme/	informe
confuse	/komfúso/	confuso
confirm	/komfírma/	confirma
emphatic	/emfátiko/	enfático

Many speakers of Spanish make no distinction between /m/ and /n/ before a boundary element, in which event they usually use the allophone [n] or [ŋ]. This makes it difficult for Spanish speakers to learn to distinguish final /m/, /n/, and /ŋ/ in English, but creates no major problem for speakers of English learning Spanish.

SPANISH CONSONANTS WHICH PRESENT NO REAL
DIFFICULTY TO THE ENGLISH LEARNER—/ş/

The /ş/ occurs only in a few dialects in Spain—chiefly in Castilian, the dialect of central Spain which owes its prestige to a long tradition of political, economic, and cultural hegemony. The /ş/ does not occur natively in any dialect of American Spanish. Because it is used by only a small minority of speakers of Spanish throughout the world, it is our preference to transcribe it in materials that are to be used for teaching by simply placing a hook beneath the symbol s, producing /ş/, avoiding the conventional symbol /θ/. This hook beneath the s can then be easily ignored by students who are imitating a speaker of any non-Castilian dialect.

The Spanish /ş/ is different from the /ş/ of English thing in that it is tenser and the tip of the tongue is farther forward. It is usually classed as "interdental," and may be so in careful speech. More often, it is in fact postdental in both languages. The differences can be heard in the items below:

English	Spanish	
thong	/ṣánka/	zanca
thought	/ṣáto/	zato
think	/ṣínko/	cinco
thimble	/ṣímbre/	cimbre
ether	/íṣe/	hice
method	/méṣo/	mezo
path	/páṣ/	paz
Beth	/béṣ/	vez
both	/bóṣ/	voz

SPANISH CONSONANTS WHICH PRESENT NO REAL DIFFICULTY TO THE ENGLISH LEARNER—/ŋy/ and /(l)y/

The palatalized nasal [ŋy] could well be assigned to the phoneme sequence /ny/. The small number of contrasts between such pairs as huraño and uranio could then be represented

$$/urányo/ \neq /uránio/$$

Such a description has much to be said for it. The contrast may, however, also be represented

$$/uráṇyo/ \neq /urányo/$$

thus considering [ŋy] to belong to a separate phoneme. Phonetically the difference is that /ŋy/ consists of an [n] articulated with the middle part of the tongue followed by palatalized release, whereas /ny/ consists of an [n] articulated with the tip of the tongue followed by a palatalized release. Not only is the articulatory and acoustic difference small, the functional yield is low almost to the point of vanishing. It rarely if ever occurs as the sole differentiation between two normal utterances in conversation. From a pedagogical point of view, the sequence /ny/ can well be taught for both; but one may, as we do, indicate the difference by placing a hook beneath the [ŋ] in the [ŋy] sequence that represents the palatal: thus, /ŋy/. From the point of view of comprehension and/or accent, all the problems discussed heretofore take precedence so long as the /ny/ and /ŋy/ are pronounced with the syllable onset on the /n/; even the failure to get this detail right amounts to little by comparison with other matters.

The /(l)y/ can be found in a few American dialect areas such as the uplands of Colombia, Ecuador, Peru, Bolivia, among educated speakers in Asunción, and in rural Castile (but not in the metropolis of the area, Madrid; it is largely for this reason that speakers from Valladolid are said to speak the "best" Spanish—they have both the /ṣ/ and the /(l)y/). In the areas where the /(l)y/ occurs, a contrast between such pairs as sella vs. Celia, which is elsewhere clearly

$$/séya/ \neq /sélya/$$

or between <u>hallas</u> vs. <u>alias</u>, elsewhere quite clearly

$$/\text{áyas}/ \neq /\text{ályas}/$$

must be interpreted as /sélya/ ≠ /sélia/, /ályas/ ≠ /álias/
or, with a phoneme /(l)y/, as

$$/\text{sé(l)ya}/ \neq /\text{sélya}/, /\text{á(l)yas}/ \neq /\text{ályas}/.$$

It makes little difference for practical purposes how one chooses to transcribe it, because the contrast has an even lower functional yield than does the /ŋy/ set. Again, in a pedagogical transcription, we prefer to write a compromise which indicates the possibility of contrast but does not insist on it: for the palatal lateral, we write /(l)y/ with parentheses around the <u>l</u> to indicate that in many dialects it does not occur at all. So long as the sequence /ly/ or /(l)y/ is taught as having the syllable onset on the /l/, there is no problem.

It may now be noted that this hook which we write in the /ş/ and the /ŋy/, and the parentheses which we write around <u>l</u> in /(l)y/, mean, for the student: "These are distinctions of minor importance in the language, and it will not harm my expression or comprehension if I ignore them." For the teacher, it means: "I can insist that my students make this contrast if I have it in my own speech and if they are doing everything else extremely well." For our critics and analytically minded colleagues, it means: "We know where the contrasts are, and we are not ignoring them—just playing them down by a minimum modification in the symbols."

THE CONSONANT SEQUENCES OF ENGLISH AND SPANISH $\boxed{6}$

Up to this point we have generally dealt with the problems which arise from the differences between the consonants of English and Spanish. It is obvious, however, that consonants also combine with each other, and that the combining habits of the two languages are quite different. From these differences come further problems.

Our procedure will be to examine Spanish consonant sequences exhaustively, since they are both fewer and less complex than are the English sequences, and to point out the problems which arise.

SYLLABLE-INITIAL CLUSTERS—/Cl/

One kind of consonant cluster which occurs at the beginning of syllables is that of a consonant followed by /l/. The consonant preceding the /l/ may be /p b k g/ or /f/. This fact may be symbolized:

/Cl/   C = /p b k g f/

Aside from the lack of aspiration of /p/ and /k/ and the phonetic characteristics of the Spanish /l/, these present no problem, since all occur in English.

English	Spanish	
plan	/plán/	plan
blank	/blánka/	blanca
Clara	/klára/	clara
Gloria	/glórya/	Gloria
floor	/flór/	flor

It may be pointed out that perhaps /tl/ is also entering the pattern: /átlas, atléta, atlántiko/ and Mexican place names /tlaskála/ "Tlaxcala," /tústla/ "Tuxtla," /masatlán/ "Mazatlán." Since /tl/ does not occur in English except with the syllable onset at the /l/, the cluster constitutes a problem of some dimensions if it is to be mastered.

SYLLABLE-INITIAL CLUSTERS—/Cr/

Another kind of syllable-initial consonant cluster in Spanish is that of a consonant followed by /r/, thus:

70

/Cr/   C = /p b t d k g f r/

The only problems again are those which arise from the specific phonetic shape of the consonants involved: lack of aspiration on /p t k/ and the flap of the /r/ (trilled, as already discussed, in /rr/). The /r/ in these clusters may be a slightly retroflex spirant in the dialects of the lower west coast of South America. Elsewhere it is a flap. All the clusters but /rr/ (the trill which we have already observed is sometimes treated by linguists as a single phoneme /R/) occur in English; the difference which must be mastered lies in the difference between the English /r/ and the Spanish /r/.

English	Spanish	
presser	/présa/	presa
bravo	/brábo/	bravo
trace	/trés/	tres
drama	/dráma/	drama
dragoon	/dragón/	dragón
credo	/krédo/	credo
grammar	/gráma/	grama
grasses	/grásas/	grasas
fresco	/frésko/	fresco
	/rrósa/	rosa

SYLLABLE-INITIAL CLUSTERS—/Cy/

C = all C except /ch y w ŋy (l)y/

It is not possible to list pairs of similar-sounding words from Spanish and English in this pattern, since at the beginning of strong and medial stressed syllables in English /Cy/ normally occurs only before the vowel /ʋ/ (actually /ʋw/ except before /r/); in Spanish it rarely occurs before /u/; /u/ is a phoneme of low frequency in Spanish. The obvious difficulty for an English speaker will be to place /Cy/ before any Spanish vowel except /u/, but he can be taught to do so by comparing a Spanish word with one in English which has the same /Cy/ cluster before /u/ instead of before a vowel more like the Spanish one. Thus, if a student cannot produce the initial cluster of /fyéra/, it may be suggested that he try English few and then "start /fyéra/ the same way."

The patterning of /Cy/ in Spanish is shown below with examples of each possible cluster:

/py/	/pyáno/	piano	/pyé/	pie	/pyóho/	piojo
/ty/	/tyára/	tiara	/tyéne/	tiene	/sintyó/	sintió
/ky/	/kyén/	quien	/kyére/	quiere	/kyósko/	quiosco
/by/	/byáhe/	viaje	/byého/	viejo	/byó/	vio
/dy/	/dyénte/	diente	/dyéta/	dieta	/dyós/	dios
/gy/	/gyár	guiar	/álgyen/	alguien	/gyó/	guio
/fy/	/fyánṣa/	fianza	/fyésta/	fiesta	/fyó/	fio
/ṣy/	/ṣyátiko/	ciático	/ṣyérra/	cierra	/koṣyó/	coció

/sy/	/syamés/	siamés	/syérra/	sierra	/tosyó/	tosió
/hy/	/máhya/	magia	/suhyéro/	sugiero	/kohyó/	cogió
/my/	/anémya/	anemia	/myél/	miel	/myópe/	miope
/ny/	/antónya/	Antonia	/nyégo/	niego	/demónyo/	demonio
/ly/	/lyár/	liar	/lyébre/	liebre	/húlyo/	Julio
/ry/	/memórya/	memoria	/baryár/	variar	/primáryo/	primario

In English, the permitted /Cy/ clusters vary somewhat from dialect to dialect. In parts of the South and in some other areas, /Cyʋw/ does not exist at all, so that words like few and hue, which are /fyʋ́w/ and /hyʋ́w/ in most dialects, are /ffw/ and /hfw/. On the other hand, certain Southern dialects have developed /Cy/ clusters in words like /kyár/ car and /kyǽr∔y/ carry. Leaving these dialects aside, we may divide the others into two large groups: those which regularly have /yʋ́w/ after the consonants /t d ş s n l/ in strong-stressed syllables, and those which do not.

/t/	Tuesday, tune
/d/	dew, duty
/ş/	thew, enthusiastic
/s/	sue, suit
/n/	new, nude
/l/	lieu, lute

American English, however, generally has /y/ after /p b f m k g/ regardless of stress: /yʋw/ or /yʋr/ with strong or medial stress, /y∔w/ or /y∔r/ with weak stress. Most dialects have /yʋw/ also after /h/, as in hue, but some Middle Atlantic seaboard dialects have only /yʋw/ in such a word exactly paralleling their /w/ instead of /hw/ in words like where.

	/yʋw/			/y∔w/, /y∔r/
/p/	pew	pewter	puritanical	popularity
/b/	beauty	bugle	bureaucracy	contribute
/f/	few	perfume	futuristic	refutation
/m/	mute	music	municipal	immunize
/k/	cute	cube	occupy	cupidity
/g/	gewgaw		argue	virgule
/h/	hue	huge		

Finally, even those dialects which do not have /yʋw/ after the alveolar consonants in stressed syllables regularly have the /y∔w/ after /l/, /n/ and /ş/ in weak-stressed syllables.

/l/	salutation, salutary
/n/	monument, granulate
/ş/	Matthew

Since /Cy/ occurs frequently before /v/ in English, but rarely before /u/ in Spanish, and since the /Cy/ cluster is obligatory in English in certain restricted environments, the English speaker will often insert /y/ into Spanish sequences of /C/ plus /u/, as in the following instances:

	English /Cyu/	Spanish /Cu/		Probable Error /Cyu/
/py/	puberty	/pubertád/	pubertad	[pyubertád]
	punitive	/punitíbo/	punitivo	[pyunitíbo]
	purify	/purifikár/	purificar	[pyurifikár]
	putrid	/pútrido/	pútrido	[pyútrido]
	popular	/populár/	popular	[popyulár]
/by/	bureaucracy	/burokráşya/	burocracia	[byurokráşya]
	butane	/butáno/	butano	[byutáno]
	distribution	/distribuşyón/	distribución	[distribyuşyón]
	tribunal	/tribunál/	tribunal	[tribyunál]
	vocabulary	/bokabuláryo/	vocabulario	[bokabyuláryo]
/fy/	fume	/fúma/	fuma	[fyúma]
	funeral	/funerál/	funeral	[fyunerál]
	fugue	/fúga/	fuga	[fyúga]
	futile	/fútil/	fútil	[fyútil]
	future	/futúra/	futura	[fyutúra]
/my/	mule	/múla/	mula	[myúla]
	municipal	/munişipál/	municipal	[myunişipál]
	museum	/muséo/	museo	[myuséo]
	music	/músika/	música	[myúsika]
	immunize	/in munişar/	inmunizar	[inmyunişár]
/ky/	Cuba	/kúba/	Cuba	[kyúba]
	cubical	/kúbiko/	cúbico	[kyúbiko]
	occupied	/okupádo/	ocupado	[okyupádo]
	occulist	/okulísta/	oculista	[okyulísta]
	particular	/partikulár/	particular	[partikyulár]
/gy/	regular	/rregulár/	regular	[rregyulár]
	regulation	/rregulaşyón/	regulación	[rregyulaşyón]
	figure	/figúrese/	figurese	[figyúrese]
	argue	/argwír/	arguir	[argyuír]
/hy/	huge	/hugár/	jugar	[hyugár]
	Huguenot	/hubilóso/	jubiloso	[hyubilóso]
	hewn	/huntár/	juntar	[hyuntár]
	Huron	/hurár/	jurar	[hyurár]

/ly/	salutations	/salutaşyónes/	salutaciones	[salyutaşyónes]
	salutary	/saludár/	saludar	[salyudár]
	emolument	/emoluménto/	emolumento	[emolyuménto]
/ny/	monument	/monuménto/	monumento	[monyuménto]
	monumental	/monumentál/	monumental	[monyumentál]
	granulate	/granulár/	granular	[granyulár]

It is not only the /Cy-/ clusters followed by /u/ that will give the English speaker problems in learning Spanish. The /Cyu/ problem results from an obligatory (or nearly obligatory) English pattern matched against a near-zero occurrence in Spanish. The other /Cy-/ problem results from the conflict between a near-zero sequence in English and an optional one in Spanish—namely, the problem of acquiring /Cy/ before vowels other than /u/. The most nearly similar English sequence is /C+yV/. Compare the following lists:

	English /C+y/	Spanish /Cy/		Probable Error /Ciy/
/p-/	recipient	/rreşipyénte/	recipiénte	[rresipiyénte]
/t-/	meteor	/metyó/	metió	[metiyó]
/k-/	trachea	/trákya/	tráquea	[trákiya]
/b-/	ambient	/ambyénte/	ambiente	[ambiyénte]
/d-/	compendious	/kompendyóso/	compendioso	[kompendiyóso]
/g-/	Guiana	/gyána/	Guiana	[giyána]
/f-/	fiasco	/fyásko/	fiasco	[fiyásko]
/ş-/	healthier	/gráşyas/	gracias	[gráşiyas]
/s-/	controversial	/kontrobersyál/	controversial	[kontrobersiyál]
/m-/	roomier	/rrúmya/	rumia	[rrúmiya]
/n-/	harmonious	/armonyóso	harmonioso	[armoniyóso]
/l-/	filial	/filyál/	filial	[filiyál]
/r-/	furious	/furyóso/	furioso	[furiyóso]

The American's tendency to insert /i/ between /C/ and /y/ in Spanish /Cy/ clusters is seriously reinforced by Spanish spelling, where the /y/ is represented by the symbol i. But since the /y/ that is represented by i is never syllabic (does not count as a syllable), whereas the /i/ that the American inserts is syllabic, the distortion is gross even if it is intelligible.

The Spanish cluster /-ry-/ is a problem because English speakers have this only rarely in weak-stressed syllables and not at all otherwise.

/máryo/	Mario
/báryo/	bario
/nórya/	noria
/baryó/	varió
/muryó/	murió
/iryó/	hirió

The /-ry-/ is here written with a hyphen before and after, because it cannot occur initially —only /rry-/ is permitted initially (see the discussion of three-consonant sequences beginning on p. 80).

SPECIAL PROBLEMS IN SPANISH /Cy-/ CLUSTERS ARISING FROM HABITS OF ASSIMILATION IN ENGLISH

/s, z, t, d/ plus /y/

The clusters /sy/, /ty/, and /dy/ occur in English only to a limited extent, even before /u/. Further, the speaker of English has many habits which make it likely that he will attempt to use his English sounds /š/, /ch/, and /ǰ/, respectively, in place of the Spanish sequences /sy/, /ty/, and /dy/.

One important factor is that in conversational English when one of the consonants /s/, /z/, /t/, or /d/ at the end of a word is followed by /y/ at the beginning of the next word, it may be assimilated to the /y/ to yield /š/, /ž/, /ch/, or /ǰ/. This usually happens when the words are pronounced closely together without the boundary element between them. It is especially frequent when the second word is you.

/sy/ → /š/	/zy/ → /ž/	/ty/ → /ch/	/dy/ → /ǰ/
miss you	please you	won't you	did you
kiss you	tease you	hit you	would you

Further support for the incorrect pronunciation of Spanish /sy/, /ty/, and /dy/ comes from phenomena which occur within words in English. For instance, the suffix spelled -ure begins with a /y/ in the pronunciation of words like tenure, figure. When the suffix added to a word or stem ending in /s/, /z/, /t/, or /d/, the result is /š/, /ž/, /ch/, /ǰ/:

press	pressure
seize	seizure
legislate	legislature
proceed	procedure

Certain words commonly pronounced with /š/, /ž/, /ch/, and /ǰ/ also have pronunciations with /sy/, /zy/, /ty/, and /dy/, which are often considered more elegant. From our present point of view, the existence of these alternate pronunciations only serves to reinforce the English speaker's feeling that in fact /sy/ and /š/, /zy/ and /ž/, /ty/ and /ch/, and /dy/ and /ǰ/ can be equated.

issue	/íšɨw/	/ísyɨw/
visual	/vížwɨl/	/vízyɨwɨl/
nature	/néychɨr/	/néytyɨr/
education	/ɛǰɨkéyšɨn/	/ɛdyɨwkéyšɨn/

These habits of the English speaker make it probable that he will fail to produce the Spanish clusters /sy/, /ty/, and /dy/ easily.

Three types of mispronunciation of /sy/, /ty/, and /dy/ are likely. (1) The English speaker will use /š/ (or, influenced by English words similar to the Spanish words, even /ž/), /ch/, or /ǰ/. (2) He will use /siy/, /tiy/, or /diy/, adding an extra vowel to break up the sequence, as with the other /Cy/ clusters discussed previously. (3) He will combine both types of error, and use /šiy/, /žiy/, /chiy/, or /ǰiy/. Which type of error is made is most influenced by similarities of Spanish words to English words. In endeavoring to correct a mispronunciation of one type, the learner often shifts to another. The following examples illustrate the three types of possibilities:

FIRST TYPE OF ERROR[1]

/sy/ → [š]

/grásyas/	gracias	→	[grášas]
/rrasyonál/	racional	→	[rrašonál]
/diskusyón/	discusión	→	[diskušón]
/sósyo/	socio	→	[sóšo]
/fasyál/	facial	→	[fašál]
/notísya/	noticia	→	[notíša]
/malísya/	malicia	→	[malíša]
/nasyonál/	nacional	→	[našonál]
/delisyóso/	delicioso	→	[delišóso]
/apresyár/	apreciar	→	[arešár]
/milísya/	milicia	→	[milíša]
/komfesyón/	confesion	→	[komɲfešón]

/sy/ → [ž]

/elisyón/	elisión	→	[eližón]
/ilusyón/	ilusión	→	[ilužón]

/ty/ → [ch]

/kwestyón/	cuestión	→	[kweschón]
/bastyón/	bastión	→	[baschón]
/bestyál/	bestial	→	[beschál]
/selestyál/	celestial	→	[seleschál]

/dy/ → [ǰ]

/kordyál/	cordial	→	[korǰál]

---

1. In these examples, /ș/ is treated as /s/ although transcribed as /ș/.

SECOND TYPE OF ERROR

/sy/ → [siy]

/soşyolohía/	sociología	→	[sosiyolohía]
/sóşyo/	socio	→	[sósiyo]
/cásyo/	Casio	→	[kásiyo]
/ofişyál/	oficial	→	[ofisiyál]
/enunşyár/	enunciar	→	[enunsiyár]

/ty/ → [tiy]

/tyéne/	tiene	→	[tiyéne]
/tyérra/	tierra	→	[tiyérra]
/tyémpo/	tiempo	→	[tiyémpo]
/tyénda/	tienda	→	[tiyénda]

/dy/ → [diy]

/dyáblo/	diablo	→	[diyáblo]
/dyána/	Diana	→	[diyána]
/dyéntes/	dientes	→	[diyéntes]

THIRD TYPE OF ERROR

/sy/ → [šiy]

/mişyón/	misión	→	[mišiyón]
/terşyáryo/	terciario	→	[teršiyáryo]
/bişyóso/	vicioso	→	[bišiyóso]

/sy/ → [žiy]

/bisyón/	visión	→	[bižiyón]
/elisyón/	elisión	→	[eližiyón]
/rrebisyón/	revisión	→	[rrebižiyón]

/ty/ → chiy

| /kwestyón/ | cuestión | → | [kweschiyón] |
| /bestyál/ | bestial | → | [beschiyál] |

/dy/ → ǰiy

| /kordyál/ | cordial | → | [korǰiyál] |

SYLLABLE-INITIAL CLUSTERS—/Cw/

C = all C except /w/, /ŋy/, and /(l)y/

This type of cluster has the widest distribution of any in Spanish, but it is limited in English. The only /Cw/ clusters that English and Spanish have in common are listed below, with examples:

	English		Spanish
/tw/	twice	/twérṣe/	tuerce
/kw/	quart	/kwárto/	quarto
/dw/	dwindle	/dwénde/	duende
/gw/	Guam	/gwám/	Guam
/ṣw/	thwack	/ṣwéco/	zueco
/sw/	swear	/swérte/	suerte
/hw/	whistle	/hwíṣyo/	juicio

The additional Spanish consonants that cluster with /w/ are /p/, /b/, /ch/, /f/, /m/, /n/, /l/, /r/, and /y/. Of these, /pw/, /bw/, /fw/, and /mw/ may be considered marginal in English: most Americans know that Puerto Rico, Buenos Aires, Fuentes, and moiré are not /pyʊ-/, /byʊ-/, /fyʊ-/, and /moy-/, but certainly the common pronunciation of place names like Buena Vista is still /byʊwnɨ vístɨ/. Perhaps because of such familiarity, perhaps because of the structural similarity of /Cw/ to /Cy/—specifically /py/, /by/, /fy/, and /my/—these four clusters are much easier for English speakers to master than /chw/, /nw/, /lw/, /rw/, and /yw/. A complete set of Spanish /Cw/ clusters is listed below:

/pw/	/pwéde/	puede	/pwérta/	puerta	/pwés/	pues
/tw/	/twérka/	tuerca	/twérto/	tuerto	/twétano/	tuétano
/kw/	/kwál/	cual	/kwénta/	cuenta	/kwóta/	cuota
/bw/	/bwéno/	bueno	/bwéy/	buey	/bwítre/	buitre
/dw/	/dwélo/	duelo	/dwéɲyo/	dueño	/dwíta/	duita
/gw/	/gwáro/	guaro	/gwélfos/	güelfos	/gwipíl/	güipil
/chw/	/chwál/	chual	/chwéko/	chueco	/chwíta/	chuita
/fw/	/fwénte/	fuente	/fwéte/	fuete	/fwímos/	fuimos
/ṣw/	/ṣwábo/	zuavo	/ṣwéko/	zueco	/ṣwíṣa/	zuiza
/sw/	/swábe/	suave	/swérte/	suerte	/swíṣo/	suizo
/hw/	/hwána/	Juana	/hwébes/	Jueves	/hwéṣ/	juez
/mw/	/mwaré/	muaré	/mwéka/	mueco	/mwérto/	muerto
/nw/	/nwébe/	nueve	/nwéṣ/	nuez	/nwéra/	nuera
/ɲyw/	/paɲywélo/	pañuelo	/buɲywélo/	buñuelo	/seɲywélo/	señuelo
/lw/	/lwégo/	luego	/lwéngo/	luengo	/lwegíto/	lueguito
/(l)yw/	/(l)ywébe/	llueve	/(l)ywéba/	llueva	/(l)ywéka/	llueca
/rw/	/ṣirwéla/	ciruela	/terwél/	Teruel	/perwáno/	peruano
/yw/	/(l)ywébe/	llueve	/(l)ywéba/	llueva	/(l)ywéka/	llueca

As with /Cy/ clusters, Spanish spelling is misleading: seeing a vocalic symbol u, the student tends to insert a vowel /u/, producing /Cuw/. That the letter u does not represent a vowel /u/ in the sequence CuV is admirably reflected in the contrast between düeto and duelo. The former has three syllables, the latter two—a fact shown in the spelling by the dieresis.

Perhaps the most difficult problem in the /Cw/ clusters is created, not by the absence of similar clusters in English, but by the conflict between Spanish /Cw/ and English /C‡w/ under weak stress. In the discussion of /Cy/ clusters above, we observed that /Cy/ occurs in English almost exclusively before /ʋw/ and /‡w/, and further that it is obligatory that /y/ appear between /C/ and /‡w/ under weak stress before another vowel:[2] gradual, evacuate, ambiguous. There are many English words with /Cy‡wV/ which have Spanish counterparts with /CwV/.

The list of correspondences below is incomplete: we have postponed three particularly troublesome sequences for separate discussion, and five of the theoretical possibilities do not exist.

	English	Spanish		Probable Error
/p-/	-------			
/k-/	evacuate	/ebakwár/	evacuar	[ebakyuwár]
/b-/	-------			
/g-/	ambiguous	/ambígwo/	ambiguo	[ambígyuwo]
/f-/	-------			
/ş-/	-------			
/m-/	Samuel	/samwél/	Samuel	[samyuwél]
/n-/	manual	/manuál/	manual	[manyuwál]
/l-/	evaluate	/ebalwár/	evaluar	[ebalyuwár]
/r-/	-------			

The three omitted consonants, /t/, /d/, and /s/, in English assimilate to a following /y/ as described earlier (p. 75)—that is, /ty/ → /ch/, /dy/ → /ǰ/, and /sy/ → /š/ or /ž/. These combining habits interfere with Spanish /tw/, /dw/, and /sw/ in examples like the ones below, where /y/ is generated before the English /‡/, as above, and assimilates to the preceding consonant:

	English	Spanish		Probable Error
		/ty/ → [ch]		
/tw/	punctual	/puntwál/	puntual	[puŋchuwál]
	tempestuous	/tempestwóso/	tempestuoso	[tempeschuwóso]
	perpetual	/perpetwóso/	perpetuoso	[perpechuwóso]
	textual	/testwál/	textual	[tekschuwál]
	perpetuate	/perpetwár/	perpetuar	[perpechuwár]
		/dy/ → [ǰ]		
/dw/	residual	/rresidwál/	residual	[rresiǰuwál]
	arduous	/árdwo/	arduo	[árǰuwo]
	gradual	/gradwál/	gradual	[graǰuwál]
		/sy/ → [ž]		
/sy/	usual	/uswál/	usual	[užuwál]
	visual	/biswál/	visual	[bižuwál]

2. If a consonant follows, the /‡w/ is often reduced to /‡/: monument /mány‡m‡nt/. It is less likely to be reduced if followed by a vowel: gradual /grǽǰ‡w‡l/.

SYLLABLE-INITIAL CLUSTERS OF THREE CONSONANTS

The first member of three-consonant initial clusters in Spanish must be a stop: /p/, /b/, /t/, /d/, /k/, /g/, /f/, or /r/. The second member must be an /l/ or /r/. The third must be a semivowel: /y/ or /w/. The sequences /tl-/, /dl-/, and /rl-/ are not permitted (see p. 70 above). The possible clusters are listed below. Not all are word-initial.

	/-ry-/	/-rw-/	/-ly-/	/-lw-/
/p-/	/pryéto/ prieto	/prwéba/ prueba	/plyégo/ pliego	/plwésti/ Pluesti
/b-/	/bryál/ brial	/brwéta/ brueta	/bíblya/ biblia	/ablwénte/ abluente
/f-/	/fryégo/ friego	/frwír/ fruir	/kantinflyár/ Cantinfliar	/flwénte/ fluente
/t-/	/tryúmfo/ triunfo	/trwéko/ trueco	--------	--------
/d-/	/bídryo/ vidrio	/drwída/ druida	--------	--------
/r-/	/rryésgo/ riesgo	/rrwído/ ruido	--------	--------
/k-/	/kryánṣa/ crianza	/krwél/ cruel	/klyénte/ cliente	/klwéka/ clueca
/g-/	/gryégo/ griego	/grwéso/ grueso	(/manglyár/) (mangliar)	(/iglwár/) (igluar)

The items in parentheses are regionalisms of restricted usage. They fill slots in the pattern which would otherwise be vacant.

These clusters do not occur in English, where all three-consonant initial clusters begin with /s-/ (which produces clusters that are of the highest order of difficulty for the Spanish speaker learning English). English speakers will invariably try to introduce an extra vowel into the sequence—that is, break the cluster into two syllables: /krwél/ ⇀ /kruwél/, /klyénte/ ⇀ /kliyénte/, and so on.

SYLLABLE-FINAL CLUSTERS

Syllable-final clusters do not normally occur in Spanish. The one possible exception to this generalization is in items like /béynte/ veinte, /ayslár/ aislar, /awnké/ aunque, /káwstiko/ cáustico, where /-yn/, /-ys/, /-wn/, and /-ws/ are clearly syllable-final. It is characteristic of /y/ and /w/, however, that they behave like consonants when they appear before a vowel, clustering with any other consonants that occur with them; but they behave like part of the nucleus of the syllable when they occur after a vowel, and must be said to cluster with the vowel rather than with any following consonant.

MEDIAL CLUSTERS

Medial clusters in Spanish are of two types: (1) INTRASYLLABIC—that is, they belong only to the second of the two syllable peaks between which they appear as medial, and (2) INTERSYLLABIC—that is, one member of the cluster belongs with the first syllable peak, the other with the second, and syllable division occurs between the members of the cluster. All the intrasyllabic clusters are syllable-initial and have been discussed above. The intersyllabic clusters consist of the limited list of syllable-final consonants (exclusive of the semivowels /y/ and /w/) /s/, /ş/, /m/, /n/, /l/, and /r/ (and less commonly a few others, like /f/), followed by any of the syllable-initial clusters examined above. An exhaustive list of these is not needed here, but a few special problems must be discussed.

MEDIAL CLUSTERS OF IDENTICAL CONSONANTS

One cluster of identical consonants is unique in that it can occur initially: /rr/. It could, of course, be analyzed as a phoneme different from /r/ rather than a cluster of two /r/'s. The arguments favoring either analysis, /r̄/ or /rr/, are technical and, from the pedagogical point of view, trivial.

In general, clusters of identical consonants signal the presence of a boundary element between them. All the forms in column B below can be interpreted as meaning either the parallel citation in column A or that in column C, whereas those in column D (containing a boundary element shown by the lengthened—i.e., doubled—consonant) are unambiguous pronunciations of the citations in column C. (Features of stress and vowel sequence are manipulated for the purpose just as they can in fact occur.)

A	B	C	D
ese lápiz	[éselápiş]	es el lápiz	[ésellápiş]
el apis	[elápis]	el lápiz	[ellápiş]
el hecho	[elécho]	el lecho	[ellécho]
él imita	[elimíta]	él limita	[ellimíta]
el oro	[elóro]	el loro	[ellóro]
Raquel ha botado.	[rrakélabotádo]	Raquel la ha botado.	[rrakéllabotádo]
tiene nana tienen Ana	[tyénenána]	tienen nana	[tyénennána]
un aire	[unáyre]	un naire	[unnáyre]
un erbio	[unérbyo]	un nervio	[unnérbyo]
ven aves ve naves	[benábes]	ven naves	[bennábes]
Dénoslo.	[dénozlo]	Dénnoslo.	[dénnozlo]
es un hombre	[ésunómbre]	es un nombre	[ésunnómbre]
todo somos	[tódosómos]	todos somos	[tódossómos]
cuánto salieron	[kwántosalyéron]	cuántos salieron	[kwántossalyéron]
uno cincuenta	[únoşinkwénta]	unos cincuenta	[únosşinkwénta]
las olas	[lasólas]	las solas	[lassólas]
las obras	[lasóbras]	las sobras	[lassóbras]
las alas	[lasálas]	las salas	[lassálas]

/l/, /n/, and /s/ seem to be the only consonants capable of doubling across a boundary element; /r+r/ is impossible because /rr/ is an initial cluster, and the /r+rr/ that might conceivably result from a final /r/ and an initial /rr/ turns out to be merely /rr/, indistinguishable from any other instance of /rr/:

/kolórróho/   coló rojo   color rojo

Infrequently, a /y/ + /y/, or /w/ + /w/ may be brought together. The result is usually simply /y/ or /w/.

/léyérta/   ley yerta
/gráwérta/   Grau-Huerta

In some dialects of Chilean Spanish, /r/ assimilates to a following /n/ or /l/ with the result that /kárlos/ Carlos is pronounced /kállos/, and /kárne/ carne is pronounced /kánne/. In such a dialect, the following pairs cannot be distinguished (both sounding like the second).

[medyóunakornáda]	[medyóunakonnáda]
medió una cornada	medió una con nada
[atúrnokéda]	[atúnnokéda]
a turno queda	atún no queda
[ibérnomás]	[ibénnomás]
y ver no más	y ven no más
[amárlapensó]	[amállapensó]
amarla pensó	a mal la pensó
[kontárlaḃyó]	[contállaḃyó]
contar la vió	con tal la vió
[animárlaḃyéha]	[animállaḃyéha]
animar la vieja	animal la vieja

MEDIAL CLUSTERS OF NON-IDENTICAL CONSONANTS

MINOR PATTERNS

The major patterns of syllable structure in Spanish allow as final consonants only /s/, /ş/, /m/, /n/, /l/, /r/, and the semivowels /y/ and /w/. It is true that other consonants may also occur, but the fact that they run counter to the major patterns is demonstrated by the kinds of simplifications and alternations that they undergo. The clusters that result from the occurrence of these minor patterns of final consonants appear largely in learned vocabulary, and even among educated speakers there is not always agreement about what the cluster should consist of.

<u>Items in which clusters tend to be reduced</u>

/-pt-/	/septyémbre/	Septiembre	→	/setyémbre/
	/séptimo/	séptimo	→	/sétimo/

/-nst-/	/instánte/	instante	→	/istánte/
/-ks-/	/eksámen/	examen	→	/esámen/
/-bm-/	/submaríno/	submarino	→	/sumaríno/

Alternation between voiced stop and voiceless stop

/-b/ ~ /-p/	/obtenér/	obtener	~	/optenér/
	/absolúto/	absoluto	~	/apsolúto/
	/abhurár/	abjurar	~	/aphurár/
/-d/ ~ /-t/	/bódka/	vodka	~	/bótka/
	/édniko/	étnico	~	/étniko/
	/admósfera/	atmosféra	~	/atmósfera/
/-g/ ~ /-k/	/tégniko/	técnico	~	/tékniko/

Alternation between altogether different clusters

/ekşétera/	etcétera	~	/etşétera/
/eklíkse/	eclipse	~	/eklípse/
/ekşelénte/	excelente	~	/esşelénte/
/ítmo/	istmo	~	/ísmo/

Clusters of Minor Patterns

/aftósa/	aftosa
/abdómen/	abdomen
/dígno/	digno
/aktíbo/	activo
/akşyón/	acción
/perspikáş/	perspicaz
/óptimo/	óptimo

MEDIAL CLUSTERS OF NON-IDENTICAL CONSONANTS
MAJOR PATTERNS

As noted above, the only frequent syllable-final consonants are /s/, /ş/, /m/, /n/, /l/, /r/, and the semivowels. When the next syllable begins with any single consonant or with any of the permitted initial clusters, the result is a medial cluster. Few of these cause any trouble for the English-speaking student other than the troubles with initial clusters that have already been discussed. The minor problems that do arise are the following.

1. In Spanish, [m] occurs in medial clusters only before the labials /p/, /b/. [ɱ] occurs before /f/. [ŋ] occurs only before the velars /k/, /g/, /h/, /+w/. [n<] occurs before /t/, /d/. [ɲ] occurs before /ch/. [n] occurs elsewhere, before /s/, /ş/, /n/, /l/, and /rr/. In other words, before a consonant the only optional choice a Spanish speaker has is to produce a nasal or not to. If he chooses to produce one, the particular shape of it—[m], [ɱ], [n<], [n], [ɲ], or [ŋ]—is obligatorily determined by the following consonant. Since the choice of nasality before a consonant is not similarly restricted in English, the

student must learn to select the appropriate nasal automatically. He must be especially warned that the orthography often fails to show the correct shape: <u>un barco</u> /umbárko/, <u>un parque</u> /umpárke/, <u>naranja</u> [naráŋha].

2. The sequence /-nt-/ in English is phonetically different from the /-nt-/ of Spanish. Compare the following similarly structured items:

English	Spanish	
Tonto	/tánto/	tanto
lentil	/lénte/	lente
pinto	/pínto/	pinto
Santa Monica	/sántamónika/	Santa Monica
quantity	/kantidád/	cantidad
Tantalus	/tántalo/	Tántalo
hunter, junta	/húnta/	junta
antidote	/antídoto/	antídoto

A widespread pronunciation of intervocalic /nt/ in American English is a single flap following a nasalized vowel. On the other hand, in the Spanish cluster /nt/, the /n/ is relatively long and distinct and the /t/ is articulated like any other /t/—not like a flap. The English flap pronunciation of this sequence can seriously distort these Spanish items.

3. Whenever the Spanish sequence /-nrr-/ occurs, the transition between /-n-/ and the following /-rr-/ generates an articulation that may be phonetically represented as $[-n^d rr-]$, because the /rr/ trill begins with the tongue tip up. The American trying to imitate the intrusive $[-^d-]$ will exaggerate it, and therefore needs to be cautioned.

$[un^d rríko]$	un rico
$[en^d rrío]$	en Río
$[kon^d rrítmo]$	con ritmo
$[sán^d rrafaél]$	San Rafael

4. A problem which should not cause any serious difficulty, but which should be called to the attention of students, results from the fact that /s/ frequently clusters with a following consonant when it appears medially in English, but in Spanish it never does—the syllable division in the Spanish sequence /-sC-/ is /-s.C-/. Compare the following examples:

English	Spanish	
respectable	/respetable/	respetable

A more serious problem, however, is the correspondence between English initial /sC-/ and Spanish /es.C-/:

English	Spanish	
squeal	/eskwéla/	escuela
scribble	/eskríbe/	escríbe
stodgy	/estádo/	estado
steal	/estíla/	estila
Slav	/eslábo/	eslavo
snow	/esnón/	esnón

THE VOWEL 7
SYSTEMS

As we did in discussing the consonant systems, for comparative purposes we could divide the vowels into two groups: (1) those where English influence would lead to misunderstanding; and (2) those where English influence would not cause misunderstanding but would produce a heavy foreign accent. The vowels, however, are all much alike in the problems they create. The basic division is not between one class of vowels and another in Spanish itself, but rather between the habits of vowel restriction (or reduction) that English imposes on syllables under weak stress and the absence of such restriction under stronger stress. In other words, the most difficult problem among Spanish vowels for the English speaker concerns the vowels under weak stress. But it is logically more satisfactory to begin our discussion with the vowel system as a whole, and then proceed to the specific problems of unstressed vowels. We therefore abandon our roughly hierarchical arrangement for the moment, returning to it subsequently to present several possible sequences organized by several different criteria.

In setting up the vowel phonemes of a language, it is useful to consider the positions—or environments—in which contrasts occur, as we have with the consonants. Actually, English has at least three vowel systems in different environments within words, whereas Spanish has only <u>one</u> system that does not vary significantly from one position in a word to another. Furthermore, the English vowel system is considerably more elaborate than that of Spanish in terms of the number of SYLLABIC NUCLEI (a vowel is the nucleus of a syllable), both SIMPLE and COMPLEX. (A simple nucleus is a single vowel. A complex nucleus [diphthong] is a single vowel followed by a glide [semivowel].) In order to examine these vowel systems, let us recall the symbols and key words from the two languages that were introduced in Chapter 4.

Five symbols are necessary for simple front vowels, two for Spanish and three for English:

[i]	sí	(Spanish)
[ɪ]	bit	(English)
[e]	sé	(Spanish)
[ɛ]	set	(English)
[æ]	sat	(English)

Five symbols are necessary for simple back vowels, two for Spanish and three for English:

[u]	su	(Spanish)
[ʊ]	soot	(English, rhyming with put)
[o]	lo	(Spanish)
[ʌ]	but	(English)
[ɔ]	sought	(English)

Only one symbol is necessary for central vowels in stressed syllables in both English and Spanish:

[a]   sot   (English),   sala   (Spanish)

One final symbol is necessary for the central unstressed vowel of English— [ɨ]—but it will not be discussed until after the system of stressed vowels has been examined.

The vowel system of English which is described below is a NORMALIZED system for American English, perhaps even idealized—that is, English has, between one dialect and another, extremely wide variation in the vowels; Spanish has almost none. This normalized system includes the vowel contrasts that are most widely shared by speakers of American English. It is merely a convenient point of departure: the varieties of standard American English which have systems different from this one will be touched upon from time to time as special problems arise in dealing with the comparable system of Spanish.

Seven simple nuclei occur in English in syllables with strong or medial stress. These seven STRESSED VOWELS or FULL VOWELS are:

[ɪ]	sit, bit, bin, fill, fizz, Rick
[ɛ]	set, bet, Ben, fell, fez, wreck
[æ]	sat, bat, ban, jazz, wrack
[a]	sot, pot, don, rock
[ɔ]	sought, bought, dawn, fall, laws, hawk
[ʌ]	putt, but, done, lull, does, luck
[ʊ]	soot, put, could, full, hook

Their articulatory positions relative to each other are shown, slightly normalized, in the following chart:

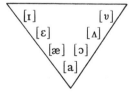 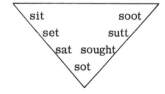 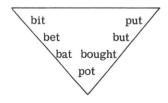

The movement of the tongue downward and backward can be felt by repeating in sequence the items on the left diagonal; the movement of the tongue upward and still farther toward the back can be felt by repeating in sequence the items on the right diagonal. The only deviation from this strictly symmetrical progression is felt in the vowel [ʌ], which is phonetically slightly more central than this normalized chart indicates, approximately as indicated below:

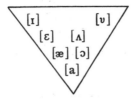

It deviates also in the fact that whereas the vowels above it and below it—[ʋ] and [ɔ], respectively—are slightly lip-rounded, it is not. Because of these two deviations from the symmetrical pattern, it is often analyzed as a central vowel (and frequently written with the phonetic symbol [ə] rather than with our symbol [ʌ]).

In examining the English vowels that are charted above, one notices a number of omissions. We have listed the vowels of sit, set, sat, sot, sought, but, soot, but we have failed to list those of sea, say, sigh, sow, soy, sew, sue. These seven are complex nuclei (diphthongs) consisting of combinations of the simple nuclei and glides, either [y] (toward a higher, tenser, fronter tongue position) or [w] (toward a higher, tenser, backer tongue position and greater lip rounding).

These appear below (note that the simple nucleus [æ] is unmatched by a complex nucleus, whereas [a] is matched by two complex nuclei, one with [y] and one with [w]):

[ɪy]   see, seat, beat, bean, feel, fees, reek
[ɛy]   say, sate, bait, bane, fail, faze, rake
[ay]   sigh, sight, bite, dine, file, eyes, like
[ɔy]   soy, quoit, loin, boil, boys
[aw]   sow, bout, down, foul, boughs
[ʌw]   sew, boat, roan, foal, foes, coke
[ʋw]   sue, boot, moon, fool, booze, Luke

The articulatory positions of the complex nuclei relative to each other are shown, again slightly normalized, in the following chart:

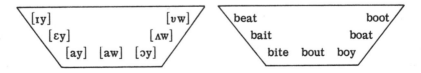

The articulatory positions of both the simple and the complex nuclei are shown below:

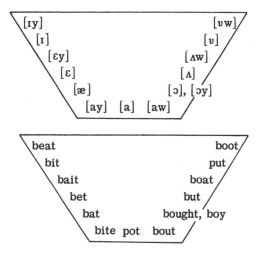

It is clear from the chart that the phonetic quality of the four simple vowels [ɪ], [ɛ], [ʌ], and [ʊ] in the environment of a following [y] or [w] is somewhat higher than their phonetic quality when not followed by [y] or [w]. In the two back vowels with [w]— [ʌw] and [ʊw]—the starting point of the vowel is both farther back and more fully lip-rounded. The difference between [ʌ] alone and [ʌ] with a following [w] is so marked, in fact, that hereafter we write them with different symbols in order to achieve a more direct one-to-one phonetic correspondence between our phonemic symbols and the actual pronunciation. We write /ʌ/ in contrast with /ow/, even though the transcription /ʌ/ vs. /ʌw/ would be adequate. The notation we are using is now summarized in a single chart.

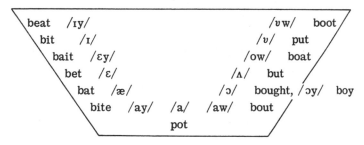

The above nuclei constitute the STRESSED VOWEL SYSTEM of English in a normalized phonemic transcription.

Not all the vowels of the system occur in all environments. Before a boundary element, for instance, the vowels /ɪ/, /ɛ/, and /ʊ/ never occur (of course, when a glide follows—/ɪy/, /ɛy/, /ʊw/—the vowel is not final, although the nucleus may be); and the vowels /æ/ and /ʌ/ are extreme' rare before a boundary element, although /æ/ some-times occurs in baa-baa (black sheep) and /ʌ/ occurs in the hesitation form that might be spelled uh. Before /r/ in those varieties of standard English which "pronounce the r" before consonants and boundary elements, certain contrasts of nuclei are often lost. The following formula shows how our normalized phonemic transcription accommodates these losses:

$$\left\{ \begin{array}{l} \left\{ \begin{array}{l} /\mathrm{ɪy}/ \\ /\mathrm{ɪ}/ \end{array} \right\} \rightarrow /\mathrm{ɪ}/ \\[2ex] \left\{ \begin{array}{l} /\mathrm{ɛy}/ \\ /\mathrm{ɛ}/ \\ /\mathrm{æ}/ \end{array} \right\} \rightarrow /\mathrm{ɛ}/ \\[3ex] \left\{ \begin{array}{l} /\upsilon\mathrm{w}/ \\ /\upsilon/ \end{array} \right\} \rightarrow /\upsilon/ \\[2ex] \left\{ \begin{array}{l} /\mathrm{ow}/ \\ /\mathrm{ɔ}/ \end{array} \right\} \rightarrow /\mathrm{ɔ}/ \end{array} \right\} \quad \text{in env. \_\_\_ /r/}$$

/a/, /ʌ/, /aw/, /ay/ all remain before /r/, and /ɔy/ does not occur at all before /r/ in the same syllable. The possibility of contrast before /r/ is therefore substantially reduced:

fear /ɪr/	/ʌr/	/ʊr/ poor
fair /ɛr/	fur	/ɔr/ four
fire /ayr/	/ar/	/awr/ hour
	far	

The nuclei above, then, constitute the special English vowel system before /r/. Many English speakers do not have /ayr/ or /awr/; rather they have /ayɨr/ and /awɨr/, which are dissyllabic (the phoneme /ɨ/ is discussed below). It is to be noted that the vowel /ʌ/ may be much centralized before /r/—in fact, the sequence /ʌr/ is similar in quality to the sequence under weak stress that will be transcribed /ɨr/. It is at this point that the stressed vowel system and the UNSTRESSED VOWEL SYSTEM come together.

It may be said that in general, and for the kind of normalized American speech we are dealing with here, there are only three areas of phonemic contrast in the unstressed vowel system: a front area, a central area, and a back-rounded area. The central area we write with /ɨ/,[1] the front with /ɨy/, and the back with /ɨw/. Thus we reject, for the present purpose, the identification of any of the members of the stressed vowel system with any of the members of the unstressed vowel system: there are phonetic similarities, but no phonemic identities, between the two systems. The unstressed vowel system is charted below:

| ɨy ɨ ɨw | | city roses value |
| | | panic sofa pillow |

---

1. This central unstressed vowel is often symbolized [ə]; the barred-i ɨ is used here, partly because the phonetic quality of the vowel is often in the range of the sound symbolized by ɨ in the transcription of the International Phonetic Association, partly because the barred-i is widely used by American linguists in approximately this sense.

Each of these unstressed nuclei has a fairly wide phonetic range. The nucleus /ɨy/ most closely resembles the nuclei /ɪy/ and /ɪ/ from the stressed vowel system. The underlined syllables under weak stress (unstressed) in the first column below are phonetically similar to the syllables under strong stress (stressed) in the second column:[2]

party	/párt ɨy/	—	tea /tíy/
many	/mέnɨy/	—	knee /níy/
busy	/bíz ɨy/	—	Z /zíy/
trivial	/trív ɨy ɨl/	—	V /víy/
equality	/ɨykwálɨt ɨy/	—	eek /íyk/, tea /tíy/
attic	/ǽt ɨyk/	—	tick /tík/, teak /tíyk/
establish	/ɨstǽblɨyš/	—	fish /fíš/, leash /líyš/

The nucleus /ɨw/, except when it is preceded by a palatal consonant (for which see below), most closely resembles the nucleus /ow/ from the stressed vowel system. The underlined unstressed nuclei of the words in the first column below are phonetically similar to the stressed syllables in the second column.

pillow	/pfl ɨw/	—	low	/lów/
motto	/mát ɨw/	—	oh	/ów/
minnow	/mín ɨw/	—	no	/nów/
Olympic	/ɨwlfmp ɨyk/	—	oh	/ów/

When it is preceded by a palatal consonant (/ch/, /y/, /ǰ/, /š/, /ž/), /ɨw/ most closely resembles the nucleus (ʊw/ from the stressed vowel systems):[3]

virtue	/vᴧrch ɨw/	—	chew	/chʊ́w/
value	/vǽly ɨw/	—	you	/yʊ́w/
gradual	/grǽǰ ɨw ɨl/	—	Jew	/ǰʊ́w/
issue	/íš ɨw/	—	shoe	/šʊw/
visual	/víž ɨw ɨl/	—	. . .	

The nucleus /ɨ/ bears a close resemblance to /ᴧ/ when it appears in open syllables: sofa /sófɨ/; but the center of its range is unlike any of the stressed nuclei: a high central unround "obscure" vowel, to be heard in the unstressed syllables of roses, battle, chasm, arbitrate, compatible—indeed, in the unstressed syllables of most of the polysyllabic

---

2. Speakers of English differ in the pronunciation of the weak-stressed nucleus /ɨy/; for some it is more like the full vowel in seedy /ɪy/, for others, like that in city /ɪ/. It is such variation that makes it difficult to identify nuclei in the unstressed vowel system with nuclei in the stressed vowel system.

3. Words such as Lulu, Sulu, wahoo, igloo; yoyo, poncho; which show a different distribution of [ʊw] and [ow] sounds may have medial stress on the final syllable; this is taken as their normalized form. In each of the three areas /ɨ/, /ɨy/, /ɨw/, some speakers of English have additional phonemic contrasts. Such contrasts are subject to great dialect variation and are not relevant to the comparison of Spanish and English; they will not be dealt with in this book.

words in English.[4] It has already been noted above that /ɨr/ and /ʌr/ are not distinguishable in many varieties of American English, so that at this point the two systems, unstressed and stressed, really merge back into one: the choice of the symbol /ʌ/ in fur, myrhh, her, vs. that of /ɨ/ in wat<u>er</u>, sail<u>or</u>, is entirely a function of stress rather than of vowel quality.

We have, then, in a normalized variety of standard American English, these syllabic nuclei, with restrictions on distribution as noted above:

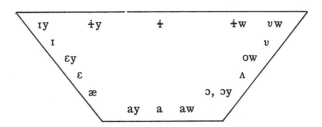

With this system as our point of reference, we may examine a few of the more conspicuous variations from it that are to be heard in different parts of North America from speakers of standard English.

1. /ɪy/: replaced by [ɨy] in stressed syllables in some dialects of the eastern seaboard (e.g., Philadelphia): <u>be</u>, <u>me</u>.

2. /ɪ/: fails to contrast with /ɛ/ before /n/ in dialects of the southern midlands (Arkansas, southern half of Missouri, Oklahoma, northwestern Texas, and in areas settled by emigrants from these areas): <u>pin</u>, <u>pen</u>, <u>again</u>, <u>hen</u>, <u>been</u>.

3. /ɛy/: replaced by [ɛɨ] in some areas of the southern Atlantic seaboard (Charleston, S. C.): <u>make</u>, <u>bait</u>.

4. /ɛ/: before /r/, expanded to a three-way contrast—<u>Mary</u>, <u>merry</u>, <u>marry</u>—along much of the eastern seaboard and in the Deep South; expanded to a two-way contrast —<u>merry</u>, <u>marry</u>—in many other areas of the East. Fails to contrast with /ɛy/ before /g/ in the Southern hills: <u>egg</u>, <u>ague</u>, <u>leg</u>, <u>Hague</u>. (See also 2, above.)

5. /æ/: replaced by [ɛɨ] in some dialects of the upper Middle West (Wisconsin, Michigan, especially among younger generation). Contrast between /æ/ and [ɛɨ] or [æɨ] is found on the Middle Atlantic seaboard: <u>can</u> ("be able") [kæn] vs. <u>can</u> ("container") [kɛɨn], [kæɨn]. Replaced by [æy] before /g/ and /š/ in the southern midlands: <u>bag</u>, <u>bash</u>.

6. /ay/: replaced before voiced consonants or a boundary element, in the Deep South by [aɨ] or by a vowel which is phonetically intermediate between /æ/ and /a/:

---

4. We are indebted in several respects to Charles A. Ferguson, William W. Gage, and Fred W. Householder for the preceding interpretation of the unstressed vowel system of English. It has certain advantages which we have not exploited, in particular the fact that it permits the elimination of the contrast between weak and medial stress (see Stockwell, review of M. Schubiger's English Intonation: Its Form and Function [1958], Language, XXXVI [1960], 544-48, and of Roger Kingdon's The Groundwork of English Intonation [1958] in International Journal of American Linguistics, XXVII [1961], 278-83). Householder symbolizes the unstressed vowels somewhat differently, but his analysis of the contrasts is virtually identical with that presented here (see, e.g., his "Accent, Juncture, Intonation and my Grandfather's Reader," Word, XIII [1957], 234-45).

mine, my, high. Replaced before voiceless consonants in eastern Canada by [ʌy]: bite, night.

7. /aw/: realized phonetically as [æw] throughout much of the midlands and South: around, about, down. Realized as [ʌw], [ɛw], or [ɨw] before voiceless consonants in Tidewater Virginia and eastern Canada: out, house, about.

8. /a/ and /ɔ/: fail to contrast in large areas—Northwest, much of the west coast, eastern Great Lakes—so that cot and caught are pronounced the same.

9. /ɔ/: replaced by [ɔw] in much of the South and Southwest: long, law.

10. /ɔy/: varies from a rather high, tight diphthong [oy] in the northeastern and especially Middle Atlantic states, and throughout much of the northern half of the country, to a substantially lower and more relaxed diphthong [ɔy] in the midland and Southern areas of the country: boy, noise, toyed.

11. /ʌ/: expanded into two contrasting nuclei before /r/ in the Middle Atlantic seaboard and Deep South: hurry [hʌr+y] vs. furry [fɨr+y]. The same contrast exists sporadically in most of the country in pairs like just (adj.) vs. just (adv.).

12. /ow/: found before /r/ in contrast with /ɔ/ in many parts of the United States: hoarse (vs. horse), four (vs. for).

13. /ʊ/: replaced by [ʊy] before palatal consonants in the region of Arkansas and Oklahoma: push.

14. /ʊw/: replaced by [ɨw] in most of the inland Northwest and sporadically elsewhere: boot, new.

15. /yʊw/: replaced by [ɪw] in many localities (e.g., southwestern Virginia and eastern Tennessee): few, beauty; replaced in some localities by [ɨw] (see also 14 above).

The above listing covers certain points where the sound systems of the dialects mentioned differ from the normalized system presented in this book. Another important type of dialect difference, however, concerns not what kind of sound system a dialect may have, but rather which vowel nuclei are used in certain words in a dialect. All American English dialects have a contrast between /ʊ/ as in foot and /ʊw/ (occasionally /ɨw/) as in boot, but there is still much variation as to which of these two nuclei will be used in items such as room, roof, coop, broom. Similarly, among speakers who do make a distinction between /a/ as in cot and /ɔ/ as in caught, there are differences in the use of these vowels in such items as dog, frog, fog, sorry.

SPANISH VOWELS

By comparison with the English vowels just presented, the system of Spanish vowels is the essence of simplicity and elegance. We will examine the Spanish vowels in detail, one by one: the following is merely an overview for perspective.

The simple vowels of Spanish are the five orthographically familiar ones:

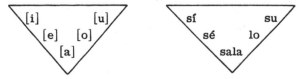

These are charted on the same principle of articulatory relation as the one we used in charting the English vowels (see chart on page 87), but note that the high and mid vowels are one notch higher in position than the corresponding high and mid simple nuclei of English. We use the following five phonetic symbols to write the vowel phonemes of Spanish: /i/, /e/, /a/, /o/, and /u/.

These vowels combine with /y/ and /w/ to form diphthongs, except that /i/ does not combine with /y/ nor /u/ with /w/:

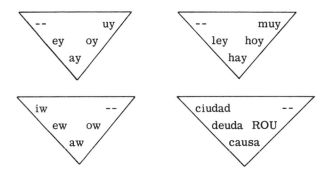

Of the eight complex nuclei produced in this way, only five are at all frequent. /ow/ is extremely rare (ROU is the abbreviation of República Oriental de Uruguay; the diphthong also occurs in a few other items like bou). /uy/ alternates with /wi/—that is, muy is pronounced either /múy/ or /mwí/. /wi/ is treated as a simple sequence of consonant plus vowel, not as a complex nucleus. /iw/ alternates with /yu/—that is, ciudad is pronounced either /siwdád/ or /syudád/. /yu/, like /wi/, is not a complex nucleus. Thus, only /ew/, /aw/, /ey/, /ay/, and /oy/ are normal, frequently occurring diphthongs. When the simple nuclei are combined in a single chart with the complex nuclei, the chart is somewhat asymmetrical:

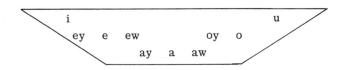

As we said before, Spanish has only one vowel system; the same nuclei, simple and complex, are found both in syllables with strong stress and in syllables with weak stress:

piríta	autór	áuto
meséra	vaivén	váina
nadár	feudál	déuda
tonó	aceitúna	acéite
futúra	oigámos	hóy

SPANISH STRESSED VOWELS—/i/

Although a distortion in the pronunciation of /i/ under strong stress will not ordinarily lead to misunderstanding, a correct pronunciation is difficult for Americans because no English vowel exactly matches the phonetic quality of the Spanish vowel. Compare English /ɪ/ and Spanish /i/:

English		Spanish
miss	/mís/	miz
sin	/sín/	sin
fin	/fín/	fin
mill	/míl/	mil
fill	/fíl/	fil
hill	/híl/	Gil
missile	/mísa/	misa

The Spanish vowel is higher, tenser, and (especially before a voiced consonant) shorter. Indeed, the difference is of such a magnitude that we must try a different comparison to get somewhat closer—namely, English /ɪy/ with Spanish /i/:

English		Spanish
me	/mí/	mí
tea	/tí/	tí
see	/sí/	sí
bee	/bí/	ví
Dee	/dí/	dí
knee	/ní/	ní

These are obviously more nearly alike. But the English /ɪy/ is a diphthong, as a rule (although some dialects always, and all dialects occasionally, have a negligible glide in the diphthong). Most English speakers begin the glide slightly higher than [ɪ], which is their normal tongue position for /ɪ/, and glide up to approximately the position of Spanish /i/. Equating English /ɪy/ with Spanish /i/ will not cause misunderstanding, but it will make some degree of accent. The American may need to be told to make the vowel shorter with his tongue high and tense; with a little attention, he can master it quickly.

SPANISH STRESSED VOWELS—/u/

The problem of Spanish /u/ is parallel in every detail with the problem of /i/: there are two English nuclei which approximate Spanish /u/, but neither is exactly like it. Compare the following:

English /ʊ/		Spanish /u/
puss	/pús/	pus
pull	/púl/	pul
full	/fúl/	ful
rook	/rrús/	rus

The English /ʋ/ is clearly lower and less tense than the Spanish /u/. But when we compare the English /ʋw/, as below:

English /ʋw/	Spanish /u/	
too	/tú/	tú
coo	/kú/	cu
pooh	/pú/	pu
boo	/bú/	bu
moo	/mú/	mu
taboo	/tabú/	tabú

we once again find diphthongization in English as compared with a pure vowel in Spanish. Specifically, Spanish /u/ is high back rounded throughout, extending its rounding into the preceding consonant, whereas the English /ʋw/ begins with little or no rounding and becomes rounded toward the end, is less tense, and in general longer than the Spanish /u/. The substitution of the English nucleus for the Spanish one will not ordinarily cause misunderstanding, but it is an obvious mark of accent.

SPANISH STRESSED VOWELS—/a/

Compare the following phonetically similar lists.

English /a/	Spanish /a/	
pot	/páta/	pata
cot	/káta/	cata
hot	/háto/	jato
hock	/háka/	jaca
lot	/láta/	lata
pock	/páka/	paca
not	/náta/	nata
Bonn	/bán/	van

Under stress, Spanish /a/ is only a slight problem. In a few American dialects the /a/ is somewhat farther back than the Spanish /a/, and before voiced consonants the English /a/ is substantially longer than the Spanish one; but in general the English /a/ under strong stress transfers successfully.[5]

SPANISH STRESSED VOWELS—/o/

The English simple nucleus /ʌ/ is unrounded and somewhat central. It cannot be compared with Spanish /o/. The nucleus that must be compared with Spanish /o/ is English /ow/:

---

5. For the minority of Americans who have an /ɔ/ vowel instead of /a/ in words like pot, cot, and so on, the nearest English analogy to Spanish /a/ is the vowel in words like father. Some Americans have only rare examples—or even none—of the /a/ vowel.

English /ow/	Spanish /o/	
cone	/kón/	con
coal	/kól/	col
goal	/gól/	gol
dose	/dós/	dos
coas(t)	/kós/	cos
no	/nó/	no
low	/ló/	lo
so	/só/	so
dough	/dó/	do
cocoa	/kóko/	coco

The comparison reveals obvious differences. The lip rounding of Spanish /o/ is consistent throughout the vowel, extending ordinarily even back into the preceding consonant (i.e., the Spanish speaker's lips are already rounded at the beginning of syllables like /kón/, /gól/, /dós/). The English /ow/ begins with slight rounding or, in many dialects, none at all, and becomes rounded (but not so much as in Spanish /o/) by the end. In addition to becoming more fully rounded, the English /ow/ changes quality: it glides from a mid-back or mid-central position to a higher, backer position, and is longer than Spanish /o/:

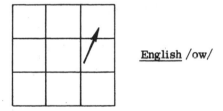

English /ow/

In Spanish, /ow/ is extremely rare, although it does occur in a few items. The substitution of English /ow/ for Spanish /o/ will therefore rarely lead to misunderstanding, but it is an obvious mark of accent.

SPANISH STRESSED VOWELS—/e/

The Spanish /e/ presents a somewhat different problem from that of other vowels. /e/ has two allophones in Spanish: a higher one, and a lower one. The lower one matches English /ɛ/ fairly closely. Compare the following lists:

English /ɛ/	Spanish /e/	
mess	/més/	mes
Bess	/béş/	vez
Tess	/téş/	tez
pesky	/péske/	pesque
dell	/dél/	del

English /ε/	Spanish /e/	
Ben	/bén/	ven
ten	/tén/	ten
den	/dén/	den

The English /ε/ matches the Spanish /e/ reasonably well before /s/ and /l/, somewhat less well before /n/. But the English /ε/ never occurs in word-final position, whereas Spanish /e/ does. The most similar English vowel that does occur finally is /εy/, and to confuse it with Spanish /e/ has unfortunate consequences:

English /εy/	Spanish /e/	
day	/dé/	de
Kay	/ké/	que
say	/sé/	se
bay	/bé/	ve
Fay	/fé/	fe
may	/mé/	me
lay	/lé/	le

Because English permits /εy/, but never /ε/, in final position, an English speaker is certain to try his /εy/ as a substitute for Spanish /e/. The problem is that Spanish itself has an /ey/ in contrast with /e/, so that the English speaker's substitution of /εy/ for /e/ will obliterate the distinction between the items below:

Spanish

/e/		/ey/	
/lé/	le	/léy/	ley
/rré/	re	/rréy/	rey
/mamé/	mamé	/maméy/	mamey

Therefore, the American has no option but to learn to produce Spanish /e/ accurately. It is higher and tenser than his /ε/, but it has no glide like his /εy/. He can be shown that Spanish /e/ starts like English /εy/ but is held steady without glide. It is generally shorter and tenser than either English /ε/ or /εy/, especially before voiced consonants.

SPANISH DIPHTHONGS—/ey/

In discussing Spanish /e/, we pointed out that English /εy/ is likely, especially at the ends of words, to be substituted for it, and that this could easily lead to misunderstanding because it might then be misheard as Spanish /ey/. The latter is, in fact, phonetically somewhat different from English /εy/:

English /ɛy/	Spanish /ey/	
lay	/léy/	ley
ray	/rréy/	rey
base	/béys/	veis
bane	/béynte/	veinte
train	/tréynta/	treinta
reign	/rreyna/	reina
pain	/péyne/	peine

The Spanish glide toward a higher fronter position is faster than the English, and extends farther. It also begins somewhat higher. They might be compared on a diagram:

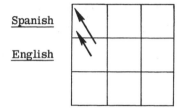

The English /ɛy/ can be remade into a successful Spanish /ey/ by making it start slightly higher, articulating more tensely throughout, making a rapid rise through the glide, and—above all—being certain that the glide is carried all the way up and forward.

SPANISH DIPHTHONGS—/ay/

Although both English and Spanish have a diphthong of this type, the phonetic difference is considerable:

English /ay/	Spanish /ay/	
eye	/áy/	hay
sigh	/sáya/	saya
bile	/báyle/	baile
bin(d)	/báyne/	vaine
tine	/táyno/	taino
knife	/náyfe/	naife
hike	/háyke/	jaique
hymen	/háyme/	Jaime
tight	/táyta/	taita

The rise of the semivowel toward a higher fronter position is noticeably shorter and slower in English than in Spanish.

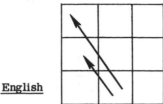

English   Spanish

English /ay/ can be remade into a successful Spanish /ay/ by articulating more tensely throughout and by being certain that the glide is carried rapidly all the way forward and up.

SPANISH DIPHTHONGS—/oy/

The comparison is much the same as described above for /ey/ and /ay/:

English /ɔy/	Spanish /oy/	
soy	/sóy/	soy
boy	/bóy/	voy
coy	/kóy/	coy
toy	/óy/	hoy

The difference is revealed by this diagram:

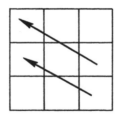

Spanish

English

English /ɔy/ (or /oy/) can be remade into a successful Spanish /oy/ by starting it noticeably higher, articulating more tensely throughout, and carrying the glide rapidly all the way up and forward.

SPANISH DIPHTHONGS—/aw/

This is by far the most frequent of the Spanish /Vw/ diphthongs. The /-w/ diphthongs are closely parallel to the /-y/ diphthongs in the problems they create: accent but not unintelligibility. Compare the following.

English /aw/	Spanish /aw/	
out	/áwto/	auto
how	/háw/	jau
couch	/káwcho/	caucho
cows	/káwsa/	causa

English /aw/	Spanish /aw/	
howl	/háwla/	jaula
chow	/cháw/	chao
route	/rráwta/	rauta
loud	/láwda/	lauda
pout	/páwta/	pauta

The glide in Spanish /aw/ is tenser, goes farther, and is faster than the glide in English /aw/, with markedly greater rounding at the end.

English 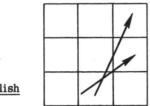 Spanish

SPANISH DIPHTHONGS—/ew/

This diphthong is relatively rare in Spanish, but it presents a difficult problem to English speakers, since there is no standard counterpart in English. (The complex nucleus /ɛw/ occurs in the speech of some Americans in place of /ow/ (no, so) or in the speech of others in place of /aw/ (house, out). In either instance, the pronunciation is regarded as unusual by most speakers.)

Spanish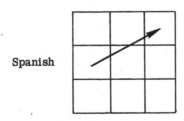

/şéwta/ Ceuta   /déwda/ deuda   /déwdo/ deudo

SPANISH DIPHTHONGS—/uy/ and /iw/

These diphthongs are of minor importance, because /uy/ alternates with /wi/:

muy → /múy/, /mwí/
cuida → /kúyda/, /kwída/

and /iw/ alternates with /yu/:

ciudad → /şiwdád/, /şyudád/
tiuque → /tíwke/, /tyúke/

Except for the extremely common form /múy/, the second alternate is the preferred form. It may be noted, however, that ciudad in some dialects has moved to a /wi/ pattern and /şwidád/ is normal in these dialects.

We have pointed out that the unstressed vowel system of English differs from the stressed vowel system, and consists of only three members: /ɨ/, as in roses, sofa; /ɨy/, as in party, panic; /ɨw/, as in nephew, pillow. Since, as we noted earlier, /ɨ/ occurs in the unstressed syllables of the majority of English polysyllabic words, and is, for practical purposes, the only English vowel under weak stress that needs to be compared with the variety of vowels which are possible under weak stress in Spanish, we might look first at the kinds of English words in which /ɨ/ automatically replaces other English nuclei whenever strong stress is replaced by weak stress. It is convenient to speak of all the nuclei that occur under strong stress as full vowels and of the vowel /ɨ/ as the reduced vowel. Note the following instances of stress alternation in English:

/ɛy/ ➤ /ɨ/

/éybɨl/	able	/ɨbílɨtɨy/	ability
/séytɨn/	Satan	/sɨtǽnɨyk/	satanic

/ay/ ➤ /ɨ/

/órgɨnàyz/	organize	/òrgɨnɨzéysɨn/	organization
/yúwnɨfày/	unify	/yòwnɨfɨkéysɨn/	unification

/æ/ ➤ /ɨ/

/æplɨkéysɨn/	application	/ɨpláy/	apply
/rɨyǽlɨtɨy/	reality	/rífɨl/	real

/ow/ ➤ /ɨ/

/kɨmpównɨnt/	component	/kàmpɨnénchɨl/	componential
/prɨpówz/	propose	/pràpɨzísɨn/	proposition

/a/ ➤ /ɨ/

/bátɨnɨy/	botany	/bɨtǽnɨkɨl/	botanical
/kámbæt/	combat (n.)	/kɨmbǽt/	combat (v.)

The above list is illustrative only; an exhaustive listing of all the alternating vowel classes of English would be lengthy and irrelevant to the present point, which is simply to demonstrate that such alternation occurs with great frequency and regularity. VOWEL REDUCTION is a phenomenon of great generality in English,[6] and it is obligatory in such a large percentage of instances that the English speaker will invariably reduce the vowels of Spanish under weak stress in the same way.

---

6. For a fuller discussion of English vowel reduction, see sections 70 and 71 of "A Guide to Pronunciation," Webster's New International Dictionary of the English Language, Second Edition (Springfield, Mass.: G. & C. Merriam, 1960), pp. xxxvii-xxxix.

This point cannot be overemphasized. It belongs at the top of the hierarchy of phonological difficulty for English students. The Spanish pronunciation of Americans is consistently marred more by this offense—the reduction of weak-stressed Spanish vowels —than by any other single detail of pronunciation except perhaps intonation. It is also an extremely difficult point to teach. The average native speaker of English simply does not perceive the phonetic difference between full and reduced vowels when they are buried in a sequence of syllables, even though he can hear the difference easily enough in isolation. He must be taught to hear the difference before he can begin to learn to pronounce Spanish unstressed vowels correctly. A comparison between lists like the following is often useful; but one should remember that it is the vowel sound, not the spelling, that is being compared:

English	Spanish	
affirm	/afirmár/	afirmar
ascend	/assendér/	ascender
aspire	/aspirár/	aspirar
assistant	/asisténte/	asistente
attentively	/aténtaménte/	atentamente
fatality	/fatalidád/	fatalidad
sagacity	/sagasidád/	sagacidad
satanic	/satániko/	satánico
parallel	/paralélo/	paralelo
submarine	/submaríno/	submarino
persist	/persistír/	persistir
serene	/seréno/	sereno
defend	/defendér/	defender
excellent	/eksselénte/	excelente
direction	/direksyón/	dirección
director	/direktór/	director
rapid	/rrápido/	rápido
placid	/plásido/	plácido
insipid	/insípido/	insípido
application	/aplikasyón/	applicación
elimination	/eliminasyón/	eliminación
supplication	/suplikasyón/	suplicación
serenity	/serenidad/	serenidad
positive	/positíbo/	positivo
difficulty	/difikultád/	dificultad
collector	/kolektór/	colector
committee	/komité/	comité
oblique	/oblíkwo/	oblicuo
obscurity	/oskuridád/	oscuridad

English	Spanish	
position	/posisyón/	posición
possession	/posesyón/	posesión
professor	/profesór/	profesor
intercollegiate	/interkolehyál/	intercolegial
suppose	/suponér/	suponer
supreme	/suprémo/	supremo
deputy	/diputádo/	diputado

In examining the lists above, one should bear in mind the fact that /ɨ/ does not exist in Spanish. The reduced vowel represented by /ɨ/ is not permitted in Spanish pronunciation of Spanish words in any instance. Yet a literate speaker of English, because he is thoroughly familiar with the writing system of English, which represents the reduced vowels with the same symbols used for full vowels, will be entirely convinced that he is pronouncing full vowels /i e a o u/ when he is in fact reducing them to /ɨ/—that is, replacing them with a totally non-Spanish vowel.

Once the English speaker has been brought to an awareness of the nature of reduced vowels under weak stress, he must learn to discriminate between the various weak-stressed vowels of Spanish. To teach him to discriminate between them, contrasts like the following can be used. When he uses them, the instructor must be extremely careful not to exaggerate the vowel under weak stress, or the whole point of the drill will be lost.

/i/		/e/	
/pitón/	pitón	/petón/	petón
/rrimár/	rimar	/rremár/	remar
/pilón/	pilón	/pelón/	pelón
/tilón/	tilón	/telón/	telón
/mi(l)yón/	millón	/me(l)yón/	mellón
/pisáda/	pisada	/pesáda/	pesada
/piríta/	pirita	/períta/	perita
/piɲyíta/	piñita	/peɲyíta/	peñita
/biníto/	vinito	/beníto/	Benito
/miséra/	misera	/meséra/	mesera

/i/		/a/	
/libár/	libar	/labár/	lavar
/pitón/	pitón	/patón/	patón
/mitád/	mitad	/matád/	matad
/chirlár/	chirlar	/charlár/	charlar
/pinṣón/	pinzón	/panṣón/	panzón
/nidár/	nidar	/nadár/	nadar
/pisándo/	pisando	/pasándo/	pasando

/i/		/a/	
/fiháron/	fijaron	/faháron/	fajaron
/siléro/	silero	/saléro/	salero
/litéra/	litera	/latéra/	latera

/i/		/o/	
/figón/	figón	/fogón/	fogón
/timó/	timó	/tomó/	tomó
/mirár/	mirar	/morár/	morar
/liméra/	limera	/loméra/	lomera
/tiríto/	tirito	/toríto/	torito
/pikíto/	piquito	/pokíto/	poquito
/ihíto/	hijito	/ohíto/	ojito
/imíto/	imito	/omíto/	omito
/pisáda/	pisada	/posáda/	posada
/miráda/	mirada	/moráda/	morada

/e/		/a/	
/bóche/	boche	/bócha/	bocha
/méses/	meses	/mésas/	mesas
/tehón/	tejón	/tahón/	tajón
/pegár/	pegar	/pagár/	pagar
/penál/	penal	/panál/	panal
/besár/	besar	/basar/	basar
/dedíto/	dedito	/dadíto/	dadito
/merkádo/	mercado	/markádo/	marcado
/paréşe/	parece	/peréşe/	perece
/seŋyóras/	señoras	/seŋyóres/	señores

/e/		/o/	
/páse/	pase	/páso/	paso
/péyne/	peine	/péyno/	peino
/léche/	leche	/lécho/	lecho
/bíne/	vine	/bíno/	vino
/pelár/	pelar	/polár/	polar
/lesyón/	lesión	/loşyón/	loción
/ternéro/	ternéro	/tornéro/	tornero
/şerríto/	cerrito	/şorríto/	zorrito
/pesáda/	pesada	/posáda/	posada
/preposişyón/	preposición	/proposişyón/	proposición

	/e/		/u/
/legár/	legar	/lugár/	lugar
/sekşyón/	sección	/sukşyón/	succión
/temór/	temor	/tumór/	tumor
/lechár/	lechar	/luchár/	luchar
/pensyón/	pensión	/punşyón/	punción
/políta/	perita	/puríta/	purita
/pechéro/	pechero	/puchéro/	puchero
/rretína/	retina	/rrutína/	rutina
/meséta/	meseta	/muséta/	museta
/pensádo/	pensado	/punsádo/	punsado

	/a/		/o/
/séra/	sera	/şéro/	cero
/pára/	para	/páro/	paro
/kúba/	Cuba	/kúbo/	cubo
/bóla/	bola	/bólo/	bolo
/mésa/	mesa	/méso/	meso
/espósa/	esposa	/espóso/	esposo
/maréa/	marea	/maréo/	mareo
/şeréşa/	cereza	/şeréşo/	cerezo
/derécha/	derecha	/derécho/	derecho
/maría/	María	/moría/	moría

	/a/		/u/
/sabído/	sabido	/subído/	subido
/papíta/	papita	/pupíta/	pupita
/barríta/	barrita	/burríta/	burrita
/maléta/	maleta	/muléta/	muleta
/karákas/	Caracas	/kurákas/	curacas
/lanéro/	lanero	/lunéro/	lunero
/marşyáno/	Marciano	/murşyáno/	Murciano
/pargáta/	pargata	/purgáta/	purgata
/kanyáda/	cañada	/kunyáda/	cuñada
/matadór/	matador	/mutadór/	mutador

	/o/		/u/
/morár/	morar	/murár/	murar
/bokál/	vocal	/bukál/	bucal
/motilár/	motilar	/mutilár/	mutilar
/tronkár/	troncar	/trunkár/	truncar
/boşón/	vozón	/buşón/	buzón

/o/		/u/	
/omíto/	omito	/umíto/	humito
/poríto/	porito	/puríto/	purito
/ploméro/	plomero	/pluméro/	plumero
/moníta/	monita	/muníta/	munita
/sotána/	sotana	/sutána/	zutana

LEXICAL INFLUENCE ON SPANISH VOWELS

The central issue of this book to this point has been that the habitual patterns of English pronunciation tend to be superimposed upon the most nearly similar Spanish phonetic sequences. This tendency is strongly reinforced if it happens that a pair of words in English and Spanish that sound similar also mean much the same thing. The semantic correspondence reinforces the phonetic correspondence to such an extent that students will almost invariably have to be corrected again and again on items that would not, from the point of view of phonological conflict alone, cause serious difficulty. The most troublesome of these are of three types: (1) English /a/ replacing Spanish /o/, (2) English /æ/ replacing Spanish /a/, and (3) English /ɔ/ replacing Spanish /aw/. These are illustrated below (with only the crucial error indicated, although a student making this error would make others at the same time):

English /a/		Spanish /o/		Probable error
/ápɨréyšɨn/	operation	/operaşyón/	operación	/aperaşyón/
/ápɨrtúwnɨtɨy/	opportunity	/oportunidád/	oportunidad	/aportunidád/
/dáktɨr/	doctor	/doktór/	doctor	/daktór/
/káŋgrɨs/	congress	/kongréso/	congreso	/kangréso/
/kántrækt/	contract	/kontráto/	contrato	/kantráto/
/kánfɨrɨns/	conference	/komferénşya/	conferencia	/kamferénşya/
/trápɨkɨl/	tropical	/tropikál/	tropical	/trapikál/
/hàndúrɨs/	Honduras	/ondúras/	Honduras	/andúras/
/kànvɨrséyšɨn/	conversation	/kombersaşyón/	conversación	/kambersaşyón/
/háspɨtɨl/	hospital	/ospitál/	hospital	/aspitál/
/fásfɨrɨs/	phosphorous	/fósforo/	fósforo	/fásforo/
/hàspɨtǽlɨtɨy/	hospitality	/ospitalidád/	hospitalidad	/aspitalidád/
/pásɨbɨl/	possible	/posíble/	posible	/pasíble/
/bàmbárdmɨnt/	bombardment	/bombardéo/	bombardeo	/bambardéo/
/prántɨw/	pronto	/prónto/	pronto	/pránto/
/práksɨmɨt/	proximate	/próksimo/	próximo	/práksimo/

English /æ/		Spanish /a/		Probable error
/spǽnɨyš/	Spanish	/espaŋyól/	Español	/espǽŋyól/
/bǽŋk/	bank	/bánko/	banco	/bǽnko/
/blǽŋk/	blank	/blánko/	blanco	/blǽnko/
/klǽs/	class	/kláse/	clase	/klǽse/

English /æ/		Spanish /a/		Probable error
/pǽs/	pass	/páse/	pase	/pǽse/
/kǽnzɨz/	Kansas	/kánsas/	Kansas	/kǽnsas/
/mɨkǽnɨyk/	mechanic	/mekániko/	mecánico	/mekǽniko/
/ǽbsɨlùwt/	absolute	/absolúto/	absoluto	/ǽbsolúto/
/ǽnyɨwɨl/	annual	/áɲyo/	año	/ǽɳyo/

English /ɔ/		Spanish /aw/		Probable error
/ɔ́tɨwbʌ̀s/	autobus	/awtobús/	autobús	/ɔtobús/
/ɔ́ṣɨr/	author	/awtór/	autor	/ɔtór/
/ɔṣɔ́rɨtɨy/	authority	/awtoridád/	autoridad	/ɔtoridád/
/ɔ́ṣɨràyz/	authorize	/awtoríṣa/	autoriza	/ɔtoríṣa/
/ɔ́tɨmǽtɨyk/	automatic	/awtomátiko/	automático	/ɔtomátiko/

Note that in the examples above, conventional English spelling—o for /a/, a for /æ/, and au for /ɔ/—strongly reinforces the error.

VOWEL CLUSTERS IN SPANISH

One vowel never follows another in English without either a consonant, a semi-vowel, or (under special conditions) a glottal stop occurring between. When, as frequently in saw edge, a glottal stop separates the two vowels, this constitutes a part of the effect of the boundary between the words. The phonological restrictions of English are such as never to permit a vowel cluster. Words that in the spelling appear to have two vowels in sequence in fact always obey this phonological restriction. Note the following instances.

mutual	/myúwchɨwɨl/
Leon	/líyàn/
harmonious	/hàrmównɨyɨs/

Even the variant pronunciations of the, or the two forms of the indefinite article a and an, are instances of the extension of this rule across word boundaries:

the apple	/ðɨy ǽpɨl/
the man	/ðɨ mǽn/
an apple	/ɨn ǽpɨl/
a man	/ɨ mǽn/

When a noun with a final vowel occurs before a verb beginning with a vowel, if the verb is one of the auxiliaries that allows contraction, the extra vowel may be eliminated:

The sofa is over here.   /ðɨ sówfɨz ðwvɨr hɨ́r/

If, in careful or emphatic pronunciation, the speaker does not contract the auxiliary, then a glottal stop [ʔ] breaks the sequence:

The sofa is over here.   [ɨ sówfɨ ʔɨ̀z ðwvɨr hɨ́r]

It is probably true that there are styles of English speech—especially in rapid, perhaps even "careless," colloquial speech—where the generalization that English permits no vowel clusters may occasionally fail to be true. In such speech, sequences like the following occur.

the other day	/ðɨʌ̆ðɨr déy/
my older brother	/mɨówldɨr brʌ̆ðɨr/

But there is little doubt that the general pattern does not permit such vowel clusters.

Although sequences of two vowels rarely occur in English—and when they do occur, a glottal stop must obligatorily break the sequence—in Spanish such sequences are extremely frequent. Furthermore, although there are several different ways of pronouncing such sequences, all equally acceptable, the one way that English speakers will try is not among them: namely, the insertion of a glottal stop between the vowels. The acceptable Spanish pronunciations of vowel clusters are detailed below.[7]

IDENTICAL CONTIGUOUS VOWELS IN SPANISH

VV → V

Whenever identical vowels appear one directly after the other, as at the end of one word and at the beginning of the next, the normal colloquial tendency is to reduce the sequence to a single vowel. This will occasionally produce ambiguity, as in the instances below.

/ii/ → /i/

Ha visto Milo?	1 2 22
Ha visto mi hilo?	/abístomílo↓/

Es mito.	2 11
Es mi hito.	/esmíto↓/

Silo tiene.	2 1 1
Si hilo tiene.	/sílotyéne↓/

/ee/ → /e/

Creo que salgo.	2 1 1
Creo que es algo.	/kréokesálgo↓/

Qué séso!	2 1 1
Qué es eso?	/késéso↓/

---

7. See also J. Donald Bowen, "Sequences of Vowels in Spanish," <u>Boletín de Filología</u>, IX (1956-57), pp. 5-14 (Santiago, Chile).

$$/ee/ \rightarrow /e/$$

Qué celado!

Qué es helado?

Qué es el hado?

$$\overset{2}{/k}\overset{1\ 1}{esel\acute{a}do\downarrow/}$$

$$/aa/ \rightarrow /a/$$

Qué va a ser?

Qué va a hacer?

$$\overset{2}{/k}\overset{1}{eb\acute{a}s\acute{e}r\downarrow/}$$

Estallando.

Está hallando.

$$\overset{1}{/esta(l)}\overset{2\ 1}{y\acute{a}ndo\downarrow/}$$

Va a ver muchos.

Va a haber muchos.

$$\overset{2\ 2}{/b\acute{a}b\acute{e}r}\overset{1\ 1}{m\acute{u}chos\downarrow/}$$

$$/oo/ \rightarrow /o/$$

Es otro.

Eso otro.

$$\overset{2\ 1\ 1}{/\acute{e}s\acute{o}tro\downarrow/}$$

No puedo ir.

No puedo oír.

$$\overset{2\ \ 2\ 1}{/n\acute{o}pw\acute{e}do\acute{i}r\downarrow/}$$

Sin olor.

Sino olor.

$$\overset{1\ \ 21}{/s\acute{i}nol\acute{o}r\downarrow/}$$

$$/uu/ \rightarrow /u/$$

Es para Tuso.

Es para tu uso.

$$\overset{2}{/\acute{e}sparat}\overset{1\ 1}{\acute{u}so\downarrow/}$$

Desuso.

De su uso.

$$\overset{1\ 2\ 1}{/des\acute{u}so\downarrow/}$$

Consumo.

Con su humo.

$$\overset{1\ 2\ 1}{/kons\acute{u}mo\downarrow/}$$

If the speaker of Spanish wishes to avoid these ambiguities (he of course need not, since context will almost always settle the doubt his audience might theoretically have), he produces a somewhat longer vowel in each of the /VV/ occurrences. Never, however, does he produce V?V, which will be the American's most likely resolution of the potential ambiguity.

NON-IDENTICAL CONTIGUOUS VOWELS

Non-identical vowels in sequence admit of three resolutions:

1. Shortening, so that the first of the two vowels is de-emphasized in favor of the second, although both remain syllabic. This may be symbolized:

$$/VV/ \rightarrow [\breve{V}V]$$

2. Reduction to semivowel, so that one of the two vowels is de-emphasized still further, becoming non-syllabic. This may be symbolized:

$$/VV/ \rightarrow /SV/, \text{ or as } /VV/ \rightarrow /VS/$$

3. Reduction to zero, so that the first of the two vowels disappears:

$$/V^1V^2/ \rightarrow /V^2/$$

These patterns are regular, except when the first of the two vowels is under strong stress. In this environment, the rules are different and will be dealt with separately after the above patterns have been illustrated:

$$V^1 \rightarrow [\breve{\imath}] \sim /y/$$

$V^1 \rightarrow$ V^2 ↓		$[\breve{\imath}] \sim /y/$	vs. $/y/$
/e/	/syésta/	si esta	siesta
/a/	/myásma/	mi asma	miasma
/o/	/myoşéna/	mi ocena	miocena
/u/	/myúra/	mi hura	miura

$$V^1 \rightarrow [\breve{e}] \sim /y/$$

$V^1 \rightarrow$ V^2 ↓		$[\breve{e}] \sim /y/$	vs. $/y/$
/a/	/kyásma/	que asma	quiasma
/o/	/kyósko/	que hosco	quiosco
/u/	/dyúrna/	de urna	diurna

The forms in the middle column above may or may not be pronounced as transcribed in the first column, whereas those in the third column <u>must</u> so appear—that is, the vowel sequences shown in the second column are resolvable either as two syllables, of which the first is shortened (solution 1, above), or as one syllable because of the reduction of the first vowel to a semivowel (solution 2, above). The appearance of the second solution should not be considered incorrect or sloppy; it is normal conversational Spanish.

Just as the front vowels /i/ and /e/ are reduced to /y/ by the second solution, the back vowels /u/ and /o/ are reduced to /w/.

$$V^1 \rightarrow [\breve{u}] \sim /w/$$

$V^1 \rightarrow$ V^2		$[\breve{u}] \sim /w/$	vs. /w/
$\downarrow$			
/i/	/swí . . ./	su isla	suiza
/e/	/swéko/	su eco	sueco
/a/	/swábe/	su ave	suave
/o/	/Cwó . . ./	su oca	quota

$$V^1 \rightarrow [\eth] \sim /w/$$

$V^1 \rightarrow$		$[\eth] \sim /w/$	vs. /w/
$\downarrow$			
/i/	/lwísa/	lo iza	Luisa
/e/	/nwés/	no es	nuez
/a/	/ywá . . ./	yo ando	yuambo

Exactly the same observations can be made about these lists as were made about the front vowels, and need not be repeated.

Other vowel sequences to be considered are those consisting of low vowel /a/ followed by high vowels and by mid vowels. /a/ followed by a high vowel permits the first solution—shortening of the /a/: but if the second solution is chosen, it is the <u>second</u> vowel which becomes a semivowel:

$$/ai/ \sim /ay/ \text{ vs. } /ay/$$

/baybén/	va y ven	vaivén

In some dialect areas such as Chile, the first of the two alternative solutions is rarely chosen, so that the pair above would nearly always be homonymous: /baybén/. This same reduction of course happens repeatedly in related forms:

/país/	país	$\rightarrow$	/paysáhe/	paisaje
/maís/	maís	$\rightarrow$	/mayséna/	maisena

With /a/ followed by /u/, the facts are parallel in every detail. Shortening of the first may occur, or the second may become a semivowel.

$$/au/ \sim /aw/ \text{ vs. } /aw/$$

/awsénşya/	a Usencia	ausencia

The second solution is consistently preferred in some dialects; the same reduction also appears in related forms:

/baúl/	baúl	$\rightarrow$	/bawlşíto/	baulcito
/rraúl/	Raúl	$\rightarrow$	/rrawlíto/	Raulito

Whenever /a/ is followed by a <u>mid</u> vowel rather than a high vowel, the possible solutions are 1 and 3, but not 2: reduction of one vowel to a semivowel. Thus <u>la eco</u> may be either [lǎéko] or /léko/, but it is always different from laico /láyko/. Other items similarly reduced include:

/lestúfa/	la estufa
/lespósa/	la esposa
/kyórés/	Qué hora es?
/lembaháda/	la embajada
/mestríta/	maestrita

Similarly, with /a/ followed by /o/, la hora may be either [lǎóra] or /lóra/, but it always different from Laura /láwra/. Other such items include:

/lortografía/	la ortografía
/loportunidád/	la oportunidad
/lórka/	la horca
/oríta/	ahorita

      In all the preceding discussion, we omitted two instances of vowel clusters which do not pattern like the others: /ei/ and /ou/. Instead of accepting solutions 1 and 2, which one would expect on the basis of pattern congruity, they permit only solutions 1 and 3, like /a/ followed by a mid vowel. Thus se izaba is regularly different from seisava /seysába/, being either [sĕisában] or /sisába/. Similarly:

/sinterésa/	se interesa
/síncha/	se hincha
/síla/	se hila
/éstíntimo/	este íntimo

Compound numerals with veinte show this reduction even in the orthography: veinte y dos ➝ veintidós. There are, however, wide variations in the reductions that occur in counting; treinta y dos may be /tréyntaydós/ or /tréyntidós/. Among the instances of reduction to zero (solution 3, above), one deserves special mention: /lasdósimédya/ is almost invariably followed by a request for clarification—that is, did the speaker mean /dós/ dos or /dóṣe/ doce?
      The sequence /ou/ is much like /ei/ except that the diphthong /ow/ happens not to occur in Spanish (with trivial exceptions like ROU). In any case, /ou/ occurs with solutions 1 and 3:

/lútil/	lo útil
/lutilíṣa/	lo utiliza
/domíngúltimo/	domingo último
/lúniko/	lo único
/tengúno/	tengo uno

NON-IDENTICAL CONTIGUOUS VOWELS WITH V^1 UNDER STRONG STRESS, V^2 UNDER WEAK STRESS

If V^2 in the sequence $/V^1V^2/$ is /i/ or /u/, it regularly becomes a semivowel /y/ or /w/ in most dialects. Some dialects, however, shift the strong stress to the second vowel and reduce the first to zero. Only the first pattern is illustrated below:

V^1		V^2 is /i/	
/é/	→	/éy/	que esté Inés
/á/	→	/áy/	está Inés
/ó/	→	/óy/	habló Inés
/ú/	→	/úy/	y tú Inés

V^1		V^2 is /u/	
/í/	→	/íw/	sí Unamuno
/é/	→	/éw/	que esté Unamuno
/á/	→	/áw/	está Unamuno
/ó/	→	/ów/	habló Unamuno

If V^2 is /e/, /o/, or /a/, then V^2 is shortened. Some dialects shift the strong stress to the second vowel and reduce the first to a semivowel or zero. Only the shortening of the second vowel is illustrated below.

V^1		V^2 is /e/	
/í/	→	[íĕ]	sí Elena
/á/	→	[áĕ]	está Elena
/ó/	→	[óĕ]	habló Elena
/ú/	→	[úĕ]	y tú Elena

		V^2 is /o/	
/í/	→	[íŏ]	sí Orlando
/é/	→	[éŏ]	que esté Orlando
/á/	→	[áŏ]	está Orlando
/ú/	→	[úŏ]	y tú Orlando

		V^2 is /a/	
/í/	→	[íă]	sí Alicia
/é/	→	[éă]	que esté Alicia
/ó/	→	[óă]	habló Alicia
/ú/	→	[úă]	y tú Alicia

CONTIGUOUS VOWELS UNDER STRONG STRESS

The usual pattern for contiguous stressed vowels is that the first strong stress is reduced to weak, and thereafter the sequence /VV́/ behaves exactly as described under the previous subsections, depending on whether the vowels are identical or non-identical. The only alternative occurs in deliberate, careful speech, where both strong stresses may remain—when there is neither shortening nor reduction to semivowel or zero; but although there is no reduction, a glottal stop is still not permitted to separate the two vowels. A few random examples of the usual pattern are these:

¿Qué anda haciendo?	/ké ánda aṣyéndo/	/kyándaṣyéndo/
¿Qué hora es?	/ké óra és/	/kyórés/
Solo entró una.	/sólo entró úna/	/sólwentrúna/
Que esté íntimo.	/ke esté íntimo/	/kestíntimo/
¿Dónde está Ana?	/dónde está ána/	/dóndestána/

SUMMARY OF SEGMENTAL ELEMENTS 8

CONSONANTS

In general, it may be said that the Spanish consonant system is much simpler than that of English. Spanish has nineteen consonants including two semivowels:

labial	inter-dental	dental	palatal	velar	
p		t		k	voiceless stops
b		d		g	voiced stop-spirants
f	ş	s	ch	h	voiceless spirants
m		n	ny		nasals
		l	(l)y		laterals
		r			vibrant
			y	w	semivowels

English has twenty-four, including two semivowels:

labial	inter-dental	alveolar	palatal	velar	glottal	
p		t	ch	k		voiceless stops
b		d	ǰ	g		voiced stops
f	ş	s	š		h	voiceless spirants
v	đ	z	ž			voiced spirants
m		n		ŋ		nasals
		l				lateral
		r				retroflex
w			y			semivowels

116

The consonants of English which are more or less directly transferable to Spanish without serious ill effects are /ch f s m n/. /p k/ can be transferred successfully only in an unaspirated variety—and the habit of aspiration is surprisingly hard to break. /t/ has, besides the problem of aspiration, a number of other difficulties to be overcome. /b d g/ can be transferred to cover half the area of Spanish /b d g/, but Spanish additionally has something which resembles English /ð/ as an allophone of /d/ and an entirely new variety of both /b/ and /g/—namely, [ƀ] and [g]—to be mastered. English /s/ and /z/ must be systematically merged into the Spanish phoneme /s/, and for some dialects a new variety of /s/—the [^{h}] or the Castilian apical—must be learned. /ny/ and /(l)y/ are new phonemes for the English speaker, but relatively easy to master and low in functional yield even after mastered. Spanish /h/ is different from English /h/, but not too serious a problem. /l/ and /r/ are major hurdles, since English is widely different on both counts. Spanish /y/ has allophones that resemble English /y/, /ž/, and /ǰ/. Spanish /w/, although it has a similar range of allophones, is not a serious problem.

Although the clusters of Spanish are both fewer in number and less varied than those of English, they nonetheless include a number of serious problems, especially /Cy-/ clusters and the three-consonant initials.

Finally, whereas the consonants of English are relatively similar from one dialect to another (the dialectal differences of English are largely confined to vowels), there are major variations in the pronunciation of consonants of Spanish from one dialect area to another. Among the Spanish consonants which undergo wide dialectal variations are /s/, /y/, /n/, /h/, and /r/. To learn first to perceive and then to ignore these differences, as the English speaker must, is no simple problem in itself.

VOWELS

It is true of the vowels, as it was of the consonants, that the Spanish system is much simpler than that of English. Spanish has five simple vowels:

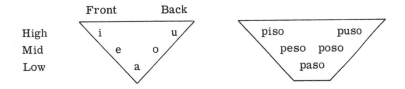

The five occur as simple nuclei, and also in combination with following /y/ or /w/. The complex nuclei so constituted are:

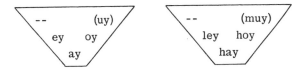

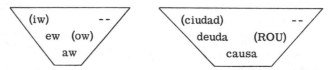

This gives a total of thirteen syllabic nuclei, but only ten of substantial frequency. Those that are not frequent are parenthesized above.

English has seven simple vowel phonemes in stressed syllables:

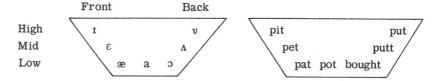

The frequent complex nuclei with /y/ and /w/ are:

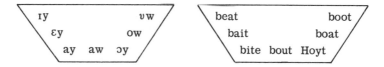

The nucleus /ow/ could be written /ʌw/. Before /r/, the syllabic nuclei which generally occur are these:

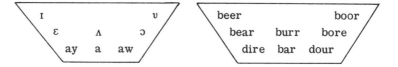

It should be noted that before /r/, /ʌ/ is centralized and /ɔ/ is raised.

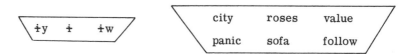

Seventeen syllabic nuclei, then, are in the prevalent pattern of American English:

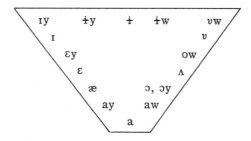

Different dialects of English may have widely different vowel systems. They may have vowel nuclei in addition to the seventeen above, particularly among the possible complex nuclei. Also, the same nucleus may appear in different dialects in different sets of words. On the other hand, there are dialects which fail to distinguish some pairs of the seventeen nuclei in the prevalent pattern, either entirely eliminating a distinction (/a/ and /ɔ/ for many dialects) or not having one in some circumstances (/ɛ/ and /ɪ/ before /n/ in some dialects). The vowels of English that are more or less directly transferable to Spanish without serious ill effects are the following:

/ɪy/	(for Spanish /í/), as in <u>sí</u>)
/ɨy/	(for Spanish weak-stressed /i/), as in ca<u>si</u>)
/ɛ/	(in syllables closed by /s/ and /l/), as in <u>desde</u>, <u>vuelto</u>)
/a/	(in all syllables under strong stress, as in <u>paso</u>)

No other reasonably direct transfers are possible, and even the four above are highly imperfect. English /ɛy/ and /ɛ/, /ʊw/ and /ʊ/, /ow/ and /ɔ/, /aw/ and /ɔ/ intersect to create serious accent problems and a few even more serious problems of intelligibility.

All Spanish diphthongs involve a glide in which the tongue moves farther than for English diphthongs. The position which is reached in Spanish diphthongs ending in /y/ is close to that for the phoneme /i/, and for diphthongs ending in /w/ close to that for /u/. In English, on the other hand, the tongue moves only part way toward the [i] or [u] position. Also, the glide is made more quickly in Spanish than in English.

The really difficult problems originate among the vowels under weak stress, where English has severe obligatory restrictions and Spanish has none. We cannot emphasize enough how disastrous the English habits of vowel reduction under weak stress are to even a modestly satisfactory pronunciation of Spanish.

Spanish shows, by comparison with English, slight dialect variation among the vowels. This is a fact of considerable linguistic interest, but it has no significant pedagogical consequences.

APPENDIX:
THE TEACHING OF
PRONUNCIATION

From the discussion that follows, no one ought to assume that we believe pronunciation should at any time be taught for long to the exclusion of grammatical and lexical structure. Complete control of the phonological restrictions of Spanish would not allow a student to communicate with anyone if the control were not accompanied by some degree of mastery of the rules of sentence formation and lexical compatibility. Our only argument is that phonological restrictions are sufficiently independent of grammatical and lexical structure that they can be mastered most efficiently by periodic concentration upon them alone, to the temporary exclusion of other levels of structure. This discussion of pedagogy should, therefore, be taken as applicable primarily during such periods of concentration.

The time when phonological training is most effective is early in the student's acquaintance with the language or with any specific fragment of it. He is unquestionably going to form some kinds of habits of pronunciation; unless they are correct habits, they will simply have to be unlearned later and replaced by correct habits. To learn incorrect habits, then unlearn them later, is inefficient for the teacher and frustrating for the student. Therefore, we believe that the best time for heavy practice on pronunciation is early in a given unit of material to be learned.

There is a school of thought which argues that pronunciation is not important enough to receive the amount of time and attention we would devote to it. Spanish spelling is, after all, good, and students need only to pronounce the language as it is spelled (observing reasonable precautions that can be summarized in a short introduction) to proceed satisfactorily. We have no sympathy with this point of view; this volume has been devoted to examining in detail the striking differences between Spanish and English pronunciation. The English-speaking habits of a lifetime, even a short one, cannot be countermanded by a few simple rules and a good spelling system. The notion that Spanish pronunciation is easy for Americans to acquire has done as much to frustrate students, disillusion tourists, and take the joy out of teaching as any other single stereotype about language learning that we know.

It is perfectly true that context will often smooth over potential confusion and misunderstanding originating in a speaker's lack of control over details of Spanish pronun-

120

ciation. It is also true that Spanish speakers are extremely tolerant of errors made by foreigners speaking their language. Neither of these facts in any way invalidates a demand for good pronunciation: it is incontrovertibly true that a communication situation which places on the hearer a heavy responsibility for phonetic guesswork will inevitably detract a proportionate amount of attention and interest from the message itself. The best pronunciation is the one that attracts least attention to itself. All who believe that the communicative function of language—as opposed to its expressive or emotive functions—is its most important function must give serious attention and ample time to eliminating all distractions from the channel of communication. Of these, inadequate pronunciation is the most obvious, one of the most persistent, and extremely difficult to eliminate.

The first step in teaching pronunciation effectively is learning when to make corrections. When to make corrections varies from student to student, from class to class, and from time to time. Certainly, some students cannot take as much correction as others, but even with those who are temperamentally capable of taking a great deal of criticism, it is bad practice to overdo correction at any one time. One must plan to come back, frequently and without fail, to any detail that still comes out wrong after a few corrections.

In making corrections, we would first strive for fluency—that is, we would rather have a student get several details wrong, but produce a sequence of syllables at normal speed, than have him produce the same syllables one at a time with every detail correct. He must concentrate on the flow of the line from the very beginning, just as in learning to swim he must move at a sufficient pace not to sink. The rough edges of his stroke can be smoothed out with practice and correction—but a correct stroke in slow motion will not keep him afloat.

Next we would concentrate on placing of stress. Misplaced stress is the most distracting single type of the many possible varieties of mispronunciation. Note the strangeness of secóndary, preparátory, confidéntial in English. This kind of mistake is, after all, a potential error in any Spanish word of two or more syllables. As long as the stress is wrong, other errors are trivial. Note such obvious examples as

| | /póngase la máskara↓/ | Póngase la máscara
Put on the mask |
| vs. | /póngase la mas kára↓/ | Póngase la más cara
Put on the more expensive one |

| | /bíste/ | viste | you saw |
| vs. | /bisté/ | bistéc | beefsteak |

After fluency and accentuation, we would concentrate on rhythm and intonation. The first part of this volume (pp. 19-34) was devoted to some of the details in these areas that need attention.

Finally, we would be concerned with vowels and consonants—but not all at once. It is important to correct the critical errors first, and to move on into less critical areas only after the critical ones have at least begun to come under habitually correct control by the students. We would focus their attention, and our correction, selectively in the following sequence:

1. The segments that cause misunderstanding
2. The segments that produce obvious accent
3. All others

The analysis offered in this volume has screened the vowels and consonants into these three different categories. A full list of them in a carefully studied order appears in Chapter 2, page 17, and is repeated below with minor elaboration to bring to a focus the main intent of the volume:

1. Weak-stressed vowels   (Obligatory reduction in English, no reduction in Spanish. English habits are extremely persistent in this detail, creating a very large number of potential misunderstandings.)

2. Strong-stressed vowels and diphthongs   (The much greater variety of English tends toward introduction of several non-Spanish syllabic nuclei. Only certain ones will produce misunderstanding. Even so, the problems involved are sufficiently interrelated that the vowel systems are best dealt with as a whole.)

3. Voiced stop-spirants   (The existence in English of contrasts—optional choices—between /d̶/ and /d/, but obligatory distribution in Spanish, and the existence in Spanish of two new allophones, [b] and [g], which do not exist in English, place these problems highest among those generated by consonantal conflicts.)

4. Vibrants and lateral continuants   (The Spanish contrast between /r/ and /rr/ does not exist in English; furthermore, the /r/ resembles, not an English /r/, but an English /t/ or /d/ in certain environments. /l/ is so different phonetically that, although it is not a problem of the magnitude of /r/ and /rr/, it is a major source of heavy accent.)

5. Voiceless stops   (The potentiality for mishearing places these above consonants like /h/ that may in fact be even more difficult to learn to produce correctly.)

6. Spirants   (/h/ is new, as a velar spirant, although the English speaker's familiar /h/ will go some distance toward adequate substitution. The distribution of the variants of /s/ is a substantial problem.)

7. Nasals and palatals

8. Semivowels

9. Consonant clusters   (Many of these are serious problems indeed. They are low in this sequence only because they cannot be corrected efficiently until the shape of their individual elements is reasonably familiar.)

During correction of segmental elements, one of course never neglects stress, rhythm, and the like. After a degree of mastery of the segments has been attained, one should return to the problems of fluency, accentuation, rhythm, and intonation in more and more complex sentences. Early in a course, when several different kinds of mistakes are made by a student simultaneously, only the errors of highest rank should be corrected. But, by the end of a period of concentration on pronunciation—varying from two weeks to a month, perhaps longer, with interruptions for the learning of basic greetings and the like—the errors that most need correcting will have been substantially removed or at least minimized. An instructor can then both focus attention on the errors of lower rank and, more important, help the student introduce his newly acquired habits of accuracy into longer and more complex sequences, moving into the study of real sentences in their full complexity, with the mind relatively free to concentrate on the really important aspects of Spanish linguistic behavior. By this time the rules of acceptable phonetic behavior—the essential link between the speaker and his audience—have been reduced largely to habit, and do not distract the learner's attention from the grammatical and lexical patterns that carry meaning. The sequence of correction will continue to apply for as long as errors are made: it is extremely important that an instructor not ignore crucial errors while correcting trivial ones.

In all the preceding discussion about when correction should take place, and about when one error should be corrected but another ignored for the time being, it has been necessary to speak as if a lesson on any given unit of subject matter could efficiently be parceled out into neat compartments: pronunciation, grammar, lexicon. Such compartmentation should be viewed rather as a matter of relative emphasis at different times. The important point is that whenever pronunciation is corrected, it can be done efficiently only by observing a reasonable hierarchy of importance. No single aspect of linguistic structure should be taught to the exclusion of others. Each aspect in turn should be highlighted by carefully arranged emphasis, and the highlighting of pronunciation should come early. Early may mean early in the course, early in each lesson in turn, early in the student's total exposure to Spanish.

The second step in teaching pronunciation effectively (the first was knowing when, in what sequence) is knowing how. The basic technique for the teaching of pronunciation is <u>mimicry</u>. The student must be encouraged to imitate without inhibition. Size of class affects this technique in only two details: as the class grows larger, more use must be made of choral imitation and repetition than of individual imitation, and the role of the audio laboratory for individual practice becomes more important. If a student imitates correctly after two or three attempts, no further teaching techniques need be brought into play. Such a student is fairly rare, however; for most students, one, two, or all three of the following techniques must be used. They should be applied in this sequence, cutting off correction at any point when it is not needed further—and always cutting off before interest has subsided, planning to return to the same problem, perhaps in another sentence, later.

1. <u>Guidance where</u>. Very often all a student needs, in order to get back on the track of correct imitation, is to know precisely where in a phrase he is making the error that has generated a negative reaction from his teacher. Indication of this is best given by isolating the offending syllable, then repeating the whole phrase or sentence for imitation. Suppose the student has said:

[ásta m∔ŋyána]   Hasta mañana

The teacher may then say:

<u>Not</u> [m∔], [ma]:   /ásta maŋyána/

But the teacher should <u>not</u> call attention to where the error occurred by stressing that syllable and distorting the normal pronunciation, thus:

/ásta ma̱nyána/

It is amazing how easily students can accurately imitate a distorted pronunciation—and the teacher, then, hearing himself perfectly echoed, must either settle for a totally wrong pronunciation which he invited or must in effect start over again and give the correct model.

        2. <u>Guidance how</u>. Suppose the student persists in his error after proper <u>guidance where</u>. Then the instructor must give some hint as to how the correct sound is produced. Early in the course, a skillful teacher will develop a stock of abbreviated devices to provide this kind of guidance. For instance, if he wants a student to produce a more rounded back vowel which the teacher has demonstrated several times along with an explanation (step 3, below), he may merely pucker out his lips; this becomes a signal to the student that he must repeat the offending sentence with adequate lip rounding of the back vowels. If the student offends by reducing an unstressed vowel several days after explanations about unstressed vowels have been given (step 3, below), it is only necessary to remind him of his error with a stock phrase, such as: "Don't reduce the unstressed vowels," or "No reduced vowels." There are many of these stereotyped corrections which would be unintelligible outside a particular class context, but in that context they are effective time savers. <u>Guidance how</u> does not include detailed phonetic explanation; that is reserved, when <u>imitation</u> and <u>guidance where</u> and <u>how</u> all fail, for step 3, below.

        3. <u>Guidance why</u>. When all else fails, one must resort to explanation. For all the high-ranking problems, explanation will almost certainly be needed at least once. In the course of the explanation, the teacher should emphasize key phrases which he will later use as catch phrases under <u>guidance how</u> when the same errors recur. The phrase <u>guidance why</u> implies the fundamental theory of linguistic error that we outlined earlier in this volume: errors stem from the interference of the habitual patterns of the student's native language, English. Explaining why an error is made consists of two steps: (1) isolating those English sounds or sequences of sounds that are most similar, phonetically, to the sounds or sequences of sounds that are proving difficult to pronounce in Spanish; and (2) modifying these in the direction of the desired Spanish sounds. Since nearly this entire volume has been devoted precisely to this point—what the differences are and how to make the explanations—they will hardly bear repetition here. There are, however, certain useful gimmicks that can often be used successfully to trick the student, as it were, into approaching the correct Spanish sequence almost without his knowing how he got there. We list these below, for whatever they may be worth.

        a. <u>To explain a flapped /r/</u>. The items in the middle column of each group must be spoken rapidly to achieve the desired effect.

		More Similar English	Less Similar English
/tárde/	tarde	totter they	tar day
/swérte/	suerte	sweater tay	swear tay
/kárta/	carta	cotter taw	car taw
/wérta/	huerta	wetter taw	wear taw
/bárgas/	Vargas	barter Gus	bar Gus
/kárne/	carne	cotter nay	car nay
/perdóne/	perdone	petter though nay	pear Doan eh

	More Similar English	Less Similar English
/fóro/ foro	photo	four oh
/máro/ maro	motto	morrow
/íra/ ira	eat a (bite)	ear a
/óra/ hora	owed a (bill)	or a
/pára/ para	pot o' (tea)	par a (hole)
/beribéri/ beriberi	Betty Betty	berry berry
/tóro/ toro	(in) toto	tore oh
/ára/ ara	oughta (with /á/)	are a
/kára/ cara	(terra) cotta	car a
/pór/ por	porter	poor
/ír/ ir	eater	ear
/pár/ par	potter	par
/sór/ sor	sewed 'er	sore
/már/ mar	moder(n)	mar
/sér/ ser	setter	Sar(ah)
/tendér/ tender	ten debtor	ten dare
/deşír/ decir	day seater	day sear
/hugár/ jugar	who got 'er	who gar
/tréşe/ trece	todáy say	trace eh
/trúke/ truque	to dó Kay	true Kay
/dríl/ dril	did éel	drill
/prónto/ pronto	put ówn toe	prone toe
/brándi/ brandy	but Ándy	brandy
/bréke/ breque	but áche eh	break eh
/krébol/ crebol	could Ábel	cray bull
/kréma/ crema	could Émma	cray ma
/gréko/ greco	good écho	Greco
/fríto/ frito	fit éat toe	free toe
/grán/ grán	git ón	gran
/gránde/ grande	git ón day	grandee

It must be emphasized that the manipulations suggested by the English pronunciations of the middle column are by no means adequate imitations of correct Spanish; they are simply somewhat closer than those in the right column, which the orthography of Spanish suggests. The closer equivalents in the middle column have the advantage only that they should require less modification in order to be rebuilt into Spanish habits than do those of the right column.

b. To explain a high front lateral /l/. The items in the middle column must be pronounced rapidly to get the desired effect.

		More Similar English	Less Similar English
/fíl/	fil	fetal	feel
/bíl/	Bill	beetle	Beal
/mél/	mel	metal, meddle	Mel
/tál/	tal	toddle	tall
/mál/	mal	mottle	mall, Moll
/kál/	cal	coddle	call
/bál/	val	bottle	ball
/kól/	col	codal	coal
/mól/	mol	modal	mole
/túl/	tul	toodle	tool

Note that although these particular Spanish words may be, in some instances, relatively rare, they provide hints about similar syllables in more common words. For instance, the last syllable of /akél/ aquél can be compared with kettle, and of /espanyol/ español with yodel.

 c. To explain the spirant allophones of /b d g/. It is useful to suggest an inebriated pronunciation of English words which have /b d g/ intervocalically: rubber, scabbard, clabber, robber, neighbor; mother, father, another, brother, lather; sugar, logger, bigger, beggar.

 d. To teach /s/ intervocalically where English suggests /z/. In words like presentar, the pressure from English /priyzént/, with /z/, is strong. Pointing out the intervocalic contrast between /s/ and /z/ in items like precedent vs. president may help the student hear the point he is missing.

 e. To teach unaspirated /p t k/. The student should practice saying English words like pea, tea, kay with a thin strip of paper closely in front of his lips and be told to "soften" his pronunciation to the point where the paper does not move. Another device is to start from English words like spy, sty, sky (which have unaspirated stops) and try to suppress the initial /s/.

 The above list is only suggestive. There must be many excellent devices we have overlooked. The devices themselves are unimportant. The principle that guidance why begins from established patterns of English, and consciously and overtly modifies them in the direction of Spanish patterns, is basic to any pedagogy that wishes to take proper cognizance of the facts of interference from the student's native language.

 Specially constructed drills can be effective devices in the teaching of pronunciation. There are, we believe, three especially useful kinds of pronunciation drills:

 1. Comparison drills. These are lists of phonetically similar English and Spanish words or phrases, to be used in establishing the precise direction that the English speaker must take in modifying his habitual patterns of pronunciation to conform to the restrictions of Spanish phonology. They are primarily for use in the task of providing guidance why, and can be used as the introduction to more specifically corrective drills.

 2. Contrast drills. These are of three types: (a) lists of items which have the same number of segments but which contrast minimally—that is, in a single segment

(piso - peso - paso - poso - puso); (b) lists of items which have identical segments, but in different orders, since position in the sequence has important effects on the allophones of the segments (doma - moda); and (c) lists which are identical except that the items in one list have a segment which is not present in the other: (oda /oda/, honda /onda/; da /da/, hada /ada/). Contrast drills are the nucleus of all productive practice on pronunciation. They have two conspicuous virtues: they focus the student's attention precisely on the crucial phonetic distinctions that he must learn to make; and they demonstrate that the distinctions are important to make, since otherwise the paired items of type a, above, would be indistinguishable and hence lead to unintelligibility.

      3. Pattern drills. In the teaching of fluency, stress, rhythm, and intonation, both the comparison drill and the contrast drill are useful, but a third type is needed to develop habitual responses in these areas where so much of the student's habitual behavior is below the level of conscious thought or control. This type consists of lists of identical suprasegmental patterns imposed on a variety of sequences of vowels and consonants.

      Drills of these three types are available, with simple explanatory notes, in our Spanish pronunciation drillbook.[1] Such drills as these, with correction of student errors in the manner described above, need only one final ingredient to achieve exceptional results in the teaching of Spanish pronunciation. This ingredient is the model.

      It is a fact—one in which American education can take no pride—that many teachers of Spanish, in both the secondary schools and the institutions of higher learning, do not pronounce Spanish well enough to provide acceptable models for their students to imitate. This does not mean that they cannot teach Spanish successfully; it means only that they must take special measures to minimize the deficiency. Among these measures are: (1) the use of exchange students as models under the instructor's supervision (some universities go to substantial lengths to make such native speakers available); and (2) the use of electronic devices to provide students with realistic models for imitation.

      What are the requisites of a good model? For an elementary class, the model probably need not have native-like pronunciation in free conversation, but he must surely be able to produce, at normal speed and with native-like pronunciation, all the sentences which the elementary class must learn. If this seems a low standard, we can only point out that it is far from being met by many teachers of Spanish. The critical phrase is of course native-like, which is difficult to define with precision. We use it to mean a pronunciation that would not, among native speakers, ever be misunderstood or call attention to itself as conspicuously accented.

      This is the minimum level of pronunciation that may be considered acceptable as the model in an elementary class. As the level of instruction rises, so also must the accuracy of the model, until there comes a point where only a native, or near-native, speaker of Spanish is acceptable.

      But the accuracy of the model is no more important than the performance of the model. We have seen many native speakers who provided a less accurate rendition of

---

      1. J. Donald Bowen and Robert P. Stockwell, Patterns of Spanish Pronunciation (Chicago: University of Chicago Press, 1960).

their language in the classroom than a moderately well-trained elementary student would. They tried to be too helpful: they slowed down their speech to a point where gross distortions of the facts of Spanish pronunciation were introduced, instead of speaking naturally; they tried to pronounce Spanish as it is spelled, introducing a contrast between b and v which no native speaker consistently uses; they used grossly exaggerated, affected, wholly unnatural intonation patterns which they would never use outside the classroom. In short, merely being a native speaker does not guarantee quality as a model.

For in addition to being accurate, the model must be realistic: he must have a realistic context in mind for every sentence, and must say each sentence in a manner appropriate to such a context. (If there is no realistic context readily imaginable for a sentence in the text, it should not be there.) Realism is one of the key factors in efficient language learning, and one of the most difficult to achieve. This point needs to be especially emphasized in the teaching of grammar and lexicon; but even in the restricted area of pronunciation, untold damage can be done to the interest and motivation of the student if he gets the impression that he is being taught an artificial pronunciation that does not in fact reflect the way real people actually talk.

If for any reason an instructor feels that his students do not have enough chance to imitate realistic Spanish, the audio laboratory may be the best solution available. (The best solution is of course smaller and smaller classes with many more hours of imitation, repetition, and practice with a native or native-like model and with skillful guidance based on understanding of the specific nature of the English-Spanish interference patterns which this book is intended to describe.) Millions of dollars have already been invested in audio laboratories in the United States, and millions more will be spent in the next ten years. But we must emphasize that time and again such laboratories are wasted; they are money thrown away on gadgetry, because so few persons know how to use them. They need not be wasted—indeed, they are probably the only practical answer to the need for providing sufficient contact time between the student and the language to assure him of an opportunity to assimilate the complex patterns of pronunciation and grammar.

The advantages of audio laboratories are well known: they can work longer hours than people; they generate no teacher morale problems out of tedious repetitive drills; they offer absolutely fixed patterns for imitation; they are easier than people to schedule; and they are somewhat less temperamental. Their limitations are also well known: they have no immediate give-and-take flexibility for adapting to the needs of a particular student at a particular moment; they will not correct the student or evaluate his readiness to pass on into further materials; they will not demand his attention and stimulate his interest; and the acoustic quality of what the student hears may be seriously limited by the fidelity of the equipment (which varies enormously).

Audio laboratories also impose serious burdens on the teacher and complicate the life of the departmental chairman because of the need for integration and standardization of laboratory work with class work. Almost nothing but wasted time and energy results from failure to integrate the laboratory practice with classroom explanations and exercises.

None of this is to suggest that audio laboratories are undesirable: they do not automatically make language teaching easier or more effective—but they do make it more nearly possible, if they are used well. For teaching pronunciation, they can be extremely effective if the kinds of exercises and the kinds of procedures that have been described above are included in the recordings that are made available in the laboratories.

In materials designed for teaching pronunciation in a laboratory, it is useful to have a system of spelling which will focus the student's hearing so that he benefits from his practice time. It is a fact of human observation in general, of hearing in particular, and especially of linguistic hearing, that we perceive what experience has taught us to perceive—we observe through a frame of reference. Spanish spelling is a good frame of reference for listening to Spanish sounds, but it can be improved considerably by being modified at certain points where special problems can be anticipated and by having its relatively few inconsistencies removed. We have suggested a MODIFIED PHONEMIC TRANSCRIPTION[2] which follows the transcription used in this volume, except that the allophones of /b d g s y/ are systematically represented: [b] - [ƀ], [d] - [đ], [g] - [g̶], [s] - [z], and [y] - [y̌], and that the shortening of vowels in sequence is marked [ĭ ĕ ă ŏ ŭ].

Neither laboratories nor textbooks nor transcriptions nor visual aids nor realia will replace the teacher. He alone can provide the elements that make for efficient language learning: guidance and correction. It is the purpose of this volume to provide him with linguistically sound information for sharpening his guidance and for focusing his correction.

---

2. We have argued this point in detail in "Respelling as an Aid in Teaching Spanish Pronunciation," Hispania XL (1957), 200-5. Since this article is readily accessible, we have not elaborated the details again here. The modified phonemic transcription suggested here is used in our Patterns of Spanish Pronunciation.

GLOSSARY

ACOUSTIC BASIS. The basis of description of speech sounds which is concerned with the physical properties of the sound waves. See ARTICULATORY BASIS.

AFFRICATE. A sound beginning as a STOP (q.v.) and ending as a FRICATIVE (q.v.)—for example, English ch.

ALLOPHONE. A variety of a specific PHONEME (q.v.) which occurs under particular circumstances. Its occurrence may be CONDITIONED (q.v.) or in FREE VARIATION (q.v.) with another allophone. For example, the English phoneme /ɪ/ has a long allophone in his /hɪːz/ and a short allophone in hit /hɪt/.

ALVEOLAR. Articulated at the gum ridge behind the upper front teeth. For example, English d is a voiced alveolar stop.

ARTICULATOR. The part of the speech apparatus which is active in the articulation of a sound; whatever part is underneath at any point where the air passage through the mouth is narrowed or closed.

ARTICULATORY BASIS. The basis of description of speech sounds which is concerned with the movements (of the tongue, lips, and so on) by the speaker producing them. See ACOUSTIC BASIS.

ASPIRATION. Audible escape of air, usually following a sound, especially a STOP (q.v.). It is often transcribed by a superscript ^{h}—for example, $[p^h]$.

ASSIMILATED. Having become more like some adjacent sound. For example, the [ɱ] allophone of Spanish /m/ in enfermo is assimilated to the following /f/.

BACK (vowel sounds). Having the narrowest point in the air passage through the mouth be in the back of the mouth, that is, along the soft palate. For example, Spanish /u/ as in futura is a back vowel.

BILABIAL. Made by closing the two lips or by bringing them close together. For example, English /b/ is a voiced bilabial stop.

BOUNDARY ELEMENT. Word or phrase boundaries which may have phonological consequences, as when two otherwise comparable sequences of two segments differ as to the way in which the speaker makes the connection between them. Thus, for example, the difference between pay line and saline.

CENTRAL (vowel sounds). Having the narrowest point of the air passage through the mouth toward the back of the hard palate: intermediate in the FRONT-BACK DIMENSION (q.v.). For example, Spanish /a/ as in sala is a low central vowel.

CLOSE TRANSITION. Absence of a BOUNDARY ELEMENT (q.v.) between VOWEL or consonant PHONEMES; the most direct connection between a given sound and the following one.

CLUSTER. A group of two or more adjacent consonants.

COMPLEX NUCLEUS. A SYLLABIC NUCLEUS (q.v.) consisting of a simple VOWEL sound followed by a GLIDE (q.v.); a diphthong. For example, Spanish /ay/ is a complex nucleus.

CONDITIONED. Predictable, given a knowledge of the surrounding sounds. For example, the occurrence of an unaspirated [p⁼] in an English word like <u>spin</u> is conditioned by the presence of a preceding /s/.

CONTINUANT. A consonant sound during which the air flow is not completely closed off at any point. For example, English /m s l/ are continuants.

CONTRAST. Difference in pronunciation which speakers use in distinguishing different utterances in a language.

DENTAL. Articulated against or just behind the upper front teeth. For example, Spanish /t/ is a voiceless dental stop.

DIALECT DIFFERENCE. Difference in linguistic system among speakers of the same language.

DIMENSION. See FRONT-BACK, HIGH-LOW, TENSE-LAX.

DIPHTHONG. A VOWEL and following GLIDE (q.v.) in the same syllable; for instance, English /ɔy/ in <u>boy</u>.

DISTINCTIVE. Serving to make stretches of speech be interpreted by a native hearer as containing different sounds.

DISTRIBUTION. The range of occurrence of a sound in terms of the environments relative to other sounds in which the given sound can occur.

EMPHASIS. The indication, by any linguistic means—such as change of stress, intonation, or word order—of the particular importance of some part of what is said.

ENVIRONMENT. The sounds which surround a given sound.

FLAP. A consonant sound in which only a single brief contact is made during the articulation. For example, a single Spanish /r/ between VOWELS is a flap.

FORCE OF ARTICULATION. Extent of muscular exertion in producing a sound.

FORTIS. Articulated with considerable muscular tension and air pressure.

FREE VARIATION. Occurrence of discriminably different sounds in the same ENVIRONMENT without such differences being DISTINCTIVE.

FRICATIVE. A consonant sound involving noise produced by impeded flow of air at some point of constriction in the speech tract. For example, English /v/ is a voiced labio-dental fricative.

FRONT (vowel sounds). Having the narrowest point in the air passage through the mouth toward the front of the hard palate. For example, Spanish /i/ as in p<u>i</u>r<u>i</u>ta is a high front vowel.

FRONT-BACK DIMENSION. The reference, in the description of vowel sounds, to the location of the narrowest part of the air passage; vowels are thereby classified as FRONT, CENTRAL, or BACK.

FULL VOWEL (in English). A vowel PHONEME which can occur with STRONG STRESS.

FUNCTIONAL LOAD. The extent of serving to distinguish utterances in a language. A phonemic CONTRAST has a HIGH functional load if the pair of sound segments in question mark the difference between a large number of utterances and a low functional load if only a few examples exist of pairs of utterances distinguished by the contrast. A PHONEME (or sequence of phonemes) has a functional load determined by all the possibilities of replacing it by any other phoneme (or sequence of phonemes) and obtaining different recognizable utterances in the language.

GLIDE. A sound adjacent to a vowel and characterized principally by direction of motion of the tongue rather than by its specific position. For example, English /y/ in /ay/, as in wise, is a glide toward a high front position.

GLOTTAL STOP. A consonant sound produced by momentary complete closure of the vocal cords.

GROOVE FRICATIVE. A FRICATIVE (q.v.) made with the tongue closer to the roof of the mouth at the sides than at the midline, so that a central trough is formed. For example, English /š/, as in shishkabob, is a voiceless palatal groove fricative.

HIERARCHY OF DIFFICULTY. A ranking of the points of comparison between two languages according to the degree to which they present obstacles to the learner.

HIGH (vowel sounds). Having the tongue fairly close to the roof of the mouth. For example, Spanish /i/ is a high front vowel.

HIGH-LOW DIMENSION. The reference, in the description of VOWEL sounds, to the closeness of the tongue to the roof of the mouth; vowels are thereby classified as HIGH, MID, or LOW.

HOLD. The middle, steadiest phase in the production of a sound.

INTERSYLLABIC (consonant or consonant clusters). Belonging partly to the preceding and partly to the following SYLLABLE. For example, the /r/ of pero has the effect of conditioning the lower allophone of the preceding /e/, yet is part of a syllable with the following /o/. The cluster /pt/ can occur only between syllables, never initially or finally.

LATERAL (continuant). A sound in the production of which a passage remains open along one or both sides of the tongue. For example, Spanish /l/ is a lateral continuant.

LAX (vowel sounds). Made with the tongue relaxed.

LEARNING THEORY. Principles of psychology concerned with the influencing of changes in behavior on the basis of experience; theory of how learning takes place.

LENIS. Articulated with relative relaxation of the muscles and slight air pressure.

LOW (vowel sounds). Having a fairly wide aperture between the tongue and the roof of the mouth—that is, with the tongue low in the mouth. For example, Spanish /a/ is a low central vowel.

MANNER OF ARTICULATION. The conditions of air flow during the production of a sound; as opposed to the POINT OF ARTICULATION (q.v.).

MEDIAL STRESS. An intermediate phonemically contrasting degree of syllabic prominence (found in English).

MID (vowel sounds). Having intermediate aperture between high and low—that is, with the tongue in a middle position in its closeness to the roof of the mouth. For example, English /ɛ/, as in e̱bb, is a mid vowel.

MINIMAL PAIR. Two words, or longer stretches of speech, which are alike except for a contrasting pair of corresponding segments in some one position—at which point one stretch has one sound and the other another—and for which this difference causes them to be distinguished by the native hearer. For example, in English, marb̲le and marv̲el form a minimal pair.

MODIFIED PHONEMIC TRANSCRIPTION FOR PEDAGOGICAL PURPOSES. A TRAN-SCRIPTION that indicates the phonetic nature of those ALLOPHONES (q.v.) which are a teaching problem for learners of a certain background; otherwise it indicates PHONEMES (q.v.).

NASAL (continuant). A sound in the production of which the passage from the throat through the nose remains open. For example, English /m/ is a nasal continuant.

NORMALIZED SYSTEM. The sound system which remains when certain phonemic CON-TRASTS, which are not found in all dialects of a language, are eliminated from consideration.

NORMALIZED TRANSCRIPTION. The TRANSCRIPTION of a NORMALIZED sound SYS-TEM.

OBLIGATORY CHOICES. Occurrence of elements (for example, sounds) in ways that can be predicted on the basis of OPTIONAL CHOICES (q.v.) already made on the same level or some other level in the structure of the language.

OPEN TRANSITION. = BOUNDARY ELEMENT.

OPTIONAL CHOICE. The appearance of one element (at a given level of the structure of a language) where some other element could have appeared without violating any constraints operating within that level.

ONSET. The first part of a sound; thus a stop may be said to have three phases: onset, hold, release.

PAIR TEST. The establishment of the fact that there exist MINIMAL PAIRS (q.v.) in which two given sounds occur in the contrasting segments.

PATTERN CONGRUITY. The tendency for linguistic systems to have classes of elements (for example, phonemes), so that most of the properties assignable to any one member of the class are common to all its members. (Thus, the class of voiceless stop phonemes of English—/p t k/—all have initial aspirated allo-phones, unaspirated allophones after /s/, all occur in initial clusters before /r/ and in final clusters before /s/ and so on.

PEAK. The most prominent part of a SYLLABLE. For instance, the phoneme /a/ is the peak of the English syllable scro̲unged /skra̲wnǰd/.

PHONEME. One of the units of pronunciation of which all utterances in a given language are composed. A phoneme is a pole of a phonemic CONTRAST (q.v.). A pho-neme may have various pronunciations under different conditions. See ALLO-PHONE.

PHONEMIC ANALYSIS. Determining the sound system of a language, by discovering the phonemic CONTRASTS (q.v.).

PHONEMIC CONTRAST. = CONTRAST.

PHONEMIC TRANSCRIPTION. A notation representing utterances of a language by indicating only the sounds significant to the native speaker. (See CONTRAST, MINIMAL PAIR.) A TRANSCRIPTION (q.v.) of a given language which represents PHONEMES. A phonemic transcription is usually written between slant lines //. Thus, English tough in the phonemic transcription of this book is /tʌf/.

PHONETIC SYMBOL. Any letter or other character used to designate a particular type of sound in a PHONETIC TRANSCRIPTION (q.v.); may be regarded as an abbreviation for a description of the method of producing a sound.

PHONETIC TRANSCRIPTION. A TRANSCRIPTION which represents speech sounds. It may be of any desired degree of detail. A phonetic transcription is usually written between square brackets [ ]. See PHONEMIC TRANSCRIPTION.

PHONETICS. The study and description of speech sounds.

PHONOLOGY. The sound system of a language, involving the system of phonemic CONTRASTS (q.v.), the limitations on occurrences of sounds, and the specification of the varieties of sound found in particular circumstances.

PHRASE. A stretch of speech making up some kind of unit, for example, a unit bounded by pauses or TERMINAL JUNCTURES (q.v.).

PITCH. High or low tone of the voice.

PITCH CONTOURS. Sequences of PITCH LEVELS (q.v.) used meaningfully in a language.

PITCH LEVELS. Significantly different degrees of vocal PITCH in a language.

POINT OF ARTICULATION. Position where the air passage through the mouth is narrowed or closed in the production of a speech sound.

REDUCED VOWEL. The (English) VOWEL PHONEME /ɨ/ which characteristically occurs in WEAK-STRESSED SYLLABLES.

RELEASE. The final part of a consonant sound, for instance the aspirated release of initial English /t/ as in teeth [tʰɨyš].

RETROFLECTION. Bending up or back of the tip of the tongue.

RETROFLEX (continuant). A consonant sound in the production of which the tongue tip is bent up or back but the air passage through the mouth is not otherwise impeded. English /r/ is generally a retroflex continuant.

SEGMENTAL ELEMENTS. Those sounds of a language which are easily considered as occurring one after the other—VOWELS, CONSONANTS, and BOUNDARY ELEMENTS—in contrast to STRESS and PITCH, which are more naturally treated as occurring superimposed on the segmental elements.

SIMPLE NUCLEUS. A single VOWEL, in contrast to a complex nucleus or diphthong.

SLIT FRICATIVE. A FRICATIVE (q.v.) made with an essentially flat aperture at the point of greatest constriction. For example, English /f/ and /š/ as in faith /fɛyš/ are slit fricatives.

SPIRANT. = FRICATIVE.

STOP. A consonant sound in whose production the air passages through the nose and mouth are simultaneously closed off.

STRESS. Relative prominence of SYLLABLES.

STRESSED VOWEL SYSTEM. The set of VOWEL PHONEMES which occur in SYLLABLES with STRONG STRESS.

STRONG STRESS. The greatest phonemically contrasting degree of syllabic prominence.

SYLLABIC NUCLEI. Simple VOWELS and diphthongs considered together.

SYLLABLE. Among various units of pronunciation found in describing the sound system of a language, the one which most closely corresponds to a single chest impulse.

TENSE (vowel sounds). Made with considerable muscular tension in the tongue.

TENSE-LAX DIMENSION. The reference in the description of VOWEL sounds to the degree of muscular tension in the tongue.

TERMINAL JUNCTURES. PHONEMES (q.v.) which are established by CONTRASTS (q.v.) in the ways in which stretches of speech can be brought to a close. Both in English and in Spanish, three terminal junctures occur: TERMINAL FALLING JUNCTURE /↓/, TERMINAL LEVEL JUNCTURE /|/, TERMINAL RISING JUNCTURE /↑/. The contrast between terminal falling juncture and terminal level juncture in English serves to distinguish pairs of utterances such as possible pronunciations of

"He knew," I answered.

$$/^2\text{hè }^4\text{knéw}^1\text{↓ }^1\grave{\text{I}}\text{ }^1\text{ánswered}^1\text{↓}/$$

He knew I answered.

$$/^2\text{hè }^4\text{knéw}^1\text{| }^1\grave{\text{I}}\text{ }^1\text{ánswered}^1\text{↓}/$$

TRANSCRIPTION. A system of notation representing utterances or partial utterances of a language. See PHONETIC TRANSCRIPTION; PHONEMIC TRANSCRIPTION.

TRILL. A VIBRANT (q.v.) with two or more interruptions.

UNASPIRATED (sound). Without ASPIRATION, that is, characterized by having no conspicuous escape of air following it.

VELAR. Articulated at the soft palate or VELUM (q.v.).

VELUM. The soft palate—that is, the back part of the roof of the mouth, not supported by superior bony structure.

VIBRANT. A sound in which the air column is interrupted by a rapid motion of the tongue across it. Vibrants are either FLAPS or TRILLS.

VOICED (sound). Characterized by vibration of the vocal cords.

VOICELESS (sound). Without vibration of the vocal cords.

VOICING. Sound quality associated with vibration of the vocal cords.

VOWEL. A sound having minimal interference with the air passage through the mouth.

VOWEL REDUCTION (in English). The appearance of /ɨ/ with WEAK STRESS where other forms of the same stem occur with FULL VOWELS under STRONG and MEDIAL STRESS. For example, able /éybɨl/ and ability /ɨbflɨtɨy/.

WEAK STRESS. The minimum phonemically contrasting degree of syllabic prominence.

ABBREVIATIONS AND SYMBOLS

C	any consonant
env.	environment
h	aspiration
N	any nasal sound
Ob	obligatory
Op	optional
V	any vowel
ẋ	weak stress
x.x	syllable division
x́	stress; strong stress
x̀	medial stress
|	terminal level juncture
x̥	non-syllabic
x̭	de-emphasized vowel, shortened in sequence with another vowel
x~x	alternates with
x̥	syllabic continuant
x<	fronter articulation; see Figure 1, p. 39.
x˻	released
x˺	unreleased
x̰	lenis; see Figure 1, p. 39, and p. 38.
x̌	voiced (ordinarily used with [t] to indicate flap)
x̌	friction y̌ w̌; palatal quality ž š ǰ č; see Figure 1, p. 39.
x=	unaspirated
/ /	encloses phonemic transcription
ọ̸	zero
↑	terminal rising juncture
⟶	"appears as," "becomes"
↓	terminal falling juncture
√	intonation pattern to be discussed as a grammatical unit
x ≠ x	"is not the same as"
#	boundary element
[ ]	encloses phonetic transcription

SUPPLEMENT:
DISTINCTIVE-FEATURE
SYSTEMS OF
ENGLISH AND SPANISH

JOHN W. MARTIN

1. The preceding account of the phonemes and allophones of Spanish and English is concerned principally with the articulation and distribution of speech sounds. In this supplement,[1] my purpose will be: first, to determine the system of distinctive articulatory features whereby the sounds of speech are given the identifying traits which serve to differentiate the higher elements (morphemes) within each language; and, second, to contrast the characteristics of the two systems. My emphasis is thus paradigmatic; I am not primarily concerned with the syntagmatic conditions under which one or another sound is used, but, rather, I desire to determine which distinctions of sound are available for differentiating meanings, how these distinctions are made, and how they are organized into a set of articulatory habits. I shall then analyze the conflict between the Spanish phonological paradigm and that of English which occasions basis learning difficulties.

In order to keep this supplement as simple and relevant as possible, dialectal variations from the "standard" pronunciations of Spanish taught in the schools of the United States receive only secondary attention.

2. The physical properties of speech sounds (PHONES) may vary without producing a corresponding variation in their roles within a given language system. Thus, a given number of repetitions of Spanish gana, for example, result in a like number of physically different articulations of each of the sounds of which that word is composed, simply because it is impossible to control all the muscular efforts which are involved in

---

1. I express my appreciation to the following for their careful reading of the manuscript and helpful suggestions: Charles A. Ferguson, William A. Stewart, Robert P. Stockwell, J. Donald Bowen, Sol Saporta. At Mr. Stewart's suggestion, the scope of the supplement was widened in order to include a number of dialectal phenomena not ordinarily taught in the schools of the United States but which are nevertheless widely heard in the Spanish-speaking world.

the pronunciation of a given sound to such an extent as to duplicate them exactly. Such physical differences between phones in the same phonetic context are called FREE VARIATIONS, and are limited to AREAS OF TOLERANCE within which they do not affect either the "accent" of the speaker or the identity of the morphemes in which they occur.

2.1 In the utterances <u>gana</u> and <u>no gana</u>, phones representing the velar consonant are produced within different areas of tolerance, and failure to keep these areas discrete affects "accent." In the first example, the velar consonant is in utterance-initial position, and in this position it is typically produced by completely blocking the air stream with the velum and the opposite part of the tongue; in the second example, the velar consonant is in intervocalic position, and in this position it is typically produced by allowing the air to pass with audible friction between the velum and the opposite part of the tongue. The difference between these two articulations, however, does not govern meaning. The corresponding phones simply occur in mutually exclusive phonetic contexts as COMBINATORY VARIANTS of a single differentiative unit; they are in COMPLEMENTARY DISTRIBUTION rather than in OPPOSITION or CONTRAST, and are recognized as being the "same" as far as the identity of a given morpheme is concerned. The areas of tolerance of such combinatory variants, as opposed to the concrete phones which are produced within them, are abstract categories called ALLOPHONES and are conventionally represented by symbols between brackets [g], [g̶].

2.2 Every phone represents a BUNDLE OF ARTICULATORY FEATURES. Spanish phones produced within the allophonic area of tolerance [g], for example, represent voice, velarity, occlusivity, and orality. Those produced within the allophonic area of tolerance [g̶] represent voice, velarity, fricativity, and orality. Occlusivity and fricativity in this instance are ALLOPHONIC FEATURES, and the occurrence of one or the other depends, as has been indicated, on the phonetic environment. Allophonic features affect "accent" but do not serve to differentiate one morpheme from another.

2.3 Features which do serve to differentiate one morpheme from another are known as DISTINCTIVE FEATURES and compose areas of tolerance called PHONEMES, which are conventionally represented by symbols between diagonals. The Spanish phoneme /g/, for example, consists of the distinctive features of voice, velarity, and orality. If for any one of these features another is substituted, the differentiative identity of corresponding phones is altered. Thus, if voicelessness is substituted for voice, the result is a phone corresponding to /k/ or /x/; if labiality is substituted for velarity, the result is a phone corresponding to /b/; if nasality is substituted for orality, the result is a phone belonging to [ŋ], an allophone or combinatory variant of /N/ (see § 9, below). Phonemes may thus be defined as abstract areas of tolerance within which phones are produced which serve to differentiate morphemes; allophones are abstract areas of tolerance within these phonemic areas, and are manifested concretely by phones which possess those features of their phonemes which are distinctive plus features which are determined by the phonetic context.

2.4 Phonemes are said to be in OPPOSITION (CONTRAST) when they have mutually differentiative function in identical environments. Thus /m/ and /n/ are in opposition in <u>mido</u> and <u>nido</u>. When phonemes fail to maintain their mutually differentiative function in identical environments, they are said to be NEUTRALIZED, and the resultant phones correspond to a larger area of tolerance—the ARCHIPHONEME—which is composed only of those features common to the neutralized phonemes. An archiphoneme is conventionally represented by a capital symbol between diagonals. The phones of an archiphoneme, like those of a phoneme, occur within allophonic areas of tolerance determined by the phonetic context. An example of neutralization is that which takes place between /m/ and /n/ in syllable-final position, producing the archiphoneme /N/, as in ampara: /aNpára/: [ampára]; un peso: /uNpéso/: [umpéso]; un dedo: /uNdédo/: [undédo]. The distinctive feature of /N/ is nasality. To this are added the allophonic features dictated by the phonetic context: bilabiality (and voice) before [p], dentoalveolarity (and voice) before [d], and so on. The resulting phones of [m] or [n] thus do not have here the differentiative capacity which they show in syllable-initial position; the difference between bilabiality and dentoalveolarity merely affects "accent," not meaning.

3. The paradigmatic structure of phonemic areas of tolerance is best studied, from an articulatory point of view, by observing the modifications of sound which are realized at various points along the air column. With respect to the consonants, those phonemic areas of tolerance which are based on the place of articulation constitute an ORDER. Since the internal organization of the orders depends upon the position of the consonants in the syllable, I shall first consider only the organization of the orders in SYLLABLE-INITIAL position, returning later to see how this organization is modified in syllable-final position.

4. The LABIAL ORDER of Spanish consists of all phonemes whose phones are articulated with both lips or with the lower lip and the upper teeth: /p/, /b/, /f/, /m/. The following chart indicates the distinctive features by which they are differentiated in syllable-initial position:

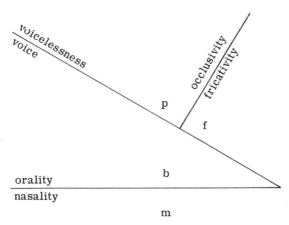

Labiality (whether bilabial or labiodental) distinguishes the phones of these phonemes from those of the phonemes of all other orders. Within the labial order, voiceless occlusives are identified as belonging to /p/; voiceless fricatives (whether bilabial or labiodental) are identified as belonging to /f/; voiced orals (whether occlusive or fricative) are identified as belonging to /b/; and nasals are identified as belonging to /m/. In no instance does the difference between bilabial and labiodental articulation of the phones of this order have phonemic significance.

Although the phones of /f/ are ordinarily articulated labiodentally, whereas those of /p/, /b/, and /m/ are ordinarily bilabial,[2] this feature is merely a reflex of their voiceless fricativity. Indeed, in many regions, bilabial phones of /f/ are regular dialectal characteristics, and are associated with a generally lenis pronunciation of all obstruents.

Phones of /b/ are ordinarily occlusive when utterance-initial, as in <u>voy</u>, or when they follow a nasal (which is always homorganic), as in <u>ambos</u>, but are characteristically fricative in other environments.[3]

5. The DENTAL (or DENTOALVEOLAR) ORDER of dialects without /θ/ consists of the following phonemes whose phones are articulated in the area of the teeth or alveolar ridge: /t/, /d/, /s/, /n/. (The dentoalveolar liquids /l/, /r/, /r̄/, along with the palatal /ʎ/, form a separate set of oppositions, and are treated in §§ 10 and 10.1, below.) The following chart illustrates the oppositions of this order:

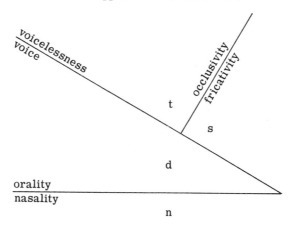

The friction of /s/ is made with the predorsum of the tongue against the lower part of the alveolar ridge (which is precisely where the occlusion of /t/ occurs, although the tip of the tongue is against the teeth), or in a manner which will be discussed in § 6,

2. Many grammarians, including those of the Real Academia (see Tomás Navarro Tomás, Hispania 3 [1921], 1-9) have attempted to impose a labiodental rather than a bilabial articulation of orthographic v. In the native Spanish phonological system, [v] occurs only as an allophone of /f/, and then only in two words known to me (see note 10, below). It is to be observed that this attempt to add a phoneme to Spanish, so that, for example, <u>tuvo</u> and <u>tubo</u> would form minimal pairs, has been made possible by two phonological circumstances: (a) syllable-initial /b/ is not <u>phonemically</u> bilabial (i.e., its area of tolerance would permit a labiodental articulation without confusion with another phoneme), and (b) the syllable-final functional yield of [v] is extremely low. (For both these points, see also note 10, below.) The pedantic pronunciation of <u>v</u> as a labiodental is inspired by the desire to have a distinctive pronunciation for a distinctive orthographic sign and by the correlative desire to preserve etymological spelling. However, a phoneme /v/ with distinctive features of voice, labiodentality, fricativity, and orality goes against the triadic system of functional oppositions which characterize the Spanish obstruents. Consequently, it has been effortlessly resisted, and, indeed, can be learned only through great effort and constant vigilance against the natural forces of the system.

3. For occlusive allophones of /b/, /d/, /g/ in other phonetic environments, see Delos Lincoln Canfield, <u>La Pronunciación del Español en América</u> (Publicaciones del Instituto Caro y Cuervo XVII, Bogotá, 1962), pp. 77-78.

below. Phones of /d/ are ordinarily occlusive when utterance-initial or when they follow a nasal (which is always homorganic) or /l/; otherwise they are characteristically frica-tive,[4] and are articulated by placing the tip or blade of the tongue in loose contact with the back surface of the upper front teeth. Since phones of /s/ are always voiceless in syllable-initial position, the difference in point of articulation between them and those of /d/ is not phonemically significant and is therefore not represented on the chart. Phones of /n/ are distinguished within this order solely by their nasality.

     5.1 In dialects with /θ/, this order consists of /t/, /d/, /θ/, and /n/ opposed as in the following chart:

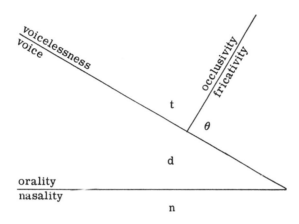

In such dialects, phones of /s/ are articulated with the tip of the tongue on the alveolar ridge in such a way as to produce a rather palatal "hushing" (as opposed to "hissing") acoustic quality, which is as characteristic of the "Castilian" dialect as is the /θ/.[5] Con-

---

    4. See note 3, above.

    5. On the articulation of phones of /s/ in dialects with and without /θ/, see Tomás Navarro Tomás, Manual de Pronunciación Española (10ª ed., Madrid, 1961), §§ 106, 107, 109, especially the following: ". . . el timbre de la s española es más grave y más palatal que el de la otra s. El oído extranjero cree hallar en nuestra s algo del timbre de la ch francesa, semejanza que en la pronunciación peculiar de algunas comarcas españolas [where we might suspect that it is a fully integrated palatal] se destaca aún mucho más que en el habla literaria y normal. La s andaluza y la de una gran parte de la América española es de tipo predorsal, aunque con notables variantes entre unos países y otros. La s apical de tipo castellano, con variantes también, se usa, según las pocas noticias que sobre esto tenemos, en parte de Méjico, de las Antillas y del Perú" (§ 106), and "En realidad, como ya queda dicho, la misma s española, en su propia estructura ápicoalveolar, muestra un cierto punto de palatalización. La s norteña refuerza este carácter palatal empleando una mayor adherencia de los lados de la lengua al cielo de la boca y disminuyendo al mismo tiempo el redondeamiento de la abertura ápicoalveolar" (§ 109). The reference to an "s apical de tipo castellano" in Mexico, the Antilles, and Peru is from P. Henríquez Ureña, "Observaciones sobre el español en América," Revista de Filología Española VIII (1921), 374-75. Without examining the entire consonantal system of the dialects in question, it is impossible to state where such an /s/ is integrated. See also Canfield, op. cit., Chap. III, for apicoalveolar /s/ in Antioquia, Colombia.

sequently, this apicoalveolar fricative is usually assigned to the oppositions of the palatal order.[6]

6. The PALATAL ORDER of Spanish in dialects without /θ/ has only one fully integrated oral member—/č/ (the lateral /ł/ is discussed in § 10, below)—phones of which are characterized by predorsal or dorsal occlusion against the palate followed by a fricative release. The nasal member of the palatal order is /ñ/. In dialects with /θ/, /s/, because of the characteristics of its phones mentioned in § 5.1, above, and discussed in note 5, above, is also assigned to this order. In dialects without /θ/, phones of /s/ are sometimes as described in § 5, above; sometimes, particularly in the coastal areas of Latin America, in southern Spain, and in the Caribbean, they consist of mere buccal friction, with the point of greatest restriction of the air flow between the dorsum of the tongue and the vault of the palate. Thus, they tend allophonically to invade the otherwise empty voiceless fricative area of tolerance of the palatal order. In syllable-final position, possibly because of the near non-existence of lexical items with syllable-final /x/ (see § 8.5, below), allophones of /s/ sometimes invade the voiceless velar fricative area of tolerance also.

Following out the parallelism which exists between the relationship of members of the labial order and the relationship of the members of the dental order, one would expect a voiced member of the palatal order to fill out the triad; indeed, certain allophones of the vowel /i/ tend to invade this otherwise empty area of tolerance. Thus, unstressed syllable-initial phones of /i/ in contact with a vowel tend, at least in emphatic pronunciation, to be occlusive (affricated) palatals, as in ¡yo! This tendency toward palatal occlusion is even stronger after a (homorganic) nasal, as in cónyuge: [kón^{d}ỹuxe] (see note 16, below, for open juncture in this word), paralleling the occlusive tendency of the voiced members of the other orders in those same phonetic environments. Consonantal fricative phones of /i/ also occur syllable-initially between vowels.

The following chart, then, shows the oppositions in the palatal order in dialects without /θ/:

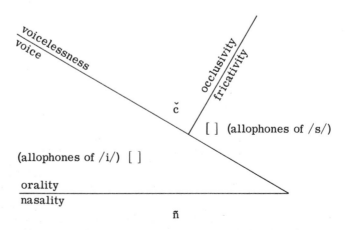

---

6. For a detailed account of the integration of the palatal order, including apicoalveolar /s/, and of the acoustic considerations involved, see Emilio Alarcos Llorach,

In dialects with /θ/, the oppositions are:

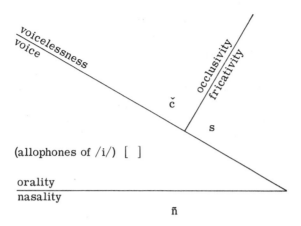

(allophones of /i/) [ ]

Within either set of palatal oppositions, phones of /ñ/ are distinguished solely by the feature of nasality.

7. The VELAR ORDER consists of all phonemes whose phones are articulated in the area of the velum: /k/, /g/, /x/. In syllable-initial position they are differentiated as follows:

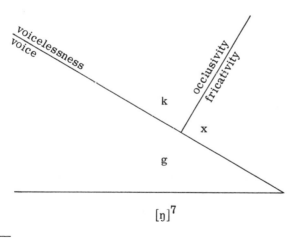

[ŋ][7]

Fonología Española (2ª ed., Madrid: Gredos, 1954) §§ 110-13. Alarcos also includes in the palatal order /y/, which he treats as a separate phoneme from /i/. For a historical treatment of the palatal order and the integration in it of the phoneme /s/ in "Castilian," see André Martinet, "The Unvoicing of Old Spanish Sibilants," _Romance Philology_ 5 (1951-52): 141-45.

7. In this analysis [ŋ] is not considered to be a separate phoneme in any dialect. See, however, O. L. Chavarría-Aguilar, "The Phonemes of Costa Rican Spanish," _Language_ 27 (1951): 236-40, where /ŋ/ is posited. I agree with Stockwell, Bowen, and Silva-Fuenzalida ("Spanish Juncture and Intonation," _Language_ 32 (1956: 641-65) that it is more economical to consider that open juncture (see _ibid._, § 107 _et seq._), before which [ŋ]—not [n]—occurs in some dialects, constitutes the phonetic context which conditions the occurrence of the allophone [ŋ].

As with phones of /b/ and /d/, phones of /g/ are occlusive when utterance-initial, and after a (homorganic) nasal, as in ángulo. Syllable-initial phones of /k/ and /x/ are distinguished by the opposition of occlusivity to fricativity and are always voiceless. Those of /g/ (whether occlusive or fricative) are distinguished by the feature of voice.

8. In SYLLABLE-FINAL position the behavior of the foregoing fricative and occlusive consonants is characterized by a high degree of neutralization within each order, so that in certain instances (treated in detail in the following sections) the differentiations are marked only by the differences between the orders.[8]

8.1 In dialects in which the phones of /f/ are labiodental rather than bilabial, the syllable-final oppositions of the LABIAL ORDER are:[9]

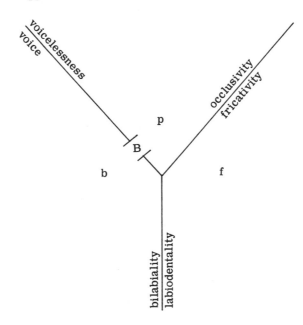

Syllable-final phones of /f/ are thus distinctively identified by the features of fricativity and labiodentality. Before voiced consonants, in accordance with the regular phonetic pattern of syllable-final fricatives, they tend to be voiced [v], as in afgano[10] (cf. phones of /s/ in mismo); in other environments, they are voiceless [f].

---

8. The most useful studies on syllable-final neutralizations in Spanish are, in addition to the work of Tomás Navarro Tomás, cited in note 5, above, that of Emilio Alarcos Llorach, cited in note 6, above (Chapter IV, "Neutralización de oposiciones,"), and that of Amado Alonso, "Una ley fonológica del español: Variabilidad de las consonantes en la tensión y distensión de la sílaba," Hispanic Review 13 (1945) 91-100, published also in his Estudios Lingüísticos (Temas Españoles), pp. 288-303, Madrid: Gredos, 1954.

9. For the syllable-final comportment of nasals, see § 9, below.

10. Since there are few words in which phones of /f/ occur in syllable-final position (such as afgano, Afganistán, nafta, naftalina, and difteria), and since only two of these show voiced allophones of /f/, the opposition of bilabiality to labiodentality has a low functional yield; nevertheless, it must be taken into account, since it forms part of the oppositional system and is analogously repeated in the comportment of other fricative phonemes.

Syllable-final phones of /p/ and /b/ are neutralized in the archiphoneme /B/ and are distinguished from those of /f/ either by occlusivity or, if fricative, by bilabiality. Before voiced consonants, as in <u>subdecano</u>, they tend to be voiced and are usually fricative [b̴], except in very deliberate speech, where they may be occlusive [b]. Before voiceless consonants, as in <u>obtener</u> and <u>absurdo</u>, they tend to be either voiceless and occlusive [p] or semivoiced[11] and fricative [b̥]. When utterance-final, they tend to be semivoiced and fricative, as in <u>Job</u>: [xob̥]. The differences between [v] and [f] and between [b̴], [b], [p], and [b̥], as indicated by the archiphoneme on the chart, do not function on the phonemic level— that is, the phones corresponding to each of these areas of tolerance are not mutually differentiative when syllable-final.

In those dialects in which the phones of /f/ are bilabial rather than labiodental, the labial phonemes are reduced to a single archiphoneme, all phones of which are bilabial, tending to be realized as [p] or [φ] before a voiceless occlusive (<u>aftosa</u>: /aBtósa/: [aptósa], [aφtósa]), as [b̴] before a voiced consonant, as in <u>afgano</u>; otherwise they are as indicated in the previous paragraph.

8.2   In dialects without /θ/, the syllable-final oppositions of the DENTAL (or DENTOALVEOLAR) ORDER are:

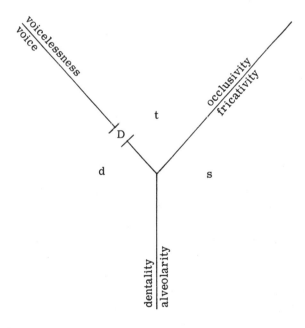

Paralleling the syllable-final comportment of /p/ and /b/, the dentals /t/ and /d/ are neutralized in syllable-final position. Before voiced consonants, phones of the resulting archiphoneme /D/ tend to be realized as fricative [đ], as in <u>admirar</u>, except in very deliberate speech, where they may be occlusive [d]. Before voiceless consonants, as in

11. Semivoiced articulation is characterized by a fading of the vibrations of the vocal cords in the midst of the pronunciation of the phone.

adquirir and *adscribir*, they tend to be either voiceless [t] or semivoiced and fricative [ɖ̥].
When utterance-final, they tend to be semivoiced or voiceless or even to disappear, as in
verdad and *usted*. As in the labial order in those dialects with labiodental phones of /f/,
the difference in point of articulation between the syllable-initial voiced phones and the
voiceless fricative phones becomes phonemically operative, so that they are distinguished
by the opposition of dentality to alveolarity.

In dialects with /θ/, syllable-final oppositions in this order, according to the
somewhat normative pronunciation described by Tomás Navarro Tomás as representing
"cultivated" speech, are as follows:

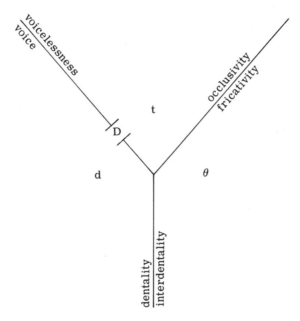

Paralleling the syllable-final pattern of phones of /f/ (§ 8.1, above), those of /θ/ before
voiced consonants in the "recommended" pronunciation tend to be voiced [z], as in *juzgar*,
and are distinguished from phones of [ɖ], belonging to /d/, as in *admirar*, by their inter-
dentality.[12] But this phonemic differentiation in syllable-final position is based only upon
the very slight (and acoustically weak) difference in point of articulation, which itself, as
we have seen, is merely a reflex of voiceless fricativity in syllable-initial position. Consequently, it is often neutralized, as is attested by relatively common identical pronunciation
of such pairs as *ved* and *vez*, or of the first syllable-final phones of *juzgar* and *admirar*,
so that the areas of tolerance of syllable-final /t/, /d/, and /θ/ are merged in /D/.

---

12. See Navarro Tomás, *op. cit.*, § 100: "En algunos tratados de español para
extranjeros se dice equivocadamente que el sonido de la *d* española es igual al de la *th*
inglesa en palabras como *their, this,* etc.; el sonido español correspondiente al de esta *th*
sonora es, como ya se dijo, § 94, el de la *z* sonora, en formas como *juzgar* - xuẓgáɹ,
hallazgo - aláẓgo; la *d*, por su parte, es un sonido menos interdental, más relajado, más
suave y más breve que la *z*." This commentary is, however, largely normative, the distinction being ignored by large segments of speakers of "Castilian" Spanish.

8.3   In dialects without /θ/, phones of the PALATAL ORDER (except for those of [ñ], an allophone of /N/ in syllable-final position; see § 9, below) are restricted to syllable-initial position. However, phones of those allophones of /s/ and /i/ which have invaded the otherwise empty areas of tolerance of this order (see § 6, above) do occur in utterance-final position (and those of /s/ also occur in syllable-final position other than utterance-final). Phones of /i/ tend in this environment toward semivoiceless friction, as in ley: [ley̌].[13] This consonantal quality is not always present, of course, but when it is, phones of [y̌] are distinguished from those phones of /s/ which consist of buccal friction by the higher point to which the dorsum rises as well as by partial voicing. This differentiation, it is to be noted, parallels that which distinguishes the unneutralized syllable-final phones of the labial and dental orders in that it is based upon a very slight difference in point of articulation.

8.4   In dialects with /θ/, phones of /s/ and those of /i/ as described in § 6, above, are the only non-nasals of the palatal order which occur in syllable-final position. As noted above, phones of [y̌] do not occur except utterance-finally. These are mutually distinguished by the difference in point of articulation in that phones of /s/ are articulated with the tongue tip farther toward the front of the mouth, while those of [y̌] are articulated with the dorsum and are produced farther back in the mouth.

8.5   In the VELAR ORDER, complete neutralization is represented by the archiphoneme /G/, whose phones are distinguished solely by velarity.[14] In utterance-final position, they are generally unreleased voiceless stops, as in cognac: [koñák̚], or semivoiced fricatives: [koñág̬], or even voiceless fricatives [koñáx]. Commonly, however, native speakers seem to find a phonemic difference between the final phones of such words as boj, borraj, reloj (when the final consonant of this word is pronounced at all) on the one hand, and those of frac, cognac, vivac on the other. There is, however, a strong counter-tendency to such phonemic differentiation, especially in utterance-final position—namely, the tendency to drop the final consonant altogether. It is to be noted, also, that such words as frac, cognac, vivac, bock, and others written with final c or k are of foreign origin, whereas the very few that are written with final j (or sometimes x) either show a strong tendency to lose the final consonant (as in reloj) or are of extremely low frequency, so that the functional yield of utterance-final velar oppositions is very small. Before a voiceless fricative or occlusive consonant, phones of the archiphoneme /G/ tend to be voiced or semivoiced fricatives, as in actor: [agtór], [ag̬tór]; examen: [egsámen], [eg̬sámen]. Before a voiced

---

13. Harold V. King, in his "Outline of Mexican Spanish Phonology," Studies in Linguistics 10 (1952) 51-62, sets up a phoneme /y/ with the following allophones: "[j], with varying amounts of voiced palatal friction, occurring initially and medially before vowels: /áya, yéga, subyúga, losyéba/." "[j^x], with varying amounts of voiceless palatal friction, occurring before pause: /mebóy#, áy#, múy#/."

14. Alarcos Llorach, op. cit., p. 154, note 1: "En final de palabra y muy pocas veces aparece /x/: boj, carcaj, herraj, realizado relajadamente y a veces sonorizado en [g] (a lo menos ante consonante sonora en el grupo sintagmático: el carcaj de Apolo) o perdido: reló . . . Véase también la nota 1 (pág. 94 de A. Alonso, art. cit. [Una ley fonológica]: 'aunque la pronunciación reloj es normal, reló se dice desde el siglo XVII; por boj y troj se prefiere boje y troje; carcaj es del vocabulario poético-mitológico; borraj es hoy bórax.'" But our present interest concerns what happens, not how often it happens.

consonant, phones of /G/ also tend to be voiced fricatives, as in <u>signo</u>: [sígno]; <u>tecnico</u>: [tégniko].

    9. Syllable-final NASAL phones are completely neutralized in the archiphoneme /N/, and take their phonetic shape through partial assimilation to the following element, except when this following element is a juncture, in which instance the realization of the archiphoneme depends upon the dialect. Thus, before a member of the labial order, the nasal is realized within the area of tolerance of /m/; before a member of the dentoalveolar order, it is in the area of tolerance of /n/, and so on. This distributional comportment of /N/ can be summarized as follows:

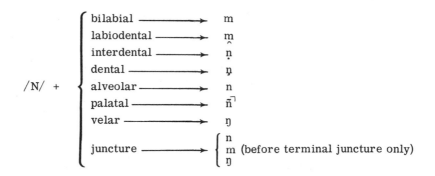

    The occurrence of internal juncture is in part dialectally determined: <u>enfermo</u> occurs both as /eN⁺féRmo/ and /eNféRmo/. In the coastal dialects, /N/ before internal or terminal juncture is realized as [ŋ]. In other dialects, /N/ before internal or terminal juncture is realized as [n]. In the Department of Valle, Colombia, /N/ is typically realized as [m] before terminal juncture, as in [kyéro pam].

    10. Phones of the LATERALS /l/ and /ʎ/ are mutually distinguished by the opposition of dentoalveolarity to palatality, and in word-final position this opposition is neutralized in the archiphoneme /L/ by the non-occurrence of phones within the area of tolerance of /ʎ/ (cf. <u>doncella</u>, <u>doncel</u>; <u>millar</u>, <u>mil</u>; and also <u>desdeñar</u>, <u>desdén</u>, which illustrate that palatal nasals follow a parallel distribution). Historically, /ʎ/ is the reflex of a longer dentoalveolar /l/—that is, a lengthened articulation of /l/ resulted in a broader contact of the tongue with the upper part of the mouth, and this broader contact, in turn, resulted in the palatal quality which this phoneme now has.

    10.1 Phones of /r/ and /r̄/ are distinguished from the laterals by apical release of air and from each other by a feature of length. In the "prestige" pronunciations which generally serve as models for school instruction, the greater length of /r̄/ is manifested by two or more contacts of the tongue against the alveolar ridge. In many dialects, however, both /r/ and /r̄/ are realized as retroflex apicoalveolar fricatives. In such dialects, length remains the distinctive feature which maintains the discreteness of these two phonemes. In word-initial position the opposition between /r/ and /r̄/ is neutralized in the archiphoneme /R/, which is always long. In syllable-final position, neutralization also takes place, and is characterized by free variation between the phones of /r/ and /r̄/, as in pardo: /páRdo/: [párdo], [párdo].[15] The only phonetic environment, then, in which /r/ and /r̄/ are in opposition is in word-medial syllable-initial position.[16]

    11. The vowels of Spanish are differentiated phonetically according to:

        (1) the height of the tongue in the oral cavity

        (2) the part of the tongue (front or back) which is in higher position

        (3) the disposition of the lips

        (4) the position of the velum

        (5) the tone of the muscles of the organs involved

If, while the vocal cords are vibrating, the tongue is allowed to rest in the bottom of the mouth and the jaws are separated with approximately four-tenths of an inch between the upper and lower front teeth, with the lips in neutral position as determined by the position of the jaws, the sound produced will represent the most open of the sounds of a continuum which can be pronounced by slowly elevating the front part of the tongue and closing the jaws as the vocal cords continue to vibrate. Another section of this continuum can be pronounced by slowly elevating the back part of the tongue from the same starting position. It is possible to vary the degree of lip rounding in producing all these vowel sounds. For discussion of Spanish vowels, it may be assumed that the lips are rounded for the whole back series, with progressively greater rounding as the tongue gets higher. The sounds of the vowel continuum may be additionally varied in accordance with the tenseness of the tongue and mouth muscles and with the position of the velum, producing tense or lax, oral or nasal sounds.

    11.1 The VOWEL TRIANGLE (§ 11.3) represents the vowel continuum from high front to low central to high back. Because of the hinged nature of the mouth, the distance between low central and high back is less than that between low central and high front. Any point on the vowel continuum may be the center of an area of tolerance of a vowel, depending upon the phonological organization of the language. Also determined by

---

15. In many dialects, a variety of neutralizations takes place between the areas of tolerance of /R/ and /L/, and the resultant LIQUID ARCHIPHONEME also neutralizes with the areas of tolerance of /s/ (carne: [kárne], [kár̄ne], [kárne], [kárˣne], [kálne], [kálne], [kásne], [kázne], [káhne], etc.) and of /i/ (golpe: [góipe]). A good survey of these neutralizations is contained in Amado Alonso: Estudios Lingüísticos: (Temas Hispanoamericanos), Chapter II,"de Geografía Fonética," 3, "-r y -l en España y América," Madrid: Gredos, 1953.

16. It might seem economical to consider that /r/ and /r̄/ are opposed in subramal and su bramar, since open juncture, if it is granted here, would seem to be evidenced precisely by the occurrence of [r̄] in -ramal. However, there are cogent reasons for assuming open juncture at certain morpheme boundaries (see Stockwell, Bowen, and Silva-Fuenzalida, op. cit.). A still-uninvestigated function of internal open juncture in Spanish would seem to be the preservation of the etymological value of prefixes and other elements. For example, desyerbar, subramal, abyección, and inyección preserve the etymological identity of des and yerba, sub and ramo, ab and -yección, in and -yección; düeto and düerno preserve the etymological identity of duo (Latin [dúo])—that is, if a phoneme has an allophone which occurs typically in initial position, and if this initial position is lost by prefixation (or, in the case of final allophones of verb stems, by suffixation), the identity of the base morpheme is preserved by open juncture and the consequent same allophone that occurs when the base morpheme is not prefixed or suffixed. In subramal, [r̄] is preserved as the normal morpheme-initial realization of /R/.

the phonological organization of the language is the size of the unutilized parts of the continuum which separate the utilized parts.

11.2   Five phonemic areas of tolerance are utilized along the vowel continuum in Spanish. Within these are contained sub-areas which are acoustically perceptible in various degrees. Open and close allophones of /e/ are frequently taught in elementary textbooks as occurring in discrete phonetic environments; open and close allophones of /o/ are less often taught; open and close allophones of /i/ and /u/ are almost universally disregarded along with the front, central, and back varieties of /a/. Although some speakers—even classes of speakers—do show a correlation of some stability between varieties of these vowels and specifiable phonetic contexts, the correlations vary sufficiently, and are frequently enough absent altogether, to make questionable the value of attempting to teach them systematically. Certainly, the allophones of vowels, to the extent that they have any importance whatever, do not approach the importance of consonantal allophones.

11.3   The areas of tolerance of /i/ and /e/ constitute the FRONT VOWEL phonemes; those of /u/ and /o/ constitute the BACK VOWEL phonemes; and that of /a/ constitutes the CENTRAL VOWEL phoneme. Phones of /i/ and /u/ belong to the HIGH VOWEL phonemes, whereas those of /e/ and /o/ belong to the MID VOWEL phonemes. Thus, /i/ is a high front vowel phoneme, /u/ is a high back vowel phoneme, /a/ is a (low) central vowel phoneme, and so on. The phonemically distinctive features, then, are POINT OF TONGUE INVOLVEMENT and TONGUE HEIGHT. Rounding and unrounding are automatic concomitants of the point of tongue involvement in Spanish and thus are not distinctive features. The following chart shows these relationships:

	Front	Central	Back
High	i		u
Mid	e		o
Low		a	

11.4   Some dialects neutralize unstressed pure-vowel phones of /i/ and /e/ and of /u/ and /o/ in the archiphonemes /I/ and /U/ respectively. This pronunciation is usually considered substandard, and is thus avoided in the classroom. There exists also another neutralization which is neither substandard nor dialectal, however, but which is also generally overlooked in our textbooks. This is the neutralization of /i/ and /e/ in /I/ and of /u/ and /o/ in /U/ after a consonant and before a stressed vowel: peor: /pIór/; poeta: /pUéta/, with consequent syllable reduction, which is often taken advantage of in verse.

11.5   The term "front" when applied to vowels is merely a relative term which is useful in the dichotomy front:back. That part of the tongue which approaches the palate in the pronunciation of the closest front vowel is really the dorsum or predorsum. Each vowel of the front series from low to high is pronounced with a part of the tongue which is a little farther forward than for the next lower vowel. Consequently, the pronunciation of sounds on the vowel continuum extends in the front vowels to a point where the tongue involves the palate, and at this point the vowels join the consonants by virtue of the resulting friction or occlusion. The same extension of the continuum occurs in the back vowels. Only the unstressed highest parts of the vowel continuum become so close as to enter the consonantal oppositions; when they do, they are always in immediate contact with a vowel and not in contact with a consonant.[17]

11.6   The highest front part has already been seen with consonantal characteristics in the palatal order, where it enters the otherwise empty area of tolerance delimited by the feature of voice, thus paralleling in some measure the phonemes /b/, /d/, and /g/. The highest back part is /u/, which also has allophones with consonantal characteristics which occur under the same conditions as described for those of /i/. The following chart résumés these relationships (the consonants are shown in their syllable-initial oppositions):

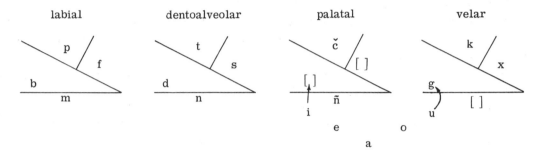

The phoneme /g/ is, of course, a consonant in its own right. When phones of /u/ are closed to such an extent as to produce friction (which is a consonantal quality), a sound that seems to belong to [g], and hence to /g/, is heard. Phonemically, this friction is not that of /g/; it can always be omitted without effect upon the identity of the morphemes in which it sometimes occurs, whereas that of /g/ cannot: agua [áǔa], [áwa]; haga: [ága].

11.7   Consonantal phones of unstressed /i/ and /u/ occur in contact with a pure vowel:

(1)   utterance-initially
(2)   utterance-internally when not in immediate contact with a consonantal phone
(3)   utterance-finally

Of these environments, the second cannot be defined without introducing another phoneme: INTERNAL OPEN JUNCTURE. A similar phoneme in English is seen in The night rate is better as opposed to The nitrate is better and The Nye trait is better.[18] Internal open juncture occurs in deshielo: /des⁺iélo/: [dezǐelo] as opposed to desierto: /desiéRto/: [desyérto]; deshueso: /des⁺uéso/: [dezǔéso] as opposed to desuello: /desuéio/ (or, in dia-

---

17. In desyerbar ([dezǐerbár]), for example, [ǐ] is in contact with [e] but not with [z], since internal open juncture (see § 11.7, below) intervenes.

18. Examples from Charles F. Hockett, A Course in Modern Linguistics, 6.1 et seq., New York: MacMillan, 1958.

lects with /ɨ/: /desuéɨo/): [desweĭo]. That is, in deshielo and deshueso the unstressed /i/ and /u/ occur before vowels but are not in immediate contact with a consonant; the open-juncture phoneme intercedes, and the vocalic phones are thus precluded.

Open juncture is not always word-internal: las hierbas: /las⁺iéRbas/: [laziérbas]; las siervas: /lasiéRbas/: [lasyérbas]; son huevos: /soN⁺uébos/: [soɲuébos]; son nuevos: /sonuébos/: [sonwébos].

Phones of /i/ and /u/ with consonantal characteristics as shown above are SEMICONSONANTS. Other phones of /i/ and /u/ are the PURE VOWEL phones, which occur only when under strong stress, as in leía, grúa, or when not in contact with another vowel, as in tímido, mudado, and the SEMIVOWEL phones, which occur only between consonants or semiconsonants and pure vowels, as in piale: /piále/: [pyále]; dueño: /duéño/: [dwéño]; reina: /Réina/: [réịna]; causa: /káusa/: [káu̯sa]. Unstressed phones of /i/ and /u/ may be separated from pure vowels by internal open juncture: piar: /pi⁺áR/: [piár]. düeto: /du⁺éto/: [duéto].[19] This fact is often taken advantage of in verse (cf. § 11.4, above).

12. Before proceeding now to consider the characteristics of the English segmental phonemes, it will be well to observe that the learner's native language is a structure in conflict with the language which he sets about to learn. The phonological aspects of that structure, along with all the other aspects, have been imposed upon him with increasing rigor throughout his childhood and on into his mature years. It is, in a sense, more meaningful to say that the native language masters the individual than that the individual masters the native language; the linguistic structure which stands behind his utterances is a facet of his culture which he has accepted in order to communicate with other members of his speech community. As a consequence of this linguistic encul- turation, the adult does not—and cannot—learn a new language in the unconscious, "natural" way that an infant does. The adult does not proceed from a tabula rasa as does the infant. He must acquire consciously a set of habits which conflicts with those he earlier acquired unconsciously.

12.1 In the phonological and phonetic aspects of language, as the infant is slowly enculturated, there evolves from the undifferentiated babble of sounds which char- acterize the pre-speech period of babyhood the increasingly rigid set of articulatory habits which characterize the differentiated sounds of the speech group to which the child belongs. As these habits take hold, other possible habits are excluded and the articulatory plasticity of childhood slowly disappears. The organs of speech become co-ordinated in habitual pat- terns with a minimum of conscious direction. Some features of sound are habitually used for differentiative purposes, but others are not. Sounds are filtered according to their

---

19. Consecutive occurrences of unstressed high vowels of the same or differ- ent series follow the same pattern as when in combination with /a/, /e/ or /o/ and not in immediate contact with a consonant or semiconsonant. Huillín is thus /uiiín/. The /u/ is unstressed and is therefore [u̯]; the first two /i/'s are also unstressed, but the first is in contact with the semiconsonant [u̯] and is therefore [i]; the second is unstressed and is in contact with a vowel, but not with a consonant or semiconsonant, and is therefore [ĭ]; the last /i/ is stressed and is therefore a pure vowel. The phonetic realization of /uiiín/ is therefore [u̯iĭín]. This phonemic representation of huillín cannot be interpreted as *[uiiín], which would correspond to */u⁺iiín/, since in this instance the /u/ would bear some degree of stress; it would not be unstressed.

differentiative functions, and auditory habits are formed, according to which some features are "heard" and others are not. These habits must be reconditioned as a new language is learned.

12.2   Instruction in the pronunciation of a foreign language, if it is to be maximally efficient, must be based upon contrastive analysis of the respective systems of distinctive features of the native and target languages. This is neither more nor less important than the contrastive analysis of the respective distributional patterns and the phonological and phonetic phenomena attendant upon those patterns in the two languages. It is, rather, a complementary study which yields additional insight into the systematic nature of the two sets of phenomena—native- and target-language sounds—and thus adds to our understanding of conflicts of habit as they are imposed by differences in total organization of the differentiative features of speech sounds.

This is not to say that the students must be taught a full phonemic analysis of their native language and of the target language; rather the teacher must be aware of the structural conflicts between the phonological system of the native language of his students and that of the target language. Through this awareness of the differences in system, he will be able to predict, understand, and help his students overcome their difficulties with the production of target-language phones. Any native speaker of the target language can, of course, detect the students' inaccuracies of pronunciation, as can skilled non-natives. It is, however, of little value to know that a pronunciation is inaccurate unless one also understands the mechanics of the inaccuracies. The teacher, to be efficient, must understand what the students must do to pronounce accurately, what systemic habits of their native language conflict with the desired new systemic habits and what part or parts of that conflict are operative in any given inaccuracy of pronunciation. This is to say that he must be fully aware of the phonological phenomena which control the dynamics of learning to pronounce a foreign language, and he must bring this awareness to bear upon the explanations and drills used in the classroom. Once the students have mastered the new system of distinctive feature oppositions by which the target language phones are produced, attention can be shifted to the equally important matter of conflicts attendant upon differences of distribution.

We are concerned here only with problems of teaching the new sounds as a system of distinctive-feature oppositions; the distributional problems and attendant phonological phenomena have been dealt with in detail in the preceding study by Stockwell and Bowen.

12.3   The structure of phonemic differentiations and allophonic behavior is in each language a single, uniquely organized mechanism; its parts resist being interchanged with those of other languages. For example, if someone fully bilingual in Spanish and English reads aloud a passage of Spanish using Spanish phones for the vowels, he will find it difficult to use English phones for the consonants; if he uses Spanish phones for the labial order, he will find it almost impossible not to use Spanish phones for the other orders; if he uses Spanish phones for the front vowels, only with great effort can he use English phones for the back vowels. Likewise, if one tries to read a passage of English using Spanish phones for the consonants, Spanish phones almost irresistibly intrude themselves for

the vowels also. When a speaker shifts from one language to another, the entire mechanism of phonemic differentiations and allophonic phenomena changes; it is as if a different machine were being used to produce a different product. For this reason, as well as
for reasons of differences in habits of distribution, students' early attempts at mastering
just a few of the sounds of a new language may be successful as they imitate them in isolation, but are not quite right when they attempt to use them in combination with other sounds
which they have not yet mastered. The two systems—target and native—simply do not mix;
the new machine refuses to function properly in any of its aspects if borrowed parts are
used anywhere in it. The proper articulation of phones of /a/ in antes, for example, is
automatically aided by the proper dental articulation of phones of /n/ and /t/. Likewise,
the proper articulation of phones of Spanish /d/ and /g/ reinforce the proper articulation
of phones of /b/; a properly pronounced phone of /u/ makes it more likely that phones of
/i/ will be accurately pronounced; and so on. The pronunciation frequently heard in the
classroom is a distortion of the English phonemic system; it results not only in a poor
approximation of Spanish sounds but also in the inhibition of the Spanish phonemic system.

12.4   Because of this highly integrated character of linguistic sound structures, it is more efficient to construct drills in the target language which will inculcate,
to the greatest extent possible, the whole system. A drill which randomly concentrates the
students' attention upon phones of /b/, /č/, /l/, /m/, /o/, /e/, /u/, for instance, is simply
not efficient, nor is any drill which leaves out of consideration the total structure of oppositional differentiations.

In order to construct efficient drills and use them productively, the teacher
must first know exactly the nature of the habits which he must teach and the nature of the
conflicts which will arise from the students' native language habits. He must then take
advantage of progress in one set of sounds, such as those of /p/, /b/, /f/, in order to
reinforce other sets, such as /t/, /d/, /s/, which are integrated with these.

12.5   The phonological systems of English and Spanish differ in that the combinations of features which make up the phonemes and allophones of the one language are
systemically different from the combinations of features which make up the phonemes and
allophones of the other. Thus, for example, Spanish /b/ is composed of the features of
labiality, orality, and voice, whereas English /b/ is composed of the features of labiality,
orality, voice, and occlusivity. That is, Spanish /b/ is either occlusive or fricative; English /b/ is occlusive only. All phones produced within the area of tolerance of the latter
are, therefore, also occlusive. The Spanish allophone [b] is composed of the features of
bilabiality, orality, voice, and fricativity. No English allophone is composed of this combination of features; Spanish [b] represents a co-ordinative habit not possessed by monolingual speakers of English. Since in English the opposition of bilabiality to labiodentality
is non-distinctive—that is, since in the labial order labiodentality is an automatic concomi-
tant of fricativity—the phones of Spanish [b] are heard by monolingual speakers of English
as phones of English /v/ and are so reproduced. Or, if a phone of Spanish [b] occurs with
very slight friction, it may have only three features which are distinctively filtered through
the English habit pattern: labiality, voice, and orality. To these, continuity is automatically
added as a replacement for the unheard fricativity of the very lenis Spanish [b], which then

becomes, for the English monolingual, automatically lip-rounded, and he interprets the sound he has heard as a phone of English /w/ and reproduces it as such.

Conflicts of habit occur also on the phonetic level, of course. The learner will tend to favor those combinations of distinctive and non-distinctive features which are characteristic of his native speech, disregarding the differences which characterize the combinations utilized by the target language. For instance, Spanish [p] of padre is much less aspirate than English [p] of patter; however, since the learner's lifelong habit has associated bilabial, voiceless oral occlusion with a relatively high degree of aspiration, he may hear, but will not reproduce except with conscious effort, the relatively low degree of aspiration which characteristically accompanies bilabial, voiceless oral occlusion in Spanish.

12.6   The phonological organization of the consonants of English is shown in the following chart:

	labial		dentoalveolar			palatal		velar	glottal
voicelessness	p	f	θ	t	s	č	š	k	h
voice	b	v	đ / d		z	ǧ	ž	g	
		occlusivity / fricativity	fricativity / occlusivity	dentality / alveolarity	occlusivity / fricativity	occlusivity / fricativity	occlusivity / fricativity	occlusivity / fricativity	occlusivity / fricativity
occlusivity-fricativity									
continuity[20]	w[21]		l[21]			r[21] retroflex / y[21] non-retroflex			
orality									
nasality	m		n			ñ[22]		ŋ	

---

20.   The continuants do not participate in the opposition of voice to voicelessness (i.e., neither of these features is distinctive for the continuants). The oral continuants are normally voiceless after aspirated voiceless stops, and both the oral and the nasal continuants tend toward voicelessness after voiceless fricatives: twin, play, pray, hue; sweet, slip, free, few; small, snow.

21.   /w/, /l/, /r/, /y/ present a front-to-back progression analogous to that of /p/, /t/, /č/, /k/; /b/, /d/, /ǧ/, /g/, and so on, and thus seem to be similarly integrated with the whole consonantal system. However, the point of articulation of /r/ is farther forward than that of /y/, but both are palatal, whereas /k/ and /g/ are velar. For purposes of comparison with Spanish, phones of /y/ and /w/ can actually be considered as consonantal allophones of /i/ and /u/, respectively. It is then seen that where the Spanish consonantal allophones of /i/ and /u/ include fricativity, those of English do not. Further, consonantal

This organization of distinctive features is a system of habits, both auditory and articulatory. The conflicts with the Spanish system on the phonological and phonetic levels are summarized in the lists which follow. The left-hand list shows the distinctive features of the Spanish phonemes, followed by the distinctive and non-distinctive features of the Spanish allophones. The underlined features in the <u>left-hand</u> list are those which are distinctive in the English system and are accordingly interpreted by learners as constituting the English phonemes and allophones shown on the right-hand side. When the learner makes a false identification—that is, when he identifies Spanish sounds according to the English differentiative system—he disregards the non-distinctive (not underlined) features of the Spanish sounds on the left-hand side; filtering what he hears through his native phonological system, he auditorily substitutes other non-distinctive features in accordance with the habitual combinations of distinctive and non-distinctive features in English. In the production of Spanish phones, the same substitutions are made as a consequence of the English habits of combining features of speech sounds.

SPANISH		ENGLISH	
/p/:	labial, voiceless, oral, occlusive	/p/	
[p]:	bilabial, voiceless, oral, occlusive, less aspirate	[p]:	bilabial, voiceless, oral, occlusive, more aspirate
[p˺]:	(same as [p], but unreleased)	[p˺]:	(same as [p], but unreleased)
/b/:	bilabial, voiced, oral	/b/, /v/, /w/ (or, if only semivoiced, /f/: cf. Sp. [b̥])	
[b]:	bilabial, voiced, oral, occlusive, less fortis	[b]:	bilabial, voiced, oral, occlusive, more fortis
[b̄]:	bilabial, voiced, oral, less fricative, less tense	[v]:	labiodental, voiced, oral, more fricative, more tense
		[w]:	labial, voiced, oral, rounded, continuant (cf. § 12.5, above)
[b̥]:	bilabial, semivoiced, oral, less fricative	[f]:	labiodental, voiceless, oral, more fricative
/f/:	labiodental, oral, less fricative	/f/ or /v/	
[f]:	labiodental, voiceless, oral, less fricative	[f]:	labiodental, voiceless, oral, more fricative
[v]:	labiodental, voiced, oral, less fricative	[v]:	labiodental, voiced, oral, more fricative
/m/:	labial, voiced, nasal, continuant (for syllable-final nasals, see /N/ at end of chart)	/m/	

---

allophones of Spanish /u/ have strong velarity and weak labiality, whereas consonantal allophones of English /u/ have weak velarity and strong labiality.

22. [ñ] may be an "incipient phoneme" in English. In some pronunciations of <u>annual</u>, for example, only two syllables are heard: [ǽ-ñɨl].

SPANISH		ENGLISH	
/t/:	dentoalveolar, voiceless, oral, occlusive	/t/	
[t]:	dentoalveolar, voiceless, oral, occlusive, less aspirate	[t]:	alveolar, voiceless, oral, occlusive, more aspirate
[t˺]:	(same as [t], but unreleased]	[t˺]:	(same as [t], but unreleased)
/d/:	dentoalveolar, voiced, oral	/d/, /đ/ (or, with light voicing, /θ/, v.Sp. [đ̥])	
[d]:	dentoalveolar, voiced, oral, occlusive, less fortis	[d]:	alveolar, voiced, oral, occlusive, more fortis
[đ]:	dental, voiced, oral, less fricative	[đ]:	dentointerdental, voiced, oral, more fricative
[đ̥]:	dental, semivoiced, oral, less fricative	[θ]:	dentointerdental, voiceless, oral, more fricative
/θ/:	(inter)dental, oral, fricative	/θ/ or /đ/	
[θ]:	(inter)dental, voiceless, oral, less fricative	[θ]:	dentointerdental, voiceless, oral, more fricative
[ẓ]:	(inter)dental, voiced, oral, less fricative	[đ]:	dentointerdental, voiced, oral, more fricative
/s/:	alveolar, oral, fricative	/s/ or /z/	
[s]:	alveolar, voiceless, oral, less fricative	[s]:	alveolar, voiceless, oral, more fricative
[z]:	alveolar, voiced, oral, less fricative	[z]:	alveolar, voiced, oral, more fricative
/n/:	dentoalveolar, voiced, nasal, (continuant) (for syllable-final nasals, see /N/ at end of chart)	/n/	
/č/:	palatal, voiceless, oral, occlusive	/č/	
[č]:	palatal, voiceless, oral, occlusive less aspirate, less fricative	[č]:	palatal, voiceless, oral, occlusive more aspirate, more fricative, lip-rounded
/i/:	(semiconsonantal allophones only)	/ǧ/, /y/ (or /ž/ or /š/, v. Spanish [ǐ̥])	
[ᵈy̌]:	palatal, voiced, oral, occlusive, occluded with front of tongue on palatal vault and sides higher, less aspirate, less fricative in the off-glide	[ǧ]:	palatal, voiced, oral, occlusive, occluded with tip of tongue on alveolar ridge and sides lower, more fricative off-glide, lip-rounded
[ǐ]:	palatal, voiced, oral, fricative, tongue not involved with alveolar ridge	[ž]:	palatal, voiced, oral, fricative, tongue tip approaches alveolar ridge, lip-rounded

SPANISH	ENGLISH

in variation with:

	SPANISH		ENGLISH
[y]:	palatal, voiced, oral, weakly fricative	[y]:	palatal, voiced, oral, continuant
[ĭ̥]:	palatal, semivoiced or voiceless, oral, fricative, tongue not involved with alveolar ridge	[š]:	palatal, voiceless, oral, fricative, tongue tip approaches alveolar ridge
/ñ/:	palatal, voiced, nasal, (continuant) (for syllable-final nasals, see /N/ at end of chart)	/ny/	
/k/:	velar, voiceless, oral, occlusive	/k/	
[k]:	velar or prevelar, voiceless, oral, occlusive, less aspirate	[k]:	velar or prevelar, voiceless, oral, occlusive, more aspirate
[k˺]:	(same as [k], but unreleased)	[k˺]:	(same as [k], but unreleased)
/g/:	velar, voiced, oral	/g/ or unidentifiable	
[g]:	velar or prevelar, voiced, oral, occlusive, less fortis	[g]:	velar or prevelar, voiced, oral, occlusive, more fortis
[ǥ]:	velar or prevelar, voiced, oral, fricative	[g]:	as above, or unidentifiable
/u/:	(semiconsonantal allophones only)	/gw/, /w/, or unidentifiable	
[gŭ]:	velar, voiced, oral, occlusive, rounded	[gw]:	(see [g], above, and [w], below)
[ŭ]:	velar, voiced, oral, fricative, rounded	unidentifiable	

in variation with:

	SPANISH		ENGLISH
[w]:	velar, voiced, oral, rounded	[w]:	labio(velar), voiced, oral continuant
/x/:	velar or prevelar, voiceless, oral, more fricative, non-labial, non-dentoalveolar, non-palatal	[h]:	glottal, voiceless, oral, less fricative
	The Spanish "liquids"—/l/, /r/, and /r̄/ are as follows:		
/l/:	alveolar, voiced, oral, lateral	/l/	
[l]:	alveolar, voiced, oral, lateral, not retroflexed	[l]:	alveolar, voiced, oral, (lateral), continuant, not retroflexed
		[ḷ]:	alveolar, voiced, oral (lateral), continuant, retroflexed
/ł/:	palatal, voiced, oral, lateral	/y/:	(v. English /l/ and /y/)
/r/:	alveolar, voiced, oral, flap (tap)	/d/	
[r]:	alveolar, voiced, oral, flap (tap)	[d̯]:	alveolar, voiced, oral, tap

SPANISH		ENGLISH
/r̄/:	alveolar, voiced, oral, multiple flap (trill)	___	no equivalent; because of previous experience with "burr" dialects, in which /r̄/ is the equivalent of /r/, this latter phoneme is usually substituted for Spanish /r̄/.

[ɹ]:	alveolar, voiced, oral, fricative	[ž̌]:	(see above)
[ɹ̥]:	alveolar, semivoiced, oral, fricative	[š̌]:	(see above)
/N/:	(syllable-final only)	/m/, /n/, /ŋ/	

| [m]: | bilabial, voiced, nasal, (continuant) | [m]: | bilabial, voiced, nasal, continuant | } /m/ |
| [m̪]: | labiodental, voiced, nasal, (continuant) | [m̪]: | labiodental, voiced, nasal, continuant | |

| [n̪]: | dental, voiced, nasal, (continuant) | [n̪]: | dental, voiced, nasal, continuant | } /n/ |
| [n]: | alveolar, voiced, nasal, (continuant) | [n]: | alveolar, voiced, nasal, continuant | |

| [ñ⁷]: | palatal, voiced, nasal, (continuant) unreleased | [n]: | same as preceding allophone |
| [ŋ]: | velar, voiced, nasal, (continuant) | [ŋ]: | velar, voiced, nasal, continuant /ŋ/ |

13. Considered as a paradigmatic system, the presentation of English consonants in the preceding section requires no serious modification for the various dialects (although some distributional problems—with /r/, for example, in the so-called "r-less" dialects—arise in some dialects). The vowels, on the other hand, present many difficulties in their dialectal variations. (The reader is referred to H. A. Gleason, Jr., An Introduction to Descriptive Linguistics, chapter 16, and especially to 16.7-16.22, New York: Holt, 1955, for an excellent but brief summary of the various interpretations of English phonemics, especially as concerns the vowels.)

13.1 In the preceding study by Stockwell and Bowen, Chapter 7, the following pattern of simple stressed-vowel nuclei is set forth:

The /ɨ/ of "jist" (see Gleason, op. cit., 16.15) is included as a high-mid central vowel if it occurs phonemically in the dialect being analyzed. To form the complex nuclei, a front upglide, usually represented by /y/, may be added to /ɪ/, /ɛ/, /a/, and /ɔ/, and a back upglide, usually represented by /w/, may be added to /a/, /ʌ/, and /ʋ/. Since the degree of upglide is not phonemically relevant, these glides may also be represented by ⌐ and ⌐, respectively.

13.2   Phonological conflicts between the English and Spanish vowel systems depend upon the phonetic realizations of the English phonemes which are incorrectly substituted for Spanish phonemes. Those involving upglides are of chief importance. The advantage of using the symbols ˅ and ˄ is that they indicate that degree of upglide (i.e., degree of closure) in the diphthongs is not phonemically controlled in English, whereas in Spanish the degree of upglide identifies different phonemes. That is, Spanish /e/, especially in open syllables, is somewhat higher and fronter than English /ɛ/ and is consequently heard and reproduced as English /ɛ˅/, which in turn has an allophonic range (i.e., area of tolerance) which embraces Spanish /e/ in the onset and /e/ or /i/ in the upglide, so that it corresponds phonemically to /ée/ or /éi/; Spanish /o/, even in closed syllables, is higher and backer than English /ʌ/ and in addition is rounded, so that it is heard and reproduced as English /ʌ˄/ (or, in closed syllables, possibly as /ʌ/), which in turn has an allophonic range which embraces Spanish /o/ in the onset and /o/ or /u/ in the upglide, so that it corresponds phonemically to /óo/ or /óu/. In addition, the Spanish pairs /ai/ and /ae/, /au/ and /ao/, and /oi/ and /oe/ correspond to only one English phoneme each —namely, the onset plus upglide /a˅/, /a˄/ and /ɔ˅/, respectively. These phenomena give rise to the following types of phonemic confusion:

The Spanish word	pronounced according to the English system as	is heard in the Spanish system as	or
le	/lɛ˅/	/lée/	/léi/
baile	/ba˅lɛ˅/	/báelee/	/báilei/
maula	/ma˄la/	/máola/	/máula/
boina	/bo˅na/	/bóena/	/bóina/
lo	/lʌ˄/	/lóo/	/lóu/

13.3   The treatment of unstressed vowels in English is a habit which when carried into Spanish produces phonetic, and sometimes phonemic, problems which have been treated in detail by Stockwell and Bowen in Chapter 7 of the foregoing study. The substitution of the English unstressed central vowel for Spanish unstressed vowels of any order or either series produces misunderstandings only to the extent that the hearer may not be able to ascertain just which Spanish vowel has been replaced by the English central vowel in unstressed position:

Has visto la [pɨsádɨ]?   (pesada, or posada, or pasada?)
Sabes [rɨmár]?   (rimar or remar?)

13.4   Another phenomenon of English, also treated in detail by Stockwell and Bowen, Chapter 7, above, is that which prohibits, in general, two contiguous vowels. On the phonetic level, hiatic consonants (the glottal stop, [y], [w]) occur to prevent such contiguity in English. Spanish has no parallels to these hiatic consonants. On the other hand, both languages utilize vowel reduction and vowel elimination, for which examples are given in Chapter 7, above.

13.5   In summary of the conflict of the vocalic systems, it is important to recognize that English-speaking students hear the stressed Spanish vowel phonemes as /ɪ˄/, /ε˄/ or /ε/, /a/, /ɔ/ or /ʌ˄/, and /ʋ˄/. That is, the phones which the students hear are filtered through the English phonemic systems and converted into English phonemes in the process of reception. Consequently, it is these English phonemes that are represented by the phones which the students produce as they imitate. If the instructor understands the distinctive features which are operative in each of the languages involved in the learning process—the native language and the target language—he can identify for the students the constituents of the target-language vowels and of the native-language vowels which the students substitute for them, thus eliminating the conflict of systems whereby the phones of the target language are filtered through the distinctive-feature system of the native language. There is no substitute for an understanding of which features are distinctive and which are not in each of the languages which the learning process brings into contact.

INDEX